CHESS
The History of a Game

CHESS
The History of a Game

Richard Eales

Facts On File Publications
New York, New York • Oxford, England

Library of Congress Cataloging in Publication Data
Eales, R. G.
  Chess, the history of a game.
  Bibliography: p.
  Includes index.
  1. Chess—History. I. Title.
GV1317.E35 1985   794.1'09   84-24685
ISBN 0-8160-1195-8

Printed in Great Britain

10 9 8 7 6 5 4 3 2 1

Contents

CONTENTS

List of Illustrations

1 (a) *Left*, Rukh. *Centre*, Shah. Two early Islamic chess pieces, Egyptian 8th–9th centuries. *Right*, Bishop. (b) Knight. (c) Rook. Three early-medieval western pieces, probably 11th century. The western adoption of the non-representational Islamic designs is clear. (British Museum)

2 (a) King, bishop, knight. (b) Seven knights. From the 'Lewis' collection of chessmen, *c.* 1150–1170. By this date characteristic western designs had evolved, a feudal state in miniature. (British Museum)

3 (a) Bishop. 14th or early 15th century, probably from south Germany. (b) Rook. 14th or early 15th century, German or Scandinavian. The basic forms were now subject to greater decoration and elaboration. Sets for practical use often broke away from this tradition in favour of a return to simpler forms. (British Museum)

4 (a) The philosopher invents the game of chess. (b) He teaches it to the king. Two woodcuts from William Caxton's *Game and Playe of the Chesse*, 1482/3. This was the second edition of Caxton's English version of Jacobus de Cessolis

5 (a) A 14th-century ivory mirror back. The literary convention of the 'romantic' chess game. (Victoria and Albert Museum). (b) Illustration from *Libro di giuocho di scacchi*, Florence 1493. This 14th-century Italian translation of Jacobus de Cessolis still had its appeal in Florence during the high renaissance

6 Title page of Thomas Middleton's satirical play, *A Game at Chess*, 1624. The chess game was partly a device to portray living characters on stage. It was taken off after protests from the Spanish ambassador

7 Title page of *The Royall Game of Chesse-Play*, 1656. Published four years before the Restoration, this image of chess could hardly be more provocative in its attitude to the Cromwellian Protectorate

(The evolution of chess notation shown in Plates 13–16 is described in Appendix One.)

Preface

A history of chess is firstly a history of chess players, and as such I hope it will interest modern players who realize that in taking up the game they are entering on a rich inheritance built up by their predecessors. But it is also an account of the changing background against which chess has evolved, the forces which have caused it to be sometimes respected and encouraged, sometimes disapproved of, or even made illegal. The long development of chess has led through many different cultures and societies. It has been variously described as a game, a sport, a science or an art. At different times its social appeal has been seen as primarily noble, intellectual, or even proletarian. In literature it has served as a metaphor for conflict through its two opposed forces, and a metaphor for order through its ranking of distinctive pieces. For these reasons I hope the book will also interest those who do not play chess well (or at all), because it deals with many important historical issues, though from an unfamiliar point of view.

No technical knowledge is needed to follow the historical arguments in the book; the development of the notation in which chess games are usually recorded is summarized in a separate Appendix. The References are confined mostly to identifying direct quotations. A fuller guide to the sources used will be found in the Bibliography. Names of authors and titles of books are given in full when first cited in the References to each chapter and in the Bibliography, thereafter abbreviated. Publication is in London unless specified otherwise. I have tried not to be too inconsistent with names, particularly Russian names, but where in doubt I have used the most familiar form (i.e. Alekhine rather than *Aljechin*). Spelling has generally been modernized in quotations from early printed books.

In the course of writing I have incurred debts too numerous to mention to scholars who have steered me away from pitfalls in their specialist areas of knowledge. I am grateful to all of them. More particularly, I am grateful to friends and colleagues who have read and commented on parts of the text, notably Gerhard Benecke, Andrew Butcher, Peter Dockwrey, D.J. Richards and Colin Russ; and to my wife Karen for help and encouragement at every stage. One special starting point of this enquiry was a discussion at the Medieval/Renaissance Seminar of the University of Kent in 1977. In another direction, I have taken encouragement from chess writers who have contributed to the history of the game, notably R.N. Coles, Harry Golombek and Raymond Keene. Finally I should like to thank Bob Wade, who invited me to submit this book to B.T. Batsford, and Peter Kemmis Betty, who has handled the subsequent arrangements with great courtesy and efficiency.

The book is dedicated to my parents, whose early encouragement enabled me both to study history and to play chess.

Richard Eales
University of Kent,
Canterbury, 1984

INTRODUCTION
Game and Histories

Why study the history of chess? The obvious task for most chess writers when they look at the past is to study the growth of skill in chess-playing. Many modern accounts of chess do just this, augmenting the picture with outline biographies of leading players, their eccentricities and their 'best games'. The sort of history produced tends to be rather truncated, because recorded chess games and biographical information do not survive in much quantity from before 1800, and only of real interest to chess players themselves. But the history of chess can go much beyond these limits. It can concern itself with chess players in general, not just chess champions, and with the changing cultural surroundings in which the game has flourished over a period of 1500 years. Once chess is put back in its historical context – noble and courtly life in the middle ages, growing leisure and education in the eighteenth and nineteenth centuries, organized sport in the twentieth – the extraordinary nature of its appeal becomes clear: no other game of such complexity has established itself in so many different cultures and civilizations. This in itself demands an explanation.

Obviously chess has meant different things to different people. At various times it has been a war game, a symbol of the social hierarchy, a minor art form, a complex of mathematical problems and an organized sport. Or rather at any one time it was a combination of several of these things, with one or another predominating. It seems to be inherently ambiguous and resistant to straightforward definitions. A recent discussion in Britain, as to whether chess ought to be subsidized by the Sports Council or the Arts Council, reflects the persistence of this difficulty as well as bureaucratic evasiveness.

The simple answer might be that chess is and always has been a game: *that* is its essential function and other attributes are largely fanciful or imaginary. To this there is a simple objection: we cannot presume that others, particularly in the past, have seen it in the same way. Had chess been perceived merely as recreation or gambling in the Arab world, it would have been more generally condemned by Islamic jurists in the early centuries, and might never have reached the west at all. Instead it was widely regarded as a training or preparation for war, and so defensible. Had chess been perceived merely as a bourgeois diversion it would hardly have attracted massive support from the early Soviet state. Instead it was regarded as a weapon for the dissemination of proletarian culture, and so worthy of encouragement. These ideas, taken individually, may be rejected, but there is still the problem of explaining why such notions have been so widely adopted. At least it is apparent from these examples that even the technical progress of chess has been influenced by the fact that it has so often been taken seriously as something other than a game.

In a more general way, modern historians and anthropologists are less prepared than most of their predecessors have been to think that labelling a social activity as a game automatically makes it less worthy of serious study. For the historian, organized leisure can be seen as the mirror image of organized work: social changes like mass education or industrialization have affected the one as much as the other. For the anthropologist, complicated games with elaborate rules, particularly when they are found in primitive societies, have obvious affinities with ritual and ceremony. The theory put forward by Johan Huizinga[1] that all civilized culture contains a common 'play element' no longer seems very convincing, but in many societies it is clear that there are complex links between game activities and supposedly serious ones; the two categories often overlap. If today a chess player is accused of taking the game 'seriously' (or too seriously!), he is being accused of taking it seriously as a competitive sport. In the past though, it may have been taken seriously for different reasons. At the end of the nineteenth century, the early American ethnographer Stewart Culin[2] argued that games of all classes were intimately linked with religious beliefs and practices, and were frequently used in divination, an idea taken up more recently by the sinologist Joseph Needham.[3] A truly comparative history or anthropology of games, which might resolve such issues, cannot even be sketched here, and it is best not to set out with such theories in advance of the facts.

The aim here is to follow the long and extraordinary history of chess, and then to see what conclusions can be drawn from it. In 1500 years as a game, chess has experienced only one major revision in its rules of play, but as a focus of social and cultural interest it has proved almost infinitely adaptable: therein lies much of its historical interest.

In modern times, it is true, no one attributes symbolic meaning to the chess pieces themselves, but the whole business of playing complex games, of which chess is the leading example, has been of great interest to psychologists. Chess has been widely used as an experimental test in the development of artificial intelligence. Some linguistic philosophers have found close parallels between the rules of complex games and the structure of language itself, as witness Wittgenstein's remark 'If you ask me: where lies the difference between chess and the syntax of a language I reply: solely in their application.'[4] Even in the twentieth century it seems, though chess is unambiguously a game, it is far from being 'merely a game'.

It may be useful at this point to sketch previous histories of chess, in order to acknowledge some debts and to redefine the purpose of the present enquiry. Also the subject is not without its inherent interest.

If one date is picked as the turning point between medieval (or earlier) myths about the origin of chess and genuine historical research, that date must be 1694, the year of the full publication of Thomas Hyde's *De Ludis Orientalibus*. The first part of this disorganized book, whose Latin text must always have been a severe challenge to the reader, is separately entitled *Mandragorias seu Historia Shahiludii*, and deals with the history of chess. Ironically Hyde based his title on one of his mistakes, his belief that the Arabic word for chess *shatranj* was derived from *satrang* meaning mandrake plant, but in general his knowledge of oriental languages was far in advance of anyone who had studied the subject previously. He was successively Professor of Arabic and Regius Professor of Hebrew at Oxford University, he was chief librarian of the Bodleian Library from 1665 to 1701, and he acted as a kind of unofficial translator for successive royal governments. Hyde's book on games, though in his own eyes a diversion from his more serious work on the scriptures, was a major antiquarian achievement. Not only did he collect a vast amount of disparate information, he also established beyond doubt the facts implicit in the older Arabic sources: that chess originated in India and then travelled by way of Persia and the Arab world to western Europe.

Mandragorias may never have had a very wide readership, though it was reprinted in 1767 along with many of Hyde's other works, but it was still a turning point, as one may see by looking at earlier references to the history of the game. Marco Girolamo Vida's popular sixteenth-century poem *Scacchia Ludus*, which seeks to explain the origin of chess by a neo-classical myth, involving a chess game among the gods and the nymph Scacchis who taught it to mortal men, was hardly historical, but it might as well have been for all the ability of contemporaries to find more convincing explanations. Arthur Saul, in *The Famous Game of Chesse-play* (1614), tried to impart to the history of chess the same kind of chronological precision which Archbishop Ussher gave to the Creation, by remarking that it 'hath been practised now 2227 years', but his conclusion rested on equally dubious evidence. He had derived from the medieval story of Jacobus de Cessolis that the name of the inventor of chess was Xerxes, equated this Xerxes with the ancient king of Persia rather than the philosopher described by de Cessolis, and so hit on his curious date of 614 BC. The only previous writers who showed something like Hyde's eagerness to collect facts about the history of the game were the early seventeenth-century Italians Alessandro Salvio and Pietro Carrera, particularly Carrera, an antiquarian who wrote copiously on Sicilian history and other subjects as well as chess. But they were more concerned with local and recent events, and lacked the linguistic knowledge to investigate the early history of the game.

Even after Hyde, writers did not easily abandon the attractive stories about the origin of chess which had been known from the Middle Ages, and understandably so, since some of them are almost as old as the game itself. But eighteenth-century writers could now at least take their legends direct from the Arabic sources, and so incorporate them into a broadly accurate historical outline. This blend of fact and fancy is well illustrated in Philip Stamma's *Noble Game of Chess* of 1745. Stamma was himself an Arabist and Translator of Oriental Languages to the British Government from 1739 to 1755, so he was well able to assess Hyde's findings. He began by saying that 'it is a popular Tradition amongst the Arabians that in Mahomet's time, Chess was invented by a Countryman of theirs called Ladjladj'. But 'their writers say they learned it from the Persians. This Account is confirmed by the Names of the Pieces, and the Terms used to this Day in playing the Game, which are Persic and foreign to their Language. The Indians are looked on as the Inventors, and some say it made its way into Persia on the following Occasion.'[5] And then Stamma launches into the story of one king challenging a rival monarch to discover the rules of chess from the board and pieces alone, which as will appear below, dates back at least to a seventh-century Persian source, the *Chatrang-namak*.

Meanwhile in France the Indian origin of chess had been supported by Fréret, in a paper read to the French Academy in 1719, before an audience including the young King Louis XV. Fréret's paper was later used by the Chevalier de Jaucourt for his article on chess which appeared in Diderot's great *Encyclopédie* (in 1755), and so it was given a much wider currency. In fact, the only obstacle to the general acceptance of this thesis lay in the determination of some classically minded scholars to see the origin of chess, as they saw the origin of most admirable things, in ancient Greece and Rome. Such men defended the idea that chess had been invented by Palamedes at the siege of Troy, regardless of the fact that it came from the same stock of medieval myths as the philosopher Xerxes. Carrera took this view in *Il Gioco degli Scacchi* of 1617 and others followed him. A further theory derived from Marco Severino, another Italian scholar dilettante, who wrote two books on the origins and meaning of chess, both posthumously published in 1690 at Naples. He contended that chess should not be identified with the Roman game of latrunculi, but was instead derived from rythmomachy, a medieval mathematical game which Severino attributed to Pythagoras. This was hardly an advance in historical understanding.

The problem arose from the fact that ancient authors often mentioned games without giving detailed information about them, so leaving endless scope for partial commentators to interpret these games as some form of chess. Many chess players welcomed such apparently flattering proofs of the game's antiquity. André Philidor decisively proved himself superior to Stamma as a chess player in the 1740s, but the first edition of his *Analyze des Echecs* in 1749 suggests that he was less aware of the true history of chess than his opponent. In his Preface he gave a long list of classical authors supposed to have praised the game: 'Herodotus, Euripedes, Philostratus, Homer, Virgil, Aristotle, Seneca, Plato, Ovid, Horace, Quintilian, Martial', and blamed some of his contemporaries for tampering with the original Greek rules 'attributed to Palamedes'.[6] Gradually however, critical scholarship made this sort of thing untenable, and the study of chess terminology in particular put the Arabic derivation of the game beyond doubt. Philidor knew many learned men, though he was not one himself, and in the 1777 second edition of his *Analyze* he omitted his earlier expansive remarks, merely saying that 'the Arabians very probably brought this game into Europe; and their authors ascribe its invention to the Indians'.[7] By 1787, when Daines Barrington read a paper to the Society of Antiquaries in London, *An Historical Disquisition on the Game of Chess*, he was able to demolish nearly all the alleged evidence for the classical origin of chess, and positively poured scorn on its supposed link with Palamedes. 'This Greek', he wrote, 'lived during the Trojan War, and was so renowned for his sagacity, that almost every early discovery was ascribed to him, insomuch that he hath been celebrated for that most notable of all inventions, viz. the eating three meals a day.'[8]

There was therefore a reasonably secure foundation for later work, and further progress was made in the next few decades. Trade and colonies led to an increased interest in India and Asia among English scholars, especially the enthusiastic amateurs, and so produced some studies of the Asiatic forms of chess. The most notable of these were Sir William Jones' *On the Indian Game of Chess* (1790), Eyles Irwin's *Account of the Chinese Game of Chess* (1793), and Captain Cox's *On the Burmha Game of Chess* (1801). After 1800 steady progress in editing and cataloguing medieval literature led to a much increased knowledge of the status of chess in the Latin west. Sir Frederick Madden, Keeper of Manuscripts in the British Museum and one of the best palaeographers of his day, was led to write an important paper on early and medieval chess pieces in 1832 by the recent discovery of the Isle of Lewis chessmen in Scotland. Later, Madden proposed to write a history of medieval chess with the leading player Howard Staunton, but nothing came of the project. Similar work was being done in other European countries, while in America, as one might expect, there was a great deal more interest in the recent history of the game. D.W. Fiske included a history of chess in America in his *Book of the First American Chess Congress* (1859) and George Allen wrote a *Life of Philidor* published in Philadelphia in 1863. This gathering of information about the game, largely undertaken by men who were at heart bibliophiles and collectors, came to a climax with Antonius van der Linde's *Geschichte und Litteratur des Schachspiels* (1874), which contains an enormous catalogue of references to chess in every possible source.

With so much useful accumulation of knowledge under way, it was unfortunate that after 1850 a few testy Victorian scholars embroiled themselves in another controversy about the origins of chess, a controversy which much resembled Staunton's acrimonious exchanges with leading players. None of the combatants doubted the oriental origins of chess put forward by Hyde and his successors, but the rise of first Persian and then Sanskrit learning made available enough evidence to re-open the debate about exactly where chess was invented, and what were its antecedents. It may be worth giving a few details of the struggle, which demonstrates what intense emotions could be roused by arcane issues of early chess. In 1850 Nathaniel Bland gave a paper to the Royal Asiatic Society, *On the Persian Game of Chess, illustrated from Oriental sources, especially in reference to the great chess, improperly ascribed to Timur, and in vindication of the Persian origin of the game against the claims of the Hindus.* As the title suggests, Bland's thesis was that the Persians had not merely acted as intermediaries in passing on the game from India to Islam, but had originated it themselves, from an earlier game played on a larger board of some kind. Writers as early as the tenth century do mention enlarged forms of the game, but none of them suggest that the ordinary chess was derived from one of them. Only one Persian manuscript, in the library of the Royal Asiatic Society,[9] does endorse this theory, but it was written in the fifteenth century or later, and indeed deals with the chess played at the court of Timur (or Tamerlane) around 1400. For this reason Bland's arguments never gained much currency, but his paper did bring to the lists the more substantial figure of Duncan Forbes, Professor of Oriental Languages at King's College, London. Forbes reverted to the Indian origins of chess and to the ordinary board of 64 squares, but he held that the 'original' chess was a game for four players, an idea first advanced by Captain Cox at the beginning of the century. He published these theories in a series of articles in the *Illustrated London News* in 1854 and 1855 written at the suggestion of Howard Staunton; then incorporated them into a larger *History of Chess* (1860).

The trouble was that in the mid-nineteenth century only a haphazard selection of Sanskrit works were known in Europe, and their dating was largely a matter of conjecture. Forbes believed that the primitive four-handed chess was mentioned in ancient Hindu scriptures and could be dated as early as 3000 BC, but later scholarship has shown that the texts in question were later than he supposed, and anyway contain no mention of chess. The four-handed game certainly existed in India, but as there are no references to it earlier than the eleventh century it was more probably an offshoot of the two-handed game rather than the other way round. News of this damning discovery reached van der Linde just as he was finishing his German history of chess in 1874. In the words of H.J.R. Murray (in 1900):

> He wrote his book and had almost finished printing it when the result of the investigations of the great German Sanskrit scholar Weber came to him as a terrible surprise. He learnt from them that his implicit trust in Forbes had been misplaced, that Forbes was in serious – almost wilful – error as to the facts upon which he had based his theories, that as a result a large portion of his own work was worthless from the point of view of historic fact, and that he had been throwing his money away. He suppressed the greater part of his work, sat down and rewrote it in the light of his new knowledge, but because he was a Dutchman, and expressed himself with all the vigour of which an angry Dutchman is capable, English chesswriters . . . have ignored his conclusions, have suppressed his facts . . . and have clung to Forbes' unfacts and have exalted Forbes' theory into fact, almost as a patriotic duty.[10]

Even now the ghost of Forbes occasionally appears to haunt popular books on the subject, and in particular the idea that chess is thousands of years old has a perennial appeal. But on the whole, as in the controversies of the eighteenth century, the facts have gradually gained the upper hand. Van der Linde's *Geschichte* of 1874, together with a supplementary volume of *Quellenstudien* in 1881, replaced Forbes as the standard authority.

In the century that has elapsed since 1880 only a handful of works has greatly advanced the study of chess history. Baron von der Lasa, long established as a theoretician of the game, wrote a general account concentrating on western history in his *Forschungen* of 1897. In 1905 there were two important monographs: by Savenkov on Russian chess and by Fiske on chess in Iceland. But the one name of central importance is that of H.J.R. Murray. Born in 1868, the eldest son of James Murray, the learned editor of the *Oxford English Dictionary*, he was brought up in a Victorian tradition of industry and dedication. From 1894 onwards he contributed a series of articles to the *British Chess Magazine* which showed his growing mastery of the subject, though they were written in the intervals of a schoolteaching career.[11] Eventually they were all poured into his *History of Chess* of 1913, 900 pages of massive scholarship and erudition which summed up the entire tradition of research going back to Thomas Hyde. Murray's achievement was made possible by his predecessors, particularly van der Linde, but he added a great deal that was new and fused the whole into a single coherent account. The very excellence of his work has had a dampening effect on the subject, for whenever historians or critics come across a mention of chess in their researches they almost invariably put in a reference to Murray's *History* and pursue the matter no further. Apart from more recent theories about early chess in China, and several books on the history and design of chess pieces, there have been few real contributions. Murray would probably have regretted more than anyone else the fact that it has taken so long for two generations of new research into history, literature and archaeology to be put at the service of the history of chess.

The present work makes no claim to emulate or replace Murray's scholarship, and is conceived on quite a different scale. Its aim is twofold: to summarize what is now known about the subject, and to suggest a number of new approaches which make chess even more relevant and valuable to the social and cultural historian than it was in 1913.

CHAPTER ONE
Origins in the East

When was the game of chess invented? This question, often asked, has acquired a sort of history of its own, stretching from Indian, Persian and medieval myth through antiquarian conjectures to something like a secure foundation in modern Oriental scholarship. The myths and conjectures will crop up repeatedly later in this history, if only because they are valuable sources of information for the mentalities of their authors and the periods in which they were invented. For the real and probably unromantic origins of the game however, they are of little use. Instead the safest procedure is to begin with the first period in which we have reliable documentary evidence for a game which must be chess, and then to follow the threads back into the labyrinth of early history.

A chronological account of the history of chess from its first invention is impossible, because no one knows for certain when or where the first invention was, so the method used here is to look in turn at each of the areas of civilization associated with its early progress: Islam, Persia, India and China. The result is not just a catalogue but a detective story, proceeding from the known to the unknown. From only one of these cultures, Islam, is there a surviving chess literature which tells us in detail about the rules of the game and how it was played. It is possible from Arabic sources to reconstruct substantial portions of treatises written as early as AD 850, the oldest known chess books. Before this date there are only incidental references to the game in Arabic, Persian, Sanskrit and Chinese literature, enough to tell us that chess existed, but not whether it had yet stabilized into the game familiar later on, or whether it was still evolving. The earliest of these texts can be placed around the year 600. Before that, there is only archaeology, and conjecture, and references to other board games which may have anticipated the appeal of chess, or resembled it, or even been its lineal ancestors. The search for the origin of chess is thus rather like the search for the 'missing link' in human evolution. Though we may narrow down the area of search, neither is likely to be found, but the pursuit is still fascinating and informative.

Islam

The first documented period in the history of chess is the Islamic world of
the ninth and tenth centuries, in particular the Court at Baghdad of the
Abbasid caliphs, who had originally come to power in the year 750. Chess
may have been known in the Byzantine empire as well in the early part of
this period, but it had almost certainly not reached western Europe till
near its end. Despite some stories in medieval romances, and the existence
in Paris of sixteen carved pieces known until quite recently as
'Charlemagne's chessmen', the contemporary western emperor (who
died in 814) and his court must have known nothing of the game. This had
not prevented chess from reaching a considerable state of sophistication in
the east: surviving literature includes not merely descriptions of chess and
its significance, but also specimen games, opening analysis and problems.
The manuscripts in which this literature is preserved date only from the
twelfth and thirteenth centuries, and most are considerably later, but they
contain sizeable extracts of works attributed to as-Suli, who became the
leading chess player at the Abbasid court in the reign of the Caliph al-
Muktafi (902–908) and died in 946, and to his pupil al-Lajlaj who died
about 970. In the later middle ages these men became semi-mythical
figures in various parts of the Arab world, credited with marvellous ability
at chess and even the invention of the game itself, but both were historical
personages. As-Suli in particular was a member of a Turkish princely
family and a successful courtier, who wrote a literary history of the
Abbasid caliphate as well as works on chess. Al-Lajlaj was known
personally to the contemporary biographer Ibn an-Nadim. The internal
consistency of the manuscripts, and their agreement with the descriptions
of early commentators confirm that they really do contain substantial
parts of the chess treatises of these tenth-century players.

From them can be learned quite a lot about the early Muslim masters'
views on chess strategy: their favourite opening formations, their tactics
in the middlegame and their selection of key endgame positions. We can
also learn, incidentally, something of the status of chess in Islamic law and
society in their day. But for a number of reasons it is hard to have much
confidence in what they can tell us about the origins and early history of
the game. The first steps back before 900, it is true, can be taken with some
confidence. Ibn an-Nadim, writing in 988, knew of a whole succession of
leading players who had composed books on chess, at least two of them, al-
Adli and ar-Razi, earlier than as-Suli. The two of them were said to have
played together before the Caliph al-Mutawakkil (847–861), when al-
Adli, who had been established for some time as the champion player, lost
to his younger rival. As-Suli knew neither, because both had died before
he came to the fore after 902, but he knew their works and made it clear

that he thought ar-Razi the stronger player, devoting much of his treatises to refuting al-Adli's ideas. By quoting al-Adli so much, if only as a foil, he encouraged later compilers to take him seriously, and this led paradoxically to many more of al-Adli's conclusions being preserved in the manuscripts. It is still much harder to reconstruct the works of al-Adli than those of as-Suli or al-Lajlaj, but it is in part possible, and this pushes back the dawn of recorded chess theory to the mid-ninth century. Before that date there are no references to books on chess, lost or not, but as-Suli names three earlier players of master class, Jabir, Rabrab and Abu'n-Na'am, implying perhaps that they succeeded one another as court champions. This would place them all in the first half of the ninth century, so there is nothing implausible about the story of a later historian who describes the Caliph al-Ma'mun watching Rabrab and Jabir play while he was on an expedition in 819.

The trail of detailed circumstantial evidence can thus be traced back to about the year 800 and the time of the famous Caliph Harun al-Rashid (786–809), where it begins to peter out. There are, it is true, many stories linking chess with the names of earlier Caliphs, men of letters and other Muslim notables, but these are almost entirely unsupported by contemporary evidence or by convincing details, like the names of chess players remembered for their contributions to the game. It is also true that there were many reasons which might have induced writers and historians to make up stories of this kind. Islamic law was and is all-embracing: from its core in the *Qur'an* early commentators developed a series of codes which regulated every aspect of life and belief. The position of chess in this great system was a dubious one. It was not forbidden by name in the *Qur'an*, probably because the game was unknown to Muhammad, but it still risked subsequent condemnation, either by analogy with activities which had been specifically forbidden like gambling, or failing that, because the prophet had never actually commended it. At the least it might be held superfluous, because it took up time which could have been devoted to necessary and praiseworthy occupations. In the words of the Prophet: 'when truth is set aside, only error remains.' When the book was not specific in such legal matters, guidance was sought from the recorded deeds or sayings of Muhammad and his early followers, so there was therefore a continual process by which 'authentic traditions' were invoked, or invented, and then discarded by more rigorous scholars.

It is against this background that the stories of early caliphs playing chess or approving of it should be judged, particularly when the stories were put about by chess players themselves. Not just the social status of the game but its legality was at stake. As-Suli included many justificatory stories of this kind in his works, of which the following is a typical example. The second caliph Omar (634–644), who was also Muhammad's father-in-law and instigated the conquest of Persia, once saw a game of chess, inquired what it was, and was told the legend that chess was invented to console a queen after a civil war between her two sons, whereupon he observed that there was nothing illegal in the game because it was linked with war. Similar stories were told of the fourth caliph Ali (656–661) and other celebrated figures. In the second place, and without any ulterior motives at all, it is easy to see why poets and historians included references to chess in their descriptions of the past, just because it was familiar in their own day: it was the same attitude as that which led western medieval writers to describe chess at the court of Charlemagne or King Arthur. These stories too, tend to be free-floating and to reappear with different figures playing the major roles. For instance, there is a story that a caliph was playing chess when a visitor was announced, so he ordered the board to be covered in case the man's religious susceptibilities were upset. But having discovered that he was quite ignorant, the caliph resumed his game, remarking that 'nothing is forbidden to the uneducated'. It occurs in three sources, with attributions to the caliphs Abd al-Malik (685–705), Walid (705–715) and Hisham (724–743). Later authors, particularly after 1400, attributed chess problems too to early historical figures, a practice which deceived many nineteenth-century scholars. Chess writers in general are rather too prepared to retail this sort of material even now. Certainly modern historians of Islam are less willing to accept tenth-century and later accounts of seventh- or eighth-century events than were their predecessors of even fifty years ago, at least not without clear traditions and convincing details. As has been suggested above, detailed evidence for chess playing does not exist before the year 800 at the earliest. The statement of the historian al-Mas'udi (d. 956) that Harun al-Rashid was the first of the Abbasid caliphs to play chess cannot be proved correct, but it is not at all implausible.

This kind of re-assessment of the sources certainly makes it impossible to say much about chess in the early period of Islam from c. 640 to c. 800, because nearly all the details usually given by historians, such as the early appearance of 'blindfold' chess, are derived from much later evidence.

Murray's remark, that 'chess had already become a popular game throughout Islam, from Spain to the banks of the Indus, before the commencement of the Abbasid caliphate'[1] in 750, now looks like mere speculation. However, it is unnecessary to go to the opposite extreme and deny the very existence of the game, in at least some parts of the Islamic world, during these first centuries. Even the most ruthless winnowing of the evidence still leaves one or two certain references to chess in Arabic works written before 800; fleeting references only, but sufficient for a clear identification. For example a line of verse written by the Arabic poet al-Farazdaq, who died in 728, runs 'I keep you from your inheritance and from the royal crown so that, hindered by my arm, you remain a Pawn among the Pawns'. The Arabic word *baidaq* has no meaning except that of a pawn in chess, so there is no ambiguity. More generally, though the names and details may be suspect, it is hard to reject the consensus of all the Arabic authors of the ninth and tenth centuries that chess had reached Islam from the Persians, who in turn had it from India. Archaeology cannot be used to confirm this, because no Arab or Persian chess pieces survive from such an early date, but philology can. The Arabic word for chess, *shatranj*, is derived from the Persian *chatrang*, which itself came from the Sanskrit *chaturanga*. Most of the Arabic words for the chess pieces too, were derived from Persian. Not for the last time, the vocabulary of chess serves as a signpost, or indicator, of the route taken by the game from one culture to another, as shown in Table 1.

Modern equivalent	Persian	Arabic	Contemporary meaning
King	Shah	Shah	King
Queen	Farzin	{ Firzan { Firz	Counsellor (later Vizir)
Bishop	Pil	Fil	Elephant
Knight	Asp	Faras	Horse
Rook	Rukh	Rukh	Chariot
Pawn	Pujada	Baidaq	Foot soldier

Table 1

Unlike the stories of chess-playing caliphs, not all the accounts of the invention of chess in Arabic writing are of purely Arabic origin. Some of them are: as-Suli for instance rejected earlier legends in favour of attributing chess to Joshua and other respectable figures from the Old Testament. Later writers in Islam pushed this theory back to Adam, who supposedly played the game to console himself for the death of Abel, or imported suitable Greek philosophers as its putative inventors, including Aristotle, Galen and Hippocrates. Later still few saw the need to go back before as-Suli or al-Lajlaj as the first recorded chess players. But some of the earliest accounts, or rather legends, of the origin of the game found in Arabic writing, do seem to have reached Islam along with the game itself, from Persia. In one case, this can be proved. To discover more about the origins of chess, it is therefore necessary to trace back these clues afforded by later writers into early Persian history.

Persia

Before it was overrun by the Arab armies in the 640s, the Persian empire had been ruled by the Sasanian dynasty since the early third century. It had its own language and script, and its own Zoroastrian religion. After the conquest Persian culture was for a time submerged, but conversion to Islam did not cause the Persians to give up their feelings of cultural superiority over their Bedouin conquerors. The extended Arab empire in the end took over many ideas and institutions from the settled civilizations it had subdued, and which became its clients or *mawali*. The *mawali*, who greatly outnumbered the true Arabs, the original inhabitants of Arabia, secured a full recognition of their status by supporting the violent revolution which led to the establishment of the Abbasid caliphate with its capital at Baghdad in 750. Meanwhile much Persian history and literature was translated into Arabic and circulated more widely in that form. This was the background against which chess spread through the Arab world between *c.* 650 and *c.* 750–800, though as emphasized above, there is so little reliable evidence that the speed of its dissemination remains a matter of conjecture. The fact that Arabic authors as early as al-Adli seem to have been unaware of the Persian derivation of the name *shatranj* and their chess terms, though they knew that the game itself was Persian, might suggest a longer period of transition than Murray and others allowed, with much being forgotten in the process, and something like a new beginning.

Nevertheless, the history of chess in Persia can be usefully approached through a much later work, the *Shahnama* or 'Book of Kings' composed by the poet Firdausi and completed in the year 1011. Though written so many years after the Arab conquest, it is in Persian, as part of the deliberate attempt to engineer a Persian literary renaissance with nationalistic overtones. It was based on all the available accounts about the Sasanian rulers, in particular the earlier sixth-century epic collection the *Khoday-nama*, which despite its translation into Arabic in the eighth century, has subsequently been lost. Where the *Shahnama* can be checked against earlier materials, it is often found to be remarkably faithful to its original sources, though this cannot be relied on, as many of the available stories of Sasanian times were no more than a shifting collection of legends. The references to chess are found in a section which celebrates the achievements of Bozorgmehr, vizier of King Khusrau Nushirwan (531–579) and himself a legendary figure. The story describes how a richly equipped envoy from the Raja of India arrives at the Shah's court:[2]

The envoy now presented a message on silk which the Rajah of India had sent to Nushirwan. Accompanying it was a chequer-board so carefully constructed and with such art that a treasure-house had been emptied for it. The message which the Indian brought from the Rajah was to this effect.

'May you live as long as the skies endure! Bid those who have been most engaged in the pursuit of science to place the chequer-board before you and let each man express his opinion as to how this subtle game is played. Let them identify each piece by name, declare how it must be moved and upon which square. They must be able to identify the foot-soldier, the elephant, and the rest of the army, such as the chariot and the horse, and the movements of the vizier and the shah. If they discover how this subtle game is played, they will have surpassed all other sages and I will then gladly send to your court the impost and tribute which you exact. If, on the other hand, the council of notable men of Iran fail utterly in this science and prove themselves to be unequal with us in it, you will no longer be able to exact from this land and territory of ours any kind of tribute or impost. You, on the other hand, will submit to the payment of tribute; for science is superior to any wealth however noteworthy.'

This appeal to intellectual chivalry having been accepted, only Bozorgmehr was equal to the task. After a day and a night in study he was able to announce his conclusions:

'The sage has invented a battlefield, in the midst of which the king takes up his station. To left and right of him the army is dispersed, the foot-soldiers occupying the rank in front. At the king's side stands his sagacious conseller advising him on the strategy to be carried out during the battle. In two directions the elephants are posted with their faces turned towards where the conflict is. Beyond them are stationed the war-horses, on which are mounted two resourceful riders, and fighting alongside them on either hand to right and left are the chariots ready for the fray.'

The Indian envoys were deeply mortified, but Bozorgmehr had not finished with them yet. He proceeded to invent the game of *nard*, usually thought to be backgammon, and sent that as a challenge to the Indian Rajah, whose Brahman courtiers were of course unable to discover its rules. The Persian victory was complete. At this point Firdausi included another myth, which described the earlier invention of the game in India. According to this the game was invented for a queen following a civil war between her two sons Gow and Talhand, in which Talhand had been killed. It was meant to serve as an explanation of his death, in that only one Shah could come off victorious, and to console the queen, in which it was only partially successful.

It is the first of the two stories in the *Shahnama*, the nationalistic myth, which is more immediately interesting, however, because it survives in another and earlier recension in an original middle-Persian work, the *Chatrang-namak*, generally now thought to have been written in the seventh century at the very end of the Sasanian period. Here again there is the story of the embassy sent to Nushirwan, though the Indian king is now called Dewasarm and his envoy Takhtaritus. Again Bozorgmehr, here called Wajurgmitr, comes off victorious and drives home his point with the invention of nard. The importance of this text is considerable. It is the only pre-Islamic (or pre-800) source which gives such details as the names of the pieces, so confirming that the chess of this period was indeed a game for two players, played on a board of sixty-four squares. It is salutary to remember how little evidence there is for such basic facts. The only other reference to chess in middle-Persian literature occurs in the *Karnamak-i Artakhsher-i Papakan*, or 'Book of the Deeds of Ardashir son of Papak', the heroic third-century founder of the Sasanian dynasty. At one point Ardashir was said to be 'more skilled than all others at ball-play, in horsemanship, in *chatrang*, in hunting, and in other accomplishments'. In this there is no more than the name to go on, but we can derive the fact that *chatrang* was an accepted noble accomplishment by the time the *Karnamak* was written in about 600, though hardly in the third century. Two references to chess in Persian sources does not seem very much, but it should be remembered that only five works of middle-Persian secular literature survive at all on any scale.

Before going on to trace the dim beginnings of chess in early India, it is worth recalling the subsequent fate of these myths and legends. Firdausi was not the only writer to be reshaping and transmitting them in the ninth century or later; many Arabic authors did the same. Thus the story of the queen's consolation after the death of her son appears in the works of the historian al-Ya'qubi, who was writing just before 900, and in several of the chess manuscripts. It was also a common idea that chess should be set in opposition to *nard*: the game of skill symbolizing human choice and free-will; the game of chance, the capricious workings of fate. Some Arabic authors, like al-Ya'qubi and al-Mas'udi, made both games of Indian origin, others followed the *Chatrang-namak* and *Shahnama* in ascribing nard to Persia, but all of them departed from the Persian tradition by regarding chess as the later and better invention. This time the Indians were the moral victors. Arabic chess writers also filled out the stock of traditions by discovering other reasons for the invention of the game: to educate a prince, to replace war, or to occupy the time of a king who, like Alexander, had defeated all his enemies within reach and was at a loss for something destructive to do. As mentioned above, they also began to link chess with names taken from Hebrew scriptures and Greek philosophy.

There is, however, one other legend which occurs in almost every one of these Arabic sources and may be of much earlier origin: the story of the 'doubling of the squares'. It is that the inventor of chess, when asked to name his reward by a grateful monarch, asked for a quantity of grain, one grain for the first square of the chessboard, two for the second, four for the third and so on. As kings will, the ruler agreed, only to discover that the quantity so produced was unimaginably large: the number of grains on the last square would be 2^{63} and the total $2^{64} - 1$ or about 18 million million million.

None of these myths and legends is historical, but all of them except those of obviously later invention point the way back to Persia and India. Only the 'embassy' story can be proved to be pre-Islamic, by the survival of the *Chatrang-namak*, but it is very likely that the 'consolation of the queen' and the 'doubling of the squares' are early too.[3] The latter was the kind of story which is likely to have been transmitted along with the decimal numbers which made such calculations possible. The compiler of a twelfth-century chess manuscript wrote, probably quoting al-Adli, 'It is universally acknowledged that three things were produced from India, in which no other country anticipated it, and the like of which existed nowhere else: the book *Kalila wa Dimna*, the nine cyphers with which one can count to infinity, and chess.' All three: the game, the *Kalila wa Dimna* (a book of literary fables) and the decimal numbers, travelled on to western Christendom by the eleventh century. Finally, the tradition enshrined in the *Chatrang-namak*, that chess was introduced from India to Persia in the reign of Khusrau Nushirwan (531–579), may be accepted as a plausible hypothesis. It could not have been much later for the game to be listed among accepted social accomplishments in the *Karnamak*, around the end of the century. Al-Mas'udi, writing in the mid-tenth century, preserved the same tradition, saying of Nushirwan that he 'had sent from India the book *Kalila wa Dimna*, the game of chess, and a black dye called hindi, which dyes the hair to its roots a permanent and brilliant black'. This theory would carry the history of chess back to the earliest date so far reached, the mid-sixth century.

India

In examining the Indian origins of chess it is as well to recognize at the outset that there are no Sanskrit literary sources earlier than the first references in Persian already discussed, at least none that can be clearly identified as chess. Of the various passages in early Sanskrit texts which have been thought at one time or another to mention chess, only two earlier than 800 are still accepted by scholars,[4] and neither of them reveals much about the game except its existence. The first of them, from

Vasavadatta, a fantasy romance written by Subandhu in about 600, may not even do so much. The relevant passage is usually rendered: 'The time of the rains played its game with frogs for chessmen, which, yellow and green in colour as if mottled with lac, leapt up on the black field squares.' A much later commentator identified this as a reference to chess, and Murray agreed, but the key word is not an accepted term for 'chessmen', and could equally well be translated more generally as 'gambling pieces'.[5] The second passage is rather more satisfactory. It comes from the *Harshacharita*, or 'Life of Harsha', written by Bana around 625. Northern India had dissolved into a number of warring states after the collapse of the Gupta empire in the mid-fifth century, and Harsha, king of Kanauj on the Ganges from 606 to 647, was the most successful of the rulers who tried to build up military empires in the succeeding period. The style of this biography written by his court poet is ornate, and too full of puns to strike the modern reader as anything other than comic, but it contains the following, in praise of the peace and order of Harsha's rule: 'Under this monarch . . . only bees quarrel in collecting dews; the only feet cut off are those in metre: only *ashtapadas* teach the positions of the *chaturanga*.'

The *ashtapada* was the sixty-four-square gaming board, *chaturanga* was the Sanskrit name for chess and also meant (here lies the pun) an army, or its formation. The meaning is therefore certain, but hardly informative. The problems presented by chess in India can only be fully grasped with the realization that there are just two more surviving references to it in the whole literature of the sub-continent up to 1000, by which time Islam had developed the formidable technical works of as-Suli and al-Lajlaj. Both are ninth century in date. The first is the *Haravijaya* ('Victory of Siva') of Ratnakara, written just before 850. In another punning passage he mentions the four elements of the chess set, or of the army: foot-soldiers, horses, chariots and elephants. The second, the *Kavyalankara* of Rudrata, was written around the end of the ninth century and contains a number of metrical puzzles: verses in which the syllables were set out in a grid pattern so as to make sense either when read consecutively, or when read according to the movements of a chess piece from square to square. This defines the move of several of the pieces, though one cannot eliminate the suspicion that the poet bent the rules in order to make his task more possible. Ratnakara and Rudrata wrote in the far north-western kingdom of Kashmir, which suggests that by their time the game had spread across northern India from the central Ganges basin where it may have originated. On the other hand, there is no evidence to support the idea that chess had reached the south by 1000, though it might have done so. Yet a further complication arises from the fact that Islamic influences were beginning to impinge on western India as early as the eighth century, preparing the way for the great destructive campaigns of

1190–1230, which spread Muslim rule across the north of the continent, to Bengal in the east. The conquerors not only destroyed a great deal, they also brought their own institutions with them, so making it dangerous to use later sources as evidence for pre-Islamic culture.

The conclusion to be drawn from all this is a depressing one. Very little is known from indigenous sources about chess in India for almost half a millennium after its first appearance around the year 600; not even enough to resolve with absolute certainty such basic problems as whether the 'original' chess was played with dice, whether it was a game for two or four players, and what were the moves of the pieces. It is therefore natural to turn to the reports of outside observers and visitors to India, even if they do not seem at first sight to be much more encouraging. The *Chatrang-namak* gave the name of the king who challenged Nushirwan as Dewasarm, which sounds Indian, but no one has managed to identify the name with a historical ruler. The later Arabic legends afford a variety of names: usually Balhait or Shihram for the king and Qaflan or Sassa ben Dahir for the philosopher who invented the game. Of this selection only Sassa (originally Khakha) and Dahir are genuinely Indian: both were rulers of the western kingdom of Sind in the seventh century, whose names reached the Arab world because they had come into contact with invading Muslim armies. They lived too late to have invented chess, or even to have transmitted it to the west. Most Muslim writers knew little about India, as can be seen from their habit of describing it as a single unitary kingdom, on the model of Persia.

It is only after 1000 that there is a direct account of Indian chess by an Arab observer, the scientist and geographer al-Biruni, who travelled in western India around the year 1030. Al-Biruni was for a time attached to the court of the ruthless Mahmud of Ghazna (997–1030) who was attempting to extend Muslim power in the area, but seems also to have employed some of his loot on literary patronage (Firdausi, author of the *Shahnama*, was another recipient). Al–Biruni's account of Indian chess is detailed and circumstantial, but it has tended to create more problems than it has solved, because most of it is given up to an account of a form of chess played by four players and with the use of dice to decide which piece could be moved. Was this the typical chess of the period in India, or even the original version of the game? A twelfth-century Arabic manuscript, probably quoting the earlier work of al-Adli, preserves the tradition that the Persians modified the game which they had received from India: 'this is the form of chess which the Persians took from the Indians, and which we took from the Persians. The Persians altered some of the rules, as is agreed.' Could these alterations have involved the re-shaping of the whole game? As has already been emphasized, there is little enough evidence on which to base a judgement.

Instead, any argument must rely on relative evidence and degrees of probability. From India, varieties of chess spread not only west to Persia and to Europe, but also north to Tibet and Central Asia, south to Malaya, and east to Burma and Indo-China. In all of these places chess survived as a game for two players, which is also the dominant form of the traditional game in India itself. It is true that there is no early evidence from any part of this diaspora, and that the Indian element, usually evidenced by one or two terms of Sanskrit origin, was often overlaid by successive waves of Muslim or European influence before reliable evidence is available. Naturally too there were some links between Persia and Central Asia, or even the Far East, at an early date. Nevertheless, it does seem that chess must have been originally exported from India as a game for two players, to have survived in that form alone over virtually the whole of Asia and beyond. There is no tradition of a contest for popularity between two forms of the game in these lands. Nor does any later Indian writer suggest that the two types of chess to be found there in his own day were anything other than variants of a common native stock. It is therefore overwhelmingly likely that the chess for four players was an elaboration of the original form never employed outside India, while even in India it never displaced the parent game. This was the conclusion of Murray and van der Linde.[6] It is easy too to see why al-Biruni found this alien form of chess so much more interesting than the familiar game for two players, and left such a detailed description of it. Unfortunately, this still leaves many unsolved problems about the early Indian chess and the possible changes effected in Persia, as it moved west. Al-Biruni described in detail some subtle variants of the game, in the placing of some of the pieces and their moves, even when he was writing about two-handed chess. Most of these do not survive in the 'native chess' of India, but they have been preserved in the traditional games of Burma and Indo-China, which suggests that his observation was accurate. It seems most likely that the earliest Indian chess was a game between two players, but that it permitted considerable fluctuations in the rules of play. The ironing-out of these variations must have been the Persian alterations in chess which al-Adli or his redactor had in mind; indeed he said himself in the same passage that the Indians place the piece called the elephant on corner squares and move it in a different way from 'the form of chess we have taken from the Persians and which is played now'. The luxuriance of Indian terminology and representational chessmen (elephants, chariots, camels, horses) may have led astray outside observers, and so explains contradictions in the sources. On one last matter, whether or not the early Indian chess was played with dice, there is simply no evidence on which to base a general conclusion. Al-Biruni saw dice being used in the four-handed game (throw two to move the chariot, three for the horse, and so on), but this is a practice which continually crops up in the history of pre-modern chess, particularly when gambling was involved. The *Chatrang-namak* described *chatrang* as a game of pure skill but the dice were not unknown in Islam, and certainly reappeared more frequently in medieval Europe. There is no clue preserved in the structure of the game to betray whether the 'original' chess was played with dice or not.

India, China and beyond

If it is so difficult to reconstruct the history of chess in India after 600, by which time it had already begun its journey to Persia and the west, it must seem quite impossible to reach any conclusions about the game's actual invention, before 600. Yet this has been a subject of almost continual controversy, and still arouses much interest. Murray quoted with approval a remark by D.W. Fiske: 'Before the seventh century of our era, the existence of chess in any land is not demonstrable by a single shred of contemporary or trustworthy documentary evidence. . . . Down to that date it is all impenetrable darkness.'[7] Can anything at all be known about this prehistoric period?

All that is known for certain in India is the existence of the two technical terms: *chaturanga* and *ashtapada*. *Chaturanga* is a very early word in its literal sense of 'four-limbed', and by the first or second century, if not earlier, it had been applied to the Indian army with its four arms of foot-soldiers, cavalry, chariots and elephants. *Ashtapada* (literally 'eight-footed') was applied to the sixty-four-square gaming board by Patanjali as early as the second century BC. The long history of these words before they can be proved to have been applied to chess in the seventh century leads to two main conclusions: the first Indian chess was explicitly framed to imitate contemporary warfare, and the board of sixty-four squares was used for some other purpose before chess was invented. At this point speculation begins. Murray's theory was that the *ashtapada* was used for another sort of game: a race game with dice and counters like backgammon or ludo, before it was appropriated by the inventor of chess. He was able to point to several references in early (pre-500) Sanskrit literature which mention the *ashtapada* in a context of gaming, and the fact that a race game was certainly played on an eight-by-eight board in the far south of India at a later date.[8] Race games are generally thought to predate related games of strategy, and backgammon itself, with its elongated two × twelve board, was known in India in the third century. Murray's idea is therefore plausible, but it cannot be proved to be the only possible solution. Some critics prefer to associate the *ashtapada* from its origins with a kind of proto-chess, of which nothing is known. Others regard both the board and the game, *ashtapada* and *chaturanga*, as derived from divinatory or astrological symbolism, which opens up a whole new field of enquiry.

The recent ideas put forward along these lines are best characterized by the evidence they employ: archaeological or documentary. It has already been pointed out that archaeology is generally of little use in studying the origins of chess because so few very early chess pieces survive. Even when promising objects are discovered it is almost impossible to prove that they are true chess pieces and not just figurines, short of a complete set or something approaching it. This objection applies in full force to some animal figures excavated in southern Uzbekistan in 1972 and dated by Russian archaeologists to the second century. True, one of them looks like an elephant and another like a camel, but this is hardly sufficient by itself to prove that they are really chess pieces. Russians have a long history of wishful thinking about the antiquity of chess in their country. Nor is the release of press pictures of these objects displayed on a modern chess board calculated to reassure the sceptic. The nomads of western and central Asia (including parts of present-day USSR, Afghanistan and Iran) have frequently acted as cultural intermediaries between the settled civilizations of India, China and Persia, so that the game of chess might have appeared there quite early in its history, but a date in the second century AD is much too early to fit with what is known from other sources. The leading Soviet chess historian I.M. Linder does not go beyond the cautious statement that the existence of a proto-chess with figurine pieces at this early date is 'plausible', but that if it did exist, its form is uncertain.[9] Even more doubts must be raised about some bone pieces excavated at Venafro in Campania in 1932, and dated by Italian archaeologists of that time to the third or fourth century.[10] The pieces are unquestionably chessmen of Arabic design, which raises severe doubts about the proposed date. The suggestion that they were brought back from the east by Roman soldiers does not inspire much confidence either.

More important are theories based on documentary evidence, which seek to clarify the origin of chess by studying all games known to be of an early date, which appear to resemble chess, and can be related to it in some way. The possible race game precedent for chess in India, with the link provided by the use of a common board, has already been mentioned. Beyond that it is hard to go. Board games in general are of course very ancient, and can be traced back to boards excavated from the first city of Ur and paintings of players in tombs of the Egyptian Old Kingdom (both about 2500 BC) but none earlier than chess can be shown to have been a game of strategy between equally matched forces made up of diverse elements: that was the real innovation that produced its peculiar complexity. Furthermore, this fact has been known for quite a long time, since the resolution of the eighteenth-century debates about classical Greek and Roman games. In view of this it is hardly surprising that new ideas have come from a different line of research: the revival of Stewart

Culin's nineteenth-century theories about the magical or religious origins of all board games. In the hands of Joseph Needham and others, this has led to the suggestion that the historical chess of seventh-century India was directly descended from a divinatory game (or ritual) in China.[11]

This so-called 'Chinese origin of chess' raises a number of problems. Chinese chess itself is well known as a variant of the game, hitherto regarded as the product of introduction from India at some date after 600. The earliest reference to its existence occurs in the *Yu Kuai Lu* of Niu Seng-Ju, written around the year 800. It has a story, supposedly set in 762, of a man who dreamt of a battle in which the moves of the forces: horses, commanders, waggons and armoured men, resembled those in Chinese chess. He awoke to find a set of chess men buried in an old tomb in a nearby wall. Further references to this game proliferate in the Sung period (after 960). The problem with Chinese chess is that it differs more from the Indian forms of the game than any of the other Asiatic derivatives, in Burma, Indo-China or Malaya. Only the Japanese chess, *shogi*, is more distant and that was a later derivation from China. The modern Chinese game is played on a board nine squares by eight, but the pieces move on the intersections of the lines rather than on the squares themselves, so that the actual playing area is ten by nine, and in medieval times was probably eleven by eleven. The pieces are not carved figurines but inscribed discs and there are also pieces, like the cannon, unknown anywhere else. Chinese chess therefore has some claim to be regarded as a game apart, and indeed in Burma and parts of Indo China it is played alongside 'Indian' chess without being confused with it. All the same there are enough features in common, like the exact parallel in the position and move of the horses, to rule out independent invention, which is anyway unlikely in the case of such a complex game. One of these games must have influenced the other.

Unlike the Persians, the Chinese do not preserve any tradition of receiving chess from India, so there is no positive documentary evidence to resolve the issue. Instead the argument has fallen back on the general indebtedness of China to Indian culture in certain respects, but even more on the central fact that Chinese chess can only be proved to be in existence by *c*. 800, almost two centuries after its appearance is documented in India and Persia. Needham opened up new possibilities by drawing attention to much earlier Chinese evidence for activities related to chess by their terminology, and so at least potentially forms of 'proto-chess'. The usual Chinese term for chess is *hsiang chhi*, but both the ideograms which make up the name are capable of a variety of meanings. *Chhi* is the usual symbol for such board games, as in *wei chhi*, another Oriental game which has become popular in the west under the name of Go. *Hsiang* has two relevant meanings: 'elephant' and 'image'; a related but different ideogram also transliterated as *hsiang* can mean diviner or counsellor. In view of this it proves nothing to find examples of the two ideograms separately. Even if they are found together, the phrase 'image-game' is still a very general one, and without contextual evidence it is hard to be sure that chess is referred to. The case is rather similar to that of the Indian *chaturanga*. In fact, as Needham has shown, there are references to *hsiang chhi* in works of the sixth century, in connection with an 'image-game' devised by the Emperor Wu Ti of the northern Chou (560–578) in 569. Not content with inventing this, the emperor wrote a treatise on it, then gathered all his officials into a palace hall and gave them lectures on the subject. Later historians were anxious to emphasize that the emperor would not have spent all this time on his *hsiang chhi* if it had merely been chess. For instance Kao Chheng wrote in about 1085: 'It had as pieces the sun, moon, stars and constellations, and was quite different from modern *hsiang chhi*.'[12] The rediscovery of Wang Pao's contemporary commentary on the emperor's treatise has merely confirmed this: Wu Ti's invention was not chess but a complex astrological ritual. Reconstruction suggests that the pieces were thrown on to the board, and divining boards (*shih*) had been used in this way in China since ancient times.

What then was the link between this type of divination and chess? Needham's theory at this point requires a leap of faith, based on the belief that the central characteristics of chess, opposed equal forces and a hierarchy of symbolic pieces, could only have come about through astrology: 'in China, and in China alone, on account of the dominance of the Yin-Yang theory of the macrocosm, could a divination technique or 'pre-game' have been devised which was both astrological and yet had a sufficient combat element to enable it to be vulgarized into a purely military symbolism.'[13] This may be compared with Culin's views on early Indian chess: 'it may be assumed that the board, if not indeed all boards upon which games are played, stands for the world and its four quarters (or the year and its four seasons) and that the game was essentially divinatory.'[14] Both of these are alarmingly general arguments with which to approach the history of a single game like chess. There are two reasons why their importance should not be over-estimated: the first is that they might be wrong, the second is that they might be irrelevant.

Thus, to find the divination theory unproven it is only necessary to believe that chess might have been invented independently, as a game of military symbolism from the beginning. No one has shown that this could not have been the case. Needham's more specific argument based on Wu Ti's 'image-game' is very vulnerable to criticism drawn from dating. If the 'image-game' was really invented in 569, it could hardly have been modified into chess proper, in India or in China, and then been well established as far away as Persia by 600. For this reason alone, it still seems more likely that true chess reached China from India, and it was only in the course of its subsequent transition to Chinese chess that it acquired the name of *hsiang chhi* and an admixture of astrological influence, a process probably completed by 800. Equally important is the point that divinatory 'proto-chess' may simply be an irrelevance. What has patronisingly been called vulgarization 'into a purely military symbolism' is the real point at which the game was invented; from that point on chess pursued its own independent existence, devoid of astrological significance. Certainly the divination theory has led Needham into error when he argues that 'if our general conclusions so far about the origin of true chess are right, we might expect to find widespread traces of astronomical symbolism clinging to it throughout later centuries. All historians of chess have agreed that this was in fact the case . . .'[15] In reality there is no such agreement, and of the five examples quoted by Needham at least three do not refer to chess at all. Nearly all the Arabic legends about chess have military or political meanings, and not divinatory ones, and although there are many hundreds of allusions to the symbolic significance of chess in the course of its later history in the medieval west, only an insignificantly tiny proportion of them have any connection whatsoever with divination or astrology.

Unless further evidence is forthcoming, it remains probable that chess was devised, as Murray thought it was, in northern India. Since the earliest evidence cannot be placed prior to 600, the provisional date of its invention must be in the sixth century; it could have been earlier, but to propose earlier dates is mere guesswork in the present state of knowledge. Only in one respect does it seem necessary to revise Murray's conclusions, and that is his contention (more explicit in his unrevised *Short History of Chess* than in his considered writing) that the game was the creation of a single individual. A gradual and cooperative process seems more likely, but we shall probably never know for certain.

The first chess players

Elucidating the early history of chess has proved a difficult task. Before 800 documentary evidence shrinks to a few ambiguous fragments. Also, before 800 chess did not possess the relative fixity of rule which it assumed in the Arab world after that date. Even to establish the basic facts of first appearance and dissemination it has been necessary to examine every change in terminology, in the moves of the pieces, and in the rules generally, and the limited information produced by this process does not seem to hold out much hope of reaching conclusions about the social status of the game in different early cultures.

It follows from what has been said already that the elements of early chess were shaped in imitation of warfare, and in particular of Indian warfare, though hardly so closely that the game could have been regarded as an adjunct of formal military training. The *chaturanga*, or four-fold army of infantry, cavalry, chariots and elephants, was traditional in northern India; Greek sources suggest that Alexander the Great faced this kind of formation on his invasion of the Indus valley in 326 BC. But from the first century onwards war chariots were little used, and by the fifth century they had become hardly more than transport waggons. Equally, Indian military theorists continued to regard the elephant corps as of vital importance down to the twelfth century or later, yet in the commonest form of Indian chess the elephants ended up as rather weak pieces. All this suggests that the game was modelled on a traditional image of war rather than close observation of contemporary reality. Like chess in Islam or medieval Europe it should probably be seen primarily as a game, albeit one with symbolic overtones, which helped to imbue it with status and prestige.

There is ample evidence that plausible conditons for the invention and practice of chess existed in fifth- and sixth-century India. The fifth-century Hun invasions destroyed the political unity of northern India, but the surviving smaller kingdoms did not lapse into barbarism. Patronage of Hindu and Buddhist intellectual centres continued, though the Buddhists suffered more from the invasions. By 500 the mathematician Aryabhata had calculated *pi* as 3.1416 and the length of the solar year as 365.358 days. The existence and nature of a leisured urban class is shown in the rather earlier *Kamasutra*. This text describes not merely sexual techniques but a whole cultivated life style, including decoration of the house and landscape gardening, patronage of the arts and literary discussion, music and board games. Outdoor games were much less common, except among children. Once invented, chess was not dependent for its survival on a high level of prosperity and formal culture. As it spread through Asia it already began to display a characteristic adaptability, both as a game and as a cultural form. In Sumatra, for instance, nineteenth-century travellers found that native players spent a few minutes making a new set for each game of chess, using a piece of bamboo or a palm leaf picked up on the spot. A simple economy or technology does not necessarily imply a simple culture, as anthropologists are only too well aware. Also, in societies less rigidly stratified than India, the game might spread more widely through the population. It is true that in none of these places so far as we know did chess develop a technical literature, and hence a more precise definition of the rules, as occurred in Islam.

There is more surviving evidence from the Arab world on which it is possible to base a judgement about the appeal of chess. The legal status of the game and the attempts made to improve it have already been described. After 750 (if not before) chess spread through the whole Muslim world, a great shifting mass of distinct states and peoples from Spain to the Indian frontier all nominally professing the Islamic religion, so it is hard to generalize about this. The concentration of the sources on famous players and courtly patronage may conceal the wider popularity of the game, but clearly any such popularity must have varied from one area to another. Only the most severe sects tried to enforce a legal ban on chess, but most orthodox (*Sunni*) Muslims insisted that non-representational pieces were used, in accordance with the scriptural ban on images, and (rather less successfully) that there was no gambling. The game retained its military symbolism, but in a rather unspecific way; without carved forms to play with and through changes in the language, the original Indian and Persian names of some of the pieces began to recede. Their meanings were still known, but not widely understood.

By the ninth and tenth centuries at least, chess was widely disseminated in the Arab world and had reached a considerable level of sophistication in the works of as-Suli and al-Lajlaj. One final problem about the Arab game is why its technical standard never progressed much beyond these writers until the introduction of European chess in modern times. As-Suli and al-Lajlaj became heroic figures whose ideas and achievements could never be surpassed, but merely handed on, as they were by the compilers of our surviving manuscripts. New collections of chess problems (*mansubat*) were made, but the problem collection had become rather more a minor literary form than a contribution to theory. Attention was focused on fictional attributions and romantic stories attached to the problems: the provinces, fortunes and wives staked on the outcome of the games they represent. One such story concerns a wife called Dilaram, who saved herself from the traditional fate worse than death by whispering the solution of a chess problem to her husband at the critical stage. This fits in very well with the normal form of the *mansuba*, in which the player to move must mate his opponent because he is threatened with mate himself and has no defence, a technique familiar to thriller writers of all ages.

Only one writer, in the fifteenth century, is known to have claimed an advance on all previous knowledge of chess. He was the author of a Persian manuscript in the library of the Royal Asiatic Society and probably the man known as Ali Shatranji, who played chess at the court of Timur. He may, as he says, have travelled throughout Iraq and Muslim India and defeated all comers, but some at least of the problems he attributed to himself were known earlier. In the event he had no successors, and his achievements turned out to be as transitory as the military conquests of his famous patron. Perhaps this failure was not altogether surprising, as in many respects no one in Latin Christendom either produced a real advance on the early Arabic theorists, not until the changes in the rules in the fifteenth century created a new point of departure. In the meantime the game made further progress geographically. By 900 or so the only part of the Mediterranean littoral ignorant of chess was that of western Europe. This state of affairs did not last very long.

CHAPTER TWO
The Symbolic Game of the Middle Ages

At some unknown date before AD 1000 chess was introduced into western Europe, and Europe was to be the cradle of its future development for most of the next thousand years. Initially, as an exotic oriental curiosity, the game must have had the appeal of the unfamiliar, but within a few generations it was more-or-less fully absorbed and took on the learning and outlook of Latin christendom. Some aspects of this, like the names and design of the chessmen, have clung to the game ever since; others have progressively been lost and must now be reconstructed by sifting surviving (often fragmentary) historical, literary and archaeological evidence. From this process of reconstruction there emerges the place of chess in the hierarchical society of the middle ages. There also emerges something much more surprising: the special significance of chess in a largely alien thought world, a significance based on myths and hidden meanings as much as on the actual practice of the game. But first it is necessary to look at the evidence for another much-debated question of origins: how *did* chess first reach the medieval West?

Introduction to the West

The surviving evidence for the introduction of chess into western Europe in the early middle ages is extremely diverse, but still leaves many questions unanswered. There are only a few references to the game in written sources from before 1050, or even 1100, and they are tantalizingly short and ambiguous. In itself there is nothing surprising about this; not very much secular literature survives from the tenth and eleventh centuries, and ecclesiastical disapproval must initially have restricted clerical interest in the new diversion. But it does mean that written records cannot be relied on to give more than preliminary clues about where and when chess was first played in the West. The earliest known literary account of the game, the so-called 'Einsiedeln Verses', can be dated with reasonable accuracy to just before the year 1000, but chess may well have been known in Europe for a generation or even a century before it reached the monastery at Einsiedeln in Switzerland, where the text was copied and preserved. Nor are the opinions of later medieval writers about the origins of the game particularly helpful. Once (after 1100 or so) chess had become accepted as a regular feature of noble life, they were generally prepared to believe that it had always been so, and to attribute it indifferently to the court of Charlemagne, the court of King Arthur, or the siege of Troy, the last being an especially popular date for its supposed invention.

The historian must therefore seek out other sources to augment his meagre store of information, though this is not easily done. A number of problems complicate the use of archaeological evidence, most of them already referred to in relation to the origins of the game. Medieval chessmen rarely survive in more than ones and twos; the seventy-eight twelfth-century pieces found on the Isle of Lewis in 1831 and now mostly in the British Museum are quite exceptional in this respect. The individual specimens are usually hard to date and to interpret. As miniature carvings they were subject to the same range of influences as other decorative art, from the taste of the patron to the technique of the artist. Primitive workmanship or design of chess pieces does not always imply a primitive understanding of the game, or its recent reception, unless this can be confirmed by other evidence. It follows that any attempt to link the stylistic sources of chess pieces with the dissemination of chess itself must be based on direct imitation; art-historical remarks like 'there is a hint of Byzantine infuence in this male profile' do not carry the argument very far. Nevertheless, used with caution archaeological and material evidence may help to fill gaps in the written records. A second means of achieving this lies in philology. By comparing the earliest known chess terms, in Latin and all the vernacular languages, and their derivation one from another, it is possible to work out at least some of the routes by which the game was originally transmitted around Europe. And by comparing this with what is known about sound changes and other shifts in the individual languages, it may also be possible to establish the dates at which chess terms first appeared in each of them, at least within broad limits. Naturally, there are difficulties with this approach too. Etymology is not a precise science, and few modern writers share the confidence of an earlier generation which led H.J.R. Murray to write of 'the laws of sound development' and of 'the relentless certainty of their action',[1] in relation to time and place.

But the linguistic evidence does make it possible to resolve one vital issue at the outset. All chess terms used in Europe at an early date – the words for the game itself, for the different pieces, and for 'check' and 'checkmate' – were derived from Arabic. They were either straightforward adoptions of Arabic words, where the original meaning was unknown or there was no suitable western equivalent (such as *rukh* into Latin *rochus*) or translations of the Arabic into European words with approximately the same sense (such as *shah* into Latin *rex*). The nomenclature will be discussed in more detail below, but this is sufficient for the present purpose; it demonstrates that chess must have reached Europe directly from Islam, where it was already flourishing, and not through the intermediate agency of the Greek Byzantine Empire. The point or points of its introduction into the West must therefore have been points of contact with the Muslim world, through trade, diplomacy, or coexistence along a frontier. At first sight it is surprising that the game did not filter into Europe through eastern Christendom, but this connection seems never to have been made; there are no hints of Greek influence in the later western terminology. The Greeks knew chess as *zatrikion*, a hellenization of the Persian *chatrang*, which suggests that they received it at an early date, certainly before 900. The Arab historian at-Tabari described a letter written by the Emperor Nicephorus to the Caliph Harun al-Rashid in 802, in which chess was mentioned, and though this hardly counts as reliable evidence of date, the story must at least have been plausible to at-Tabari and his readers in the early years of the tenth century. Only a generation later, and still before the earliest dateable references in the West, al-Mas'udi (d. 956) mentioned Byzantine chess as an established fact.

Various explanations might be suggested for the failure of the Greeks to pass on the game to their Latin co-religionists in this period. The first is that although chess was evidently known in Byzantium, it may never have been very popular there. Murray lists only four traceable allusions to *zatrikion* in medieval Greek literature: an early but undated work on the interpretation of dreams, the *Alexiad* of Anna Comnena and a commentary by John Zonares on the canons of the eastern church (both twelfth century), and a fifteenth-century history by Michael Ducas.[2] Yet despite this paucity, and the fact that Zonares only mentions chess in order to condemn it as contrary to ecclesiastical law, the question of the game's popularity in the Eastern Empire remains an open one. Writing at a time when this literature was little investigated, and still less appreciated, Murray freely admitted that he drew his information from a few seventeenth- and eighteenth-century glossaries and reference books. The growth of modern Byzantine scholarship has made it clear just how much more material there is to be examined, and modern writers who quote Murray's few examples as though they were based on a survey of all the available evidence seriously distort the position.

More research is needed but it is likely that chess was much more common in Byzantium than is usually supposed. There is no real reason to think that ecclesiastical hostility was effective in suppressing the game in the East while it failed in the West. The best-known reference in a Byzantine source is that in Anna Comnena's history of the reign of her father, the Emperor Alexius I (1081–1118). She mentions that he was in the habit of playing chess with members of his court on awaking in the morning, and does not imply that this was a special eccentricity on his part, though she was well aware that the game was of Persian origin, 'invented by the luxurious Assyrians and brought thence to us'.[3]

The second way of explaining why chess did not reach Europe from Byzantium lies in the whole context of cultural contacts between East and West, and so is equally relevant to the process by which it did eventually reach Europe, from Islam. It is a paradoxical but well-established fact that even in the period of the crusades more new learning came to the West from the Muslim 'enemy' than through eastern Christian civilization. This was true not only of science and mathematics, some of which like chess originated in India, but also of classical literature. The Aristotelian texts which were to revolutionize European philosophy were first translated into Latin in the twelfth century from Arabic, and the main translating centres were in areas of cultural coexistence: Spain and Sicily, and to a lesser extent the Latin states founded in Palestine by the crusaders. In this respect the period 1050 to 1100 was something of a watershed, as it witnessed movements of Christian expansion into these very areas: the Spanish 'Reconquest' after 1050, the Norman conquest of Sicily (1061–91) and the First Crusade (1096–99). But even before 1050 the first tentative signs of transmission were becoming apparent. Gerbert of Aurillac, later Pope Sylvester II, built up a great reputation as an arithmetician in the 970s and 980s on the strength of a few years study in Spain. The introduction of arithmetic into Europe forms a plausible analogue for the introduction of chess, as both involved a transfer of practical skill, but probably of explanatory texts as well. If the resemblance is accepted it would again point to Spain and southern Italy as the most likely areas of reception in the first instance. Following the same reasoning, it is correspondingly less likely that chess was brought to the West by links of trade or diplomacy. Trade routes may have acted as channels for the movement of new technical ideas, though the point is debatable, but not usually for the transfer of complex intellectual activities like chess, which were largely restricted to the clergy and aristocracy during the early Middle Ages.

In the main, the documentary evidence bears out these hypotheses. What was for a long time thought to be the earliest reference to chess in a western document occurs in the will of Ermengaud I, Count of Urgel on the Spanish marches, by which he gave his chessmen to the monastery of St Gilles (probably St Gilles at Nîmes near Montpellier) 'for the use of the church'. The will is dated 1008, and there is no reason to doubt this, though Murray suggested 1010 as an alternative. The widow of Ermengaud's elder brother, the Countess Ermessind, made a similar gift to the same church in her will of 1058, though this time the chess pieces were specifically said to be 'of crystal'. By a striking coincidence a collection of rock-crystal pieces of an early date have survived in a Catalonian church treasury, and are now in the diocesan museum at Lerida. These so-called Ager Chessmen follow the typical Islamic non-representational design, despite their Christian provenance, and are probably very similar to those involved in the eleventh-century wills. So far as it goes this evidence suggests the introduction of chess on the Christian side of the Spanish frontier sometime before the year 1000.

But early evidence also survives from other parts of Europe. The *Versus de scachis*, a ninety-eight-line poem describing the game and its rules, survives in two manuscripts (one incomplete) at the Swiss monastery of Einsiedeln, now a Baroque showpiece. Murray assigned the poem tentatively to the eleventh century, but a more recent examination of the manuscripts has dated one of them with a high degree of probability to the 990s, even earlier than the first Spanish will.[4] How then did the game appear in central Europe by this time? There were diplomatic contacts between the German Emperor Otto I (936–973) and the caliphs of Cordova in the 950s and 960s. Also, styles of manuscript illumination in Swiss monasteries, especially Reichenau on Lake Constance, less than fifty miles north of Einsiedeln, show definite signs of Byzantine influence in this period, or so it is believed. But these associations are tenuous ones and there is no corroborative evidence to link them with chess. It seems much more likely that the game came to this region from Italy. Otto I and his successors, especially Otto III (983–1002), made strenuous efforts to extend their power in Italy, and also patronized the abbey at Einsiedeln and other centres on the Alpine routes leading south from their main power base in Germany. The Latin epic *Ruodlieb*, which contains a reference to chess, was probably written by a monk at Tegernsee in south Germany, another monastery closely linked with the imperial family. *Ruodlieb* was once dated about 1030, but is now usually placed around 1050 or a little later. It is also relevant that there are a number of surviving chess pieces heavily influenced by Arabic forms, which appear to be of an early date and to come from southern Italy. Sicily itself was in Muslim hands throughout the tenth century. Taken together, this leads to the conclusion that the game probably reached Italy as well as Spain before the end of the millennium.

Such information as can be derived from the study of chess terminology is mostly consistent with dissemination from Spain and Italy in this way, but the interpretation of the linguistic evidence presents a number of problems. The words for most chess terms, such as the names of the pieces, are unknown before the thirteenth century in the European vernacular languages. This means that in the early and formative period, c. 1000–1200, it is only possible to compare regional variations in the Latin vocabulary of the game, and not those in the spoken dialects of lay society. The one exception to this is the name 'chess' itself. The French *Chanson de Roland*, which attained its final form soon after 1100, contains a reference to *esches*; and a High German glossary compiled in the eleventh and twelfth centuries includes the word *scahzabel*. Both are related to the Latin *scachus* (or *scaccus*), which meant 'check' and 'chessman' as well as 'chess'. All of these formed one large family, from which are descended the modern French *échecs*, German *Schach*, English *chess*, and cognate terms in most European languages. Nevertheless the whole family might be said to be descended from an illegitimate ancestor, because the Latin *scachus* cannot possibly be derived from the Arabic word for chess, *shatranj*. Instead, by a transfer of meaning which eludes explanation, it comes from the Arabic *shah* or king: the name of one of the pieces. Murray regarded this shift from *shah* to *scachus* as important evidence for dating the introduction of the game into the West. The *sh*-sound was then unknown in Europe, so when Hebrew or Arabic words which incorporated it were adopted in Latin, a replacement had to be found. From classical times to the sixth or seventh century this replacement was *s*- (so that *shah* would have been rendered as *sah*), but thereafter it became *sc*-, as in *scachus*. Later still, by the twelfth and thirteenth centuries, the *sh*- sound began to establish itself in the West, and words like *shah* had no need to undergo a sound change on their reception. But the argument only pins down the first appearance of *scachus* within very broad limits (c. 800–1100) and so adds little to the documentary sources. It is hard to see from this how Murray was led to the conclusion that 'philological evidence requires' chess to have been known in Europe by 900.[5] More recent research has found nothing to confirm his view.

Turning to the Latin vocabulary in use in the eleventh and twelfth centuries to describe the different chess pieces, Table 2 gives some idea of the mixture of translations and adoptions on which it was based.

Again, it is unclear how far this material can be made to throw light on the first introduction of chess in the West. Murray claimed to see in the terms given below 'two well-marked systems of nomenclature': one shown by the retention of Arabisms like *ferzia*, *alphicus* and *rochus*, the other by their translation into supposed equivalents of western origin.[6] The first was characteristic of chess in Spain, and to a lesser extent in France and England; the second was characteristic of the game in Germany, and to a lesser extent Italy and England. Only later, after 1200,

Modern equiv- alent	Arabic term		Pre-1200 Latin terms	
King	Shah	(King)	Rex	(King)
Queen	Firz ⎫ Firzan ⎭	(Vizir or Wise Man)	1 Regina 2 Femina 3 *Ferzia*	(Queen) (Lady)
Bishop	(Al-)Fil	(Elephant)	1 Comes 2 Senex ⎫ Calvus ⎭ 3 *Alphicus*	(Count or Companion) (Old Man or Counsellor)
Knight	Faras	(Horse)	Eques ⎫ Caballarius ⎬ Miles ⎭	(Knight)
Rook	Rukh ⎫ Rokh ⎭	(Chariot)	1 *Rochus* 2 Marchio	(Marquess)
Pawn	Baidaq	(Foot-man)	Pedes	(Foot-man)

Table 2

(The italicized terms seem to have been used only in chess, and almost all medieval writers were ignorant of their original meanings)

did the two systems overlap and merge together. All of this fits in very conveniently with the theory of the game's dual introduction from Spain and Italy. Unfortunately, the evidence simply will not stand up to this weight of interpretation. It is not at all clear that there were 'two well-marked systems', as almost all the variant terms can be found in mixed use in the earliest surviving sources. The tendency for the unfamiliar Arabic words to be translated was apparent almost from the beginning, though the process was carried further as the game spread northwards, particularly in Germany. Moreover, Murray overlooked one obvious reason for the heavily Arabic nomenclature later found in Spain: the existence of *continuing* Muslim influence on Iberian culture, persisting long after the first introduction of chess there. The *Libro del Acedrex* of King Alfonso x of Castile, on which he relied for evidence of the Spanish terms, is not only a later source (compiled in 1283), but one based on a Muslim collection of chess problems. Renewed contacts of this kind helped to distance Spain and Portugal from the rest of Europe. It was only in the Iberian Peninsula that chess was known by a name derived from the Arabic *shatranj*, which became in Spanish *acedrex*, modern *ajedrez*. Consequently, if the nomenclature does suggest any frontiers between zones of influence in European chess, it is the division between Spain and everywhere else which emerges most sharply.

The philological evidence is therefore quite compatible with the conclusions already reached about the reception of the game in the West, but it does not provide independent or conclusive proof of their correctness. It may yield more interesting conclusions when examined from other points of view. For example, the translations of Arabic terms were already shifting chess away from the 'purely military symbolism' (of king, vizir, elephant, horse, chariot and foot soldier) characteristic of the Indian and Muslim game. The appearance of unwarlike figures: the queen, and sometimes bishops, counts or counsellors as well, make it resemble a picture of the state in miniature rather than an army in the field. This was to be of the greatest importance later on, when chess was used as a basis for theorizing, and sermonizing, about the ranks and degrees of Christian society.

Even before this happened, the new identity of some of the chess pieces was reinforced by the design of the men used in actual play. The non-representational Arabic forms found in the earliest western sets gradually became more naturalistic in the course of the eleventh and twelfth centuries. Their characteristic humps and projections were turned into human or animal heads, and the outlines of the pieces were more freely moulded. Eventually the point was reached where the Arabic conventions were abandoned altogether and original forms emerged, shaped in imitation of the new meanings which had been assigned to the different pieces. This kind of fully developed romanesque set can be found in the 'Lewis Chessmen'. Seventy-eight pieces were found on the Isle of Lewis in the Outer Hebrides in 1831, of which sixty-seven are now in the British Museum and eleven in the Museum of National Antiquities of Scotland; no one knows why they were deposited on Lewis in the first place. They originally belonged to four different sets, though five major pieces and forty-five pawns have been lost. Each of the sets consisted of kings, queens, bishops, knights and 'warders' (armed men); the pawns were designed as inanimate objects resembling decorated milestones. The latest critical study suggests that these chessmen, which are carved in walrus ivory, a traditional material of the northern world, were made in Scandinavia around the mid-twelfth century. 'Stylistically they should be placed between about 1135 and 1170 and the fashion of the mitres suggests a date no earlier than about 1150.'[7] The appearance of bishops, with or without the latest fashion in mitres, is of some interest, because there are no references to chess bishops in the documentary sources until after 1200 (see Table 2). It is quite possible that image preceded change of terminology, and that the existence of representational chessmen led to contemporary meanings being applied to the pieces, even when they still retained meaningless, Arabic-derived names. In Spanish, for instance, *ferzia* was mistakenly thought to be the same word as *alferez* ('standard-bearer'), and there were similar instances of bogus attributions springing from the appearance of the carved shapes. The Lewis men are unique, in their quality and in the numbers that have been preserved, but there are enough surviving examples from elsewhere in Europe, particularly Germany and Norman Sicily, to show that the change to representational forms was a general and influential one.

There remains one last theory about the introduction of chess into the West which must be considered. It is based mostly on archaeological evidence. Some historians, impressed by the discovery of apparently early chessmen in northern Europe, particularly some crude whalebone pieces of a strongly Arabic type found at Witchampton in Devon during the 1920s, have argued that the game may have reached the Vikings directly from Islam rather than via Christian Europe. This assumes that chess could have travelled from one culture to the other along Varangian trade routes, which followed the rivers of Russia from Sweden to Byzantium and Persia. It would be dogmatic to rule out the possibility altogether, but the evidence in its favour is extremely problematical. The Witchampton pieces are primitive in design, and have sometimes been dated as early as the tenth century, but this is far from certain; crude workmanship is not always explained by an early date. The chess references in the Norse sagas may mention tenth- and eleventh-century kings, but they were all written after 1200.

Some general considerations are also relevant here. Though there were trade and other links between them, the Swedish 'Vikings' (Varangians) who colonized eastern Europe should not be confused with the Danes and Norwegians who migrated westwards to Britain, Iceland and elsewhere. This makes the suggested route of communication even more tenuous. Secondly, amidst natural admiration for the far-flung trading and raiding activities of the Vikings, one may lose sight of the fact that they were often impervious to the cultures of the peoples they encountered, until their own traditional religion and values began to weaken in the face of Christian conversion in the eleventh century. It is likely that chess replaced more ancient board games of the northern world as part of the same process. The chess nomenclature as it later emerged in the Scandinavian languages is entirely consistent with derivation from the south (probably through Germany), so that even if there was a primitive Viking chess, it must quickly have been overlaid by other influences. It is also relevant that while Russian historians have claimed very early dates for the introduction of the game there (Savenkov in 1905 tried to push this back to the fifth or sixth century), confirmatory evidence is lacking before the twelfth or thirteenth centuries. Much the same may be said of the thesis that chess was brought to Europe by Jewish converts (the Khazars) migrating westwards from what is now southern Russia. Though medieval Jewish communities all over Europe certainly knew and played chess, there is no evidence, even a hint of a tradition, that they were the first to introduce it.[8] In view of all this the verdict must be 'not proven'. The northern route for the introduction of chess into Europe remains an attractive theory, but theory is not turned into fact merely by frequent and enthusiastic repetition.

So how and when did chess enter the medieval West? All conclusions must be treated with caution, but it seems certain that the game came into Spain as part of the general cultural exchanges between Muslim and Christian in the Peninsula, and almost certain that a similar process took place in Italy. The onus of proof still rests on those who want to suggest additional areas of reception. In view of the first appearance of documentary sources around the year 1000, and the philological and archaeological evidence, a target date in the tenth century seems in order.

Chess in Medieval Society

The study of origins presents special difficulties; if only because there is so often an element of chance involved in the question of which contact or which experiment eventually proved fruitful. It may be more profitable to consider why chess, once arrived in Europe, spread across it so rapidly that around 1200 the game was played with roughly the same rules 'from the Indus to the Atlantic and from the Sahara to Iceland'.[9] Certainly this implies that there was a demand for a game like chess from its earliest appearance, a demand sufficient to change it from an oriental curiosity into a regular feature of noble and courtly life, within at the most two centuries and probably much less.

Some clues to this can be derived from the other recreations of the emergent western aristocracies. The further back one goes into the early Middle Ages, the more life was lived out of doors and predominantly in the hours between dawn and dusk, but even then chamber recreations and board games in particular were not unknown. Cards did not appear until the fourteenth century, but dice were already familiar. They could simply be thrown, in order to bet on the result, but they could also be applied to the game of backgammon or 'tables' (in medieval Latin *tabula*), in which there was an element of skill as to how the player used each throw in moving his pieces, or *tabulae*, on the board. Like 'cards', backgammon or tables in the Middle Ages was not a single game; Murray has identified over twenty-five variant games played on the 2 × 12 backgammon board, and there were probably more.[10] *Tabula* was often coupled with chess in medieval sources and so it has very frequently been mistranslated as 'draughts'. There is no basis for this error, despite the fact that both games were played with round flat counters. Draughts was a variant of chess played on the chessboard and so of later introduction; there are only half a dozen references to it before 1500. By contrast tables was a classical survival known in the West since the Roman period, and still played in southern Europe and France during the eleventh century, at the time of the first introduction of chess.

But there were also 'pre-chess' board games in the Germanic and Celtic areas of northern Europe. The game of *fidchell* appears in Irish epics going back to the eighth or ninth century, while the Welsh equivalent, *gwyddbwyll*, is mentioned in the famous collection of early stories called by the general name of the *Mabinogion*. Little is known of their modes of play, but both were certainly games of skill. In the Norse world of the ninth and tenth centuries there was also a characteristic board game, called *hnefatafl*. It seems to have been played between unequal forces on a square board with a central point. One side, consisting of a king and a number of supporting pieces, began in the centre and had the objective of trying to reach the outer edge; the other side, which had about twice as many pieces, tried to hem them in and capture them first. The size of the board and the number of men varied, but the principle was always the same. Before they knew chess, it was this game which the Vikings took with them to Ireland, England and elsewhere; and which is mentioned in the earliest saga literature. A complete 7 × 7 board was excavated at Ballinderry in West Meath in 1932, and fragments of similar ones have been found on other Viking sites, including the ninth-century Gokstad Ship. One last family of games which existed in most of Europe before the advent of chess was that of merels (Latin *merellus*; Arabic *qirq*, and hence in some Spanish sources *alquerque*). These were essentially superior forms of 'noughts-and-crosses', played on a lattice board with the object of putting three or more pieces into alignment. The players entered their men, and then continued to move them until one side or the other was victorious. Like tables, such games can be dated back into ancient times.

This little digression should at least have established one important point. Chess did not become popular in the eleventh and twelfth centuries because it came to people who thought it wholly original, or who had never seen board games before. Rather, chess succeeded by displacing the existing range of games; because it was inherently more complex and interesting or because it was introduced as one aspect of a new dominant culture. This second process might involve actual conquest, as in the Norman invasion of England, or just conversion and imitation, as in Scandinavia. The consequences for the older games were naturally severe. *Fidchell* and *gwyddbwyll* disappeared so completely that there is now no evidence from which they can be reconstructed. *Hnefatafl* was no longer played in noble society, because it drops out of the literary sources, but it may have survived among lower-status groups. It reappeared in a simplified form as the folk game of 'fox and geese' during the sixteenth and seventeenth centuries. Murray also found valuable evidence for reconstructing the original rules from a variant called *tablut*, which had survived among the Lapps and was recorded by the botanist Linnaeus in 1732.[11] But tables continued to be played alongside chess, if only because it was so much better adapted for gambling. So too did merels, though increasingly regarded as simple and uncultivated; its demotion to the modern children's game of 'noughts-and-crosses' being the end result. Combined boards for all three games were still quite common in the Middle Ages, and became known in English, confusingly, as 'a pair of tables'. They usually consisted of a flat square box with a chess-board on one side and a board for merels on the other, while the whole box could be opened flat to play backgammon. But in general chess tended to blot out the earlier games which it replaced, and with which it had most in common. The story of 'Peredur' in the *Mabinogion* includes a magic *gwyddbwyll* set in which the pieces moved of their own accord. When Chrétien de Troyes adapted this into French in the late twelfth century (as 'Percival') he took over the idea, but rendered the game quite naturally as chess, probably not even realising that a different game had originally been intended. The change-over was effectively complete by his day.

In fact evidence for the spread of chess across Europe increases rapidly after 1050. Murray collected about fifty references to the game in twelfth-century sources, and more have been discovered since. The Norman Conquest probably brought chess to England, though it is just possible that it was known there earlier. Certainly the royal Exchequer at Westminster, which was created sometime after 1106, was referred to as the '*scaccarium*' (standard medieval Latin for chess-board) in a writ of Henry I issued before 1118. It took its name from the chequered cloth, on which financial calculations could be carried out in full view of the sheriff whose account was being investigated, the treasurer who presided, and the members of the court. The *Dialogue of the Exchequer*, written by the Treasurer Richard of Ely in about 1177, makes this quite clear:

> For just as on the chess-board the men are arranged in rows, and move or stand by definite rules and restrictions, some pieces in the foremost rank and others in the foremost position; here too some preside, others assist, and

nobody is free to overstep the appointed laws. . . . Again, just as on a chess-board battle is joined between the kings, here too the struggle is mostly between two men, namely the treasurer and the sheriff . . .[12]

Elsewhere in northern Europe, the same process was taking place. Whatever might be thought about the earlier evidence, the Lewis chessmen show that the game was familiar in Scandinavia and on the main Viking trade routes by 1150. By this date at the latest therefore, chess was played right across Europe from the Mediterranean to the far north. It had displaced earlier pursuits at a time when the dominant groups in western society, the lay aristocracy and the higher clergy, were becoming much more culturally homogeneous and inclined to follow common codes of behaviour. This was very important. Economic growth, greater political security, more readily available education; all of these developments, however tentatively at first, helped to promote chess as one element among many in a new leisured way of life. This way of life was more sophisticated, more affluent, and above all more widely available, than ever before in medieval times.

How then was chess transmitted from one group or one nation to another in the early Middle Ages? Various mechanisms seem to have been involved, some of them dependent on literacy and others not. A number of short didactic texts have survived, describing the rules of the game from first principles, and apparently intended for those who had not encountered it before. The 'Einsiedeln Verses' of *c.* 1000 have already been referred to, and a second poem of this kind, called variously *Ludus scacorum* or *Elegia de Ludo Scachorum*, survives in about ten manuscripts. One of them, unknown to Murray, dates from 1050–1100 and so attests to the poem's early date, though its place of composition is unknown. A third set of verses is preserved in a manuscript written at Winchester in the first half of the twelfth century. By this time the genre was apparently quite well established, and a number of further works were composed between 1150 and 1250. The best known of all perhaps, was a digression on chess included in the mid-thirteenth-century Latin verse romance the *Vetula*, attributed to Ovid in the Middle Ages but probably written by the contemporary Richard de Fournival. The early scientific writer Alexander Neckam also devoted a chapter to chess in his treatise 'On the Natures of Things' (*De Naturis Rerum*) at the end of the twelfth century; he described the game and its rules after the manner of the poetic accounts before going on to condemn it for being passionate and frivolous.

It is striking that all of these descriptions of chess originated within the world of clerical learning, and the earliest of them have a specifically monastic provenance: at Einsiedeln, Winchester, or in the case of one manuscript of the *Ludus scacorum*, Bridlington Priory in Yorkshire. This suggests that the game had sufficient appeal to overcome the initial hostility of the ecclesiastical hierarchy, and that the clergy may even have had a special role in spreading knowledge of it. Like higher learning in general, chess first established itself within the confines of the monasteries, and then spread outwards into the multiplying schools and universities of the twelfth century. Naturally it was hardly at the core of the monastic or academic curriculum, but clerics were now more inclined to stray outside the narrow demands of religious education. The earliest chess treatises often formed parts of miscellaneous compilations, in which especially inquisitive or daring monks recorded things which had interested them: proto-science and mathematics, astrology, unofficial history, and excerpts from dubious classical literature. Some of these subjects later found their way into more broadly-based teaching in the schools, but at first they were regarded as of only marginal value if not actually subversive, by the powerful ecclesiastical corporations. It follows that such texts were not dear to the hearts of official archivists and that only a very small proportion of them have survived. This was certainly true of the chess treatises, with the exception of those which were incorporated in larger and more familiar works like those of Neckam and Fournival. Some of the manuscripts referred to above were only preserved accidentally, by being pasted into the bindings of later books and subsequently recovered. The corollary of a poor survival rate is that such texts *may* originally have been very numerous.

There is other evidence too to suggest that chess had a specific appeal to the medieval clergy. The frequent repetition of ecclesiastical bans early on, followed by a progressive relaxation, indicates clearly that the church authorities were unable to control or suppress the game. Manuscripts dealing with it written by churchmen for their own use increase in number over the years. In the second half of the thirteenth century one of the earliest known European collections of chess problems was copied at two English monasteries, Abbotsbury and Cerne Abbey in Dorset. Also, at the same time as they were taking up chess, twelfth-and thirteenth-century clerks were adopting another diversion recently invented by one of their own number: *rhythmomachy*, or 'the philosopher's game'. This was a game played on an enlarged chess-board eight squares by sixteen, with twenty-nine white pieces and twenty-eight black ones. The pieces were squares, circles and triangles, each bearing a number, and the rules included captures determined by arithmetical relationships between groups of men. The whole game was therefore extremely complicated and never really rivalled chess, though it lasted through the Middle Ages and was advocated in one or two printed books during the sixteenth century. But its first appearance around 1100 and early popularity provides valuable evidence for the intellectual climate of the period, and in particular the fascination exerted by new and arcane forms of learning.

Intellectual diversions had a dual appeal to such circles of educated men: first for their inherent interest as recreational activities, and second for their possible symbolic meanings. In the case of *rhythmomachy* this was numerical and geometric symbolism, both common in twelfth-century thought; in the case of chess it was usually political and moral meanings that were found.

But chess also spread rapidly through lay society, by means which did not depend so much on the transmission of written texts. This was achieved as soon as the game was included in the formal upbringing of noble youths, a process of training which became steadily more elaborate and demanding as the ideal of courteous knighthood permeated European society. Already at the beginning of the twelfth century, in his 'Clerk's Instruction' (*Disciplina Clericalis*), Petrus Alfonsi listed the seven knightly accomplishments as: 'riding, swimming, archery, boxing, hawking, chess and verse writing'.[13] Petrus Alfonsi (1062–*c*.1125), a Spanish Jew converted to Christianity in 1106, was an ideal link-man between the two cultures and a representative of twelfth-century new learning. Later in his life he went to England, where he acted as King Henry I's personal physician and passed on his knowledge of Arabic astronomy to at least one pupil, Walcher Prior of Malvern. The 'Clerk's Instruction' itself consisted mostly of Oriental stories like those in the Indian and Persian *Kalila wa Dimna*. Even this striking example of cultural transmission was not unique: a slightly later poem on chess in Hebrew is usually attributed to Abraham ibn Ezra (1092–1167), a Spanish rabbi who travelled widely and probably died in London. There were obviously opportunities here for the exchange of ideas. Many clerks and intellectuals, like Petrus Alfonsi, were not monks but mixed freely with knights and courtiers, sharing many of their attitudes and characteristic pursuits. But it remains true that once chess had gained a foothold in secular society it could spread of its own accord, without any need for the further intervention of the learned. Young men of good birth might be taught such accomplishments by tutors, but it is more likely that they learned by imitating their elders; it was for this reason that men were so eager to have their sons brought up in noble households, where things were correctly done. The great heroes of medieval Romance literature, as it developed in the century after 1150, were all said to have learned chess as part of their education: Tristan in Gottfried von Strassburg's German 'Tristan' poem, Alexander in the French decasyllabic 'Alexander Romance', and Lancelot in the 'Prose Lancelot'. The same was true of a host of minor figures, and the game frequently appears for no special literary purpose, but simply as an adjunct of courtly life. In view of the sheer quantity of such references, it is reasonable to accept them as an accurate reflection of contemporary society. The appearance of chess-boards and sets in royal and aristocratic wills and inventories from the twelfth century onwards, together with the survival of contemporary chessmen, helps to support this conclusion.

The question of how the game fitted into everyday life in monasteries and noble households, how frequently it was played and how seriously it was regarded, is rather harder to answer. Detailed descriptions of chess playing and its social context tend to occur only in literary sources, and these raise particular problems of interpretation, for when the game is not merely mentioned in passing, but contributes to the story or its meaning, we may be dealing with literary conventions which had a life of their own and could diverge from contemporary reality. Thus it was an especially common idea in medieval romances that lovers met over games of chess. Tristan and Iseult were playing at chess during their sea voyage from Ireland to Cornwall, when they accidentally drank the love potion which caused them so much trouble later on. Lancelot and Guinevere, among others, arranged assignations on the pretext of playing chess. In the thirteenth-century '*Huon of Bordeaux*', the hero played against a king's daughter, having agreed that if he lost he would be executed but if won he could spend the night with the princess and receive a hundred marks as well. Here it seems that the whole tradition was already being parodied. Yet the convention was a persistent one, and continues to crop up in later works. The chess game between Ferdinand and Miranda in *The Tempest* is probably an echo of it. Such scenes were frequently portrayed in decorative art; on carved boxes, mirror handles and similar articles especially. Was it a reflection of reality: that the game did indeed provide opportunities for private conversation in the otherwise limited privacy of noble households? It may be so, though the point cannot be proved from non-literary evidence.

Chess also appears in narrative literature, even more commonly, as a cause or justification for quarrels between characters. King John and Fulk in *Fulk fitz Warin*, Renaud and Berthelot in *Renaus de Montaubon*, King Knut and Earl Ulf in the *Olaf Saga* by Snorri Sturluson; all fell out over games of chess, whether by accident or design, and twice with fatal consequences. These three literary examples, though they have a wide geographical spread (England, France and Iceland), all date from the thirteenth century, but they are representative of many similar incidents in sagas, romances and historical epics from the twelfth century to the fifteenth. Sometimes even the boards and pieces themselves were pressed into service as offensive weapons, if they happened to be within reach. Duke Richard of Normandy in *Renaus de Montaubon* and Gawain in Wolfram von Eschenbach's *Parzival* (*c.* 1200–1215) each put up a gallant fight against considerable odds by this means. The problem for the historian is the same as before: did this extraordinary trail of victims have any counterpart in real life, or should it be consigned to the world of make-believe with Renaud's magic horse Bayard, which carried four men into battle at once? The clipped judicial phrases of the 'London Eyre Roll' for the year 1276 suggests that homicidal chess was not quite so fantastic as that. The roll covers crown pleas in the city between 1251 and 1276, and among 300 or so pleas, the game was mentioned in two:[14]

[16 August 1254] William de Wendene of Essex was playing chess with Robert son of Bernard, a knight of Essex, in Robert's house in the ward of Ralph Sperling when a quarrel arose between them. Robert the knight's squire intervened with the intention of striking William because he was arguing with his master and William, perceiving this, struck Robert in the stomach with a knife so that he died. William at once fled and took sanctuary.

[1263–1264] David de Bristoll and Juliana wife of Richard le Cordwaner were playing chess together in Richard's house, with several others present. A quarrel arising between them, David struck Juliana in the thigh with a sword, so that she died forthwith. He at once fled.

Reassuringly, a random sampling of other medieval legal records has not yielded more than a few isolated episodes of the same kind, so it seems reasonable to conclude that the habits of chess players with regard to sex and violence reflected the values of the society in which they lived, and that the game itself played only a small part in determining their behaviour. And in some circles at least the game had its modern reputation for being quiet and peaceful. In 1459 Margaret Paston wrote to her husband John:

I sent your eldest son to my Lady Morley to have knowledge what sports were used in her house. . . . And she said that there were no disguisings nor harping nor luting nor singing, nor no loud disports, but playing at the tables and chess and cards. Such disports she gave her folks leave to play and none other.[15]

But literary sources can serve as the starting point for some other and more fruitful lines of enquiry. A mass of references in medieval writing makes it clear that chess was normally played for a stake, as were most games. Muslim attempts to enforce the Prophet's ban on gambling had never had more than qualified success, and western rulers rarely attempted to legislate in this way at all, leaving the matter to local laws and customs. An activity so universal among the ruling class could not in any case be suppressed very easily, and it was uncommon for penalties to be imposed except in the church and clerical institutions like the universities. So, as early as the mid-eleventh century, this was being exploited for poetic effect in the epic *Ruodlieb*. The knight Ruodlieb, while acting as an emissary to a foreign court, is induced to play many chess games with the king and his courtiers while they try to discover his instructions, 'to learn the unknown moves he will make'. One of their devices to embarrass Ruodlieb is to play for high stakes and press him to accept his winnings in order that he might feel in their debt:

At first I refused, indeed I thought it unworthy
For me to make money like that, or for them to be fleeced by me.
I said 'I am not accustomed to growing rich by gaming.'
They said 'While you're with us, live as we do;
When you get home, there you can live as you please.'
When I'd shown enough reluctance, I accepted –
Fortune gave me the advantage, honourably.[16]

The final justification has an authentic ring to it. This pattern of court life is confirmed in later household accounts, like those of Henry VII of England and Charles VII of France which record losses at chess, among other games. A volume in the fifteenth-century library of Charles Duke of Orleans even contained a note to say that he had won it at chess. Also, the diverse chess problem collections, which survive from about 1250 onwards, are full of references to the stakes involved in the game. Part of the popularity of problems arose specifically from the fact that they were well adapted for gambling, avoiding what the Castilian *Libro del Acedrex* of 1283 referred to as 'the weariness which players experience from the long duration of the game when played right through'. By contrast with this, the problemist could demonstrate a position on the board and at once invite onlookers to bet on the likely outcome, or to choose which side they would play against the proposer, who naturally knew the solution in advance and counted on winning most of his bets. For the same reason, well-known problems could be slightly altered to make them insoluble or to change the result, in hopes of deceiving the unwary. A proportion of the positions in almost all medieval problem collections were made deliberately unsound, and some texts contained advice on how to perform this delicate operation. One Florentine manuscript of the fifteenth century begins with an especially fine catalogue of hustlers' devices, from the obvious ploy of losing the first few games, on to really complicated ways of raising the betting as high as possible. More reputable writers regularly condemned this sort of professional sharping, which carried the normal practice of playing for a stake beyond what was socially acceptable.

This at once raises another question: socially acceptable to whom? Is it possible, in other words, that the way in which the game was played and regarded changed because of its changing appeal; because it spread downwards from the lay aristocracy and higher clergy to lesser men, and in particular to the inhabitants of the towns who were not bound by courtly codes of behaviour? The problem collection included in the Florentine manuscript referred to above was made by an author who called himself simply 'a citizen of Bologna' ('*civis Bononiae*'). Here the literary evidence is ambiguous: sometimes implying that the game was exclusive, as when Huon of Bordeaux is detected through his chess playing ability while travelling disguised as a servant, and sometimes that it was more widely known, as when the young Tristan is abducted by a band of Norwegian merchants in whose ship he was playing a casual game. It is interesting that the idea of merchants playing chess was no longer incongruous as early as *c.* 1200, though the Isle of Lewis hoard testifies to the fact that chess pieces were being traded in the Scandinavian world as much as half a century earlier. Of the two cases from the 'London Eyre Roll' of 1276 cited above, the first concerns men from Essex, at least one of whom was of knightly status, while the parties in the second were both members of city families. But although the process of diffusion began before 1300, it does indeed seem to have gone further in the fourteenth and fifteenth centuries. Chess was mentioned in the civic statutes of a whole roll-call of leading towns in the later Middle Ages, in Italy, Germany and Flanders. Usually it was exempted from the ineffective bans on less desirable pursuits, but even when it was forbidden this can be seen as an indirect testimony to its persistent popularity. There are similar references in the statutes of many late medieval universities.

Nevertheless, the social appeal of chess should not be exaggerated. The evidence simply will not support H.J.R. Murray's claim that 'during the latter part of the Middle Ages, and especially from the thirteenth to the fifteenth century, chess attained to a popularity in Western Europe which has never been excelled, and probably never equalled at any later date'.[17] Popularity can be assessed in various ways, but it does not seem inappropriate to recall the hierarchical nature of medieval society, with its ninety per cent peasant population, and to apply a few statistical tests. As Murray himself pointed out, chess was 'in the main a game of the upper classes', and hence of a very small section of society in numerical terms. Aristocratic and gentry families amounted to much less than one per cent of the population, even with a generous allowance for their domestic households and retainers. The game may have spread more widely among the clergy, but it is unlikely that it reached the mass of parish priests, who frequently shared the life style of the peasants to whom they ministered. In any case, the active clergy did not make up more than two per cent of medieval populations, except in exceptional small samples. Nor should the extension of the game's appeal to towns, though real enough, be used as the basis for airy generalizations about the rise of middle class culture. It is true that the late fourteenth-century English sermonist Robert Rypon attacked poor men and craftsmen who wasted their time on activities like chess when 'all those learning a craft should make it their sole aim to seek the means of providing food and clothing for themselves',[18] but his voice was an isolated one. In general, the popular preacher's guides do not mention the game at all, and this silence, more than Rypon's view that chess was inappropriate for the lower orders, suggests that they did not very often play it.

The chess moralities, which will be described below, were essentially cultivated and up-market literary productions, rather than popular sermons. The evidence of wills and inventories leads to the same conclusion; those of the noble and wealthy frequently mention chess sets and boards, but those of lesser men like artisans and yeoman farmers rarely do so. People of this class may have possessed sets too cheap to be worth recording, and there does seem to have been a revival in the manufacture of simpler non-representational pieces in the fourteenth and fifteenth centuries, but many wills are so detailed as to rule out even this possibility. Not all chess pieces were elaborately carved or made out of expensive materials, but they were often regarded as luxury items. A statute of 1464 included chessmen in a list of expensive and superfluous goods which were no longer to be imported.

It is therefore difficult to follow Murray in his assumption that chess experienced an extraordinary and unparallelled popularity in the later Middle Ages, which subsided during the sixteenth and seventeenth centuries. It seems more likely that the tendency of the game to spread was held in check by its inherent complexity, both in equipment and in rules, and that it never came close to displacing the cruder forms of gaming, which had a much greater appeal for the mass of the population. Playing cards also seem to have been expensive and arcane when they first appeared in Europe during the fourteenth century, but later proved much more adaptable in this respect. As far as chess is concerned, it appears that the aristocratic image of the game hardly changed in the late Middle Ages, or indeed for centuries afterwards. The attempts of the mid-fifteenth-century 'citizen of Bologna' to use chess problems as the basis for casual gambling may seem to run counter to this conclusion, but we do not know enough about the social status of those who copied and used his collection to be sure; many other chess problem manuscripts were prepared for noble and ecclesiastical patrons. In any case, the conclusion is a relative one based on fragmentary evidence, and does not rule out the possibility of exceptions, in Italy or elsewhere. But in general, just as chess had spread through European feudal society between 1000 and 1200, with the rise of a more complex and uniform noble culture based on greater wealth and stability, so in the subsequent centuries it spread to those who had enough leisure, means and education to imitate aspects of the noble life style. This kind of emulation, by leading townsmen and others, implied a blurring of some distinctions in the upper ranks of society, but hardly a radical upheaval. Considering the violence of forces for economic change between 1350 and 1475, with endemic plague reducing the whole European population by as much as fifty per cent, it is remarkable how powerful and adaptable medieval class values proved to be. Most of them were transmitted to the succeeding period and included activities like chess, which drew their prestige and appeal from being regarded as essentially and originally aristocratic.

To conclude this section, it is worth surveying briefly the status of chess in medieval law. At first the canon lawyers of the church were deeply suspicious of the game. There was a long established ban on *alea* – gambling games or games of chance – for the clergy, so the initial and quite natural reaction of such men was to regard chess as merely another form of *alea*, like dice or tables. In 1061 or 1062 the leading reformer Peter Damian, Cardinal Bishop of Ostia, described in a letter how he had upbraided a certain bishop of Florence for playing chess:

> He however made a shield of defence for himself from the difference in the names and said, '*Scachus* is one thing, *alea* another. That authority therefore banned dice-play but allowed chess by its silence.' To this I replied, 'The decree does not mention *scachus* but both types of game were included under the name of *alea*.'[19]

As in practice chess was played for a stake the bishop was unable to get out of his penance, which involved washing the feet of twelve poor men. In the 1130s St Bernard forbade chess to the recently established order of Knights Templar, who he wished to be monks as well as knights; the advance guard both of a new Christian society and of the crusading campaigns against Islam. Over the succeeding centuries intermittent attempts were made to enforce such bans among the clergy, especially in relatively closed communities like monasteries and university colleges. The manuscript evidence summarized above makes it clear that these efforts were mostly unsuccessful. In the fourteenth century John Wyclif included the game among secular habits which were leading most contemporary clergy to sin and damnation, 'they will not travail fast in their ghostly office, after Christ and his apostles, that full busily have taught them; therefore they fall to nice plays, at tables, chess and hazard, and beat the streets, and sit at the tavern untill they have lost their wit.'[20] By his day it does not appear that the ecclesiastical authorities in most of Europe were even trying to apply the law rigidly, in the spirit of Peter Damian and the earlier reformers.

The reason for this moderation of clerical attitudes is not difficult to find. The game had become so popular with the rulers and leaders of secular society, and the church depended so much on reaching an accommodation with these men, that outright condemnation seemed hardly politic. The status of chess gradually rose in the eyes of the church, along with that of other socially necessary activities like war and usury, and only a ruler pious above and beyond the call of duty, like St Louis of France, ever attempted to extend restrictions on the game to laymen (in 1254). Clerical writers of the twelfth century, like Alexander Neckam, were quite prepared to condemn chess as vain and frivolous, but later authors were usually more cautious, especially after the appearance of successful chess sermons in the thirteenth century. The game came to seem not merely prestigious but also didactic and potentially useful. Thus

John Bromyard, in his fourteenth-century 'Art of Preaching' (*Summa Predicantium*), classed the desire to play well at chess among sins of pride but did not condemn the game itself. The problem was eventually solved by a series of new scholastic distinctions: games of skill were sharply marked off from games of chance and were regarded as legal, sometimes even for the clergy. The winner need feel under no compulsion to repay his stake, which was usually part of the penance enjoined on those who confessed to gambling. This attitude was characteristic of most late medieval lawyers and commentators, zealots like Wyclif and his followers apart, and amounted to a satisfactory compromise. If fortune could not 'give the advantage honourably' as Ruodlieb had claimed, then at least skill could do so, in the eyes of a more tolerant church.

Status and symbol

The discussion so far has dealt with the 'real' social history of chess in the Middle Ages: its geographical spread, appeal to different groups and place in everyday life. But in medieval literature, chess could also be regarded as having hidden or concealed meanings, and so prevalent did this idea become that in the end it may have added to the game's attractiveness for both lay and clerical audiences. Allegorical writing of one kind or another never lost its popularity during the Middle Ages. If it were common for lovers or disputants to be portrayed playing chess, then it was only a slight extension of that convention to make the chess game itself parallel the course of the love-affair or the quarrel. The king's daughter in '*Huon of Bordeaux*' and Baudrains in the fourteenth-century *Voeux du Paon* each lose their heart to an attractive opponent, and naturally lose the game as well. King Knut's attempt to cheat during his game against Earl Ulf in the *Olaf Saga*, by taking back a losing move, prepares the reader for his treacherous assassination of the earl on the following day. The chess episode in *Ruodlieb* fits into this pattern also.

Other poets and historians found or devised more general correspondences between events in chess and events in their narratives. In the famous thirteenth-century poem the *Roman de la Rose*, the attempts of Conradin grandson of the Emperor Frederick II and his ally Henry of Castile to conquer the Kingdom of Sicily in 1268 are mocked in this way:

> These two like foolish boys lost rooks, queens, pawns and knights in the game and fled from the board, because they were so afraid of being captured in the game. And yet they need not have feared a mate, because no check could be given to anyone who fought without a king. No opponent at chess can check or mate, on foot or on horseback, pawns, bishops, knights, queens or rooks.[21]

The analogy is developed over about seventy lines to hammer home the point that as neither Conradin nor Henry were kings, so neither was a real rival to Charles of Anjou, who had already made himself the ruler of Sicily. There is no doubt where the sympathies of the poet Jean de Meun lay, but yet he was able to claim with heavy irony that he was not distorting the truth of the matter, for this is indeed the rule in chess, as everyone knows.

The whole episode is reminiscent of a tale told by Alexander Neckam about King Louis VI of France (1108–1137). While fighting against his rival Henry I of England, he was forced to flee from the field of battle. An English knight pursued him, seized the reins of his horse and called out that the king was taken. Louis replied that not even in chess can the king be captured, and drove home his point by bisecting the knight with his sword. Here again, both the combative element in the game and the hierarchy of the different pieces are exploited in the narrative, though not in a very serious way. Finally, in his early poem *The Book of the Duchess*, written to commemorate the death of Blanche Duchess of Lancaster in 1369, Chaucer compared her death with the loss of his queen (*fers*) in a game against Fortune:

> At the ches with me she gan to pleye;
> With hir false draughtes dyvers
> She staal on me, and tok my fers.
> And whan I sawgh my fers awaye,
> Alass! I kouthe no lenger playe,
> But seyde, "Farewd, swete, ywys,
> And farewel al that ever ther ys!"[22]

This is typical of many other poetic contests, in which man plays chess against Fate or Death and inevitably comes off second best.

Various elements in chess were thus pressed into service as literary images, but none of the examples quoted so far, with the possible exception of the *Roman de la Rose*, seems to hint at meanings inherent in the game itself. The comparison between chess and love for instance, though just possibly based on contemporary social life, is otherwise an artificial allegory. Only one medieval work tried to treat it really seriously: a fourteenth-century imitation of the *Roman de la Rose* called the *Eschez amoureux*. This 'Amorous Chess', a vast and sprawling poem of unknown authorship, centres on a chess game between the poet and his lady in the Garden of Pleasure, and runs to a total of over 30,000 lines. The game itself, though it is described in such detail that most of its moves can be reconstructed, takes up only about 500 of them, but it is preceded by a lengthy introduction in which the board and every one of the thirty-two pieces and pawns is assigned a separate meaning. Each had a distinctive shape and was made from a characteristic material, to represent a moral quality of men or women. The lady's two knights, for instance, were fashioned from sapphires and bore as badges a unicorn and a hare to stand for female modesty and timidity. The poet's first pawn, who represented idleness, carried a shield on which was shown a withered tree, for reasons not altogether clear. It is scarcely surprising that the original verse was soon linked with a prose commentary in which some of the finer points were explained. To a modern reader the whole conception seems forced and unconvincing, and as the poem never gained much popularity it is possible that medieval audiences reacted in the same way. Even the industrious versifier John Lydgate left unfinished his English translation *Reson and Sensuallyte* sometime in the early fifteenth century, breaking off suddenly at the fourth pawn on the poet's side with twelve pieces still to go.

The same can be said about most extended treatments of chess in medieval literature. Richard de Fournival's *Vetula*, for instance, contains a passage in which the chessmen are given astronomical meanings: the king is the sun, the queen Venus, the bishop Jupiter, the knight Mars, the rook the moon, and the pawn Saturn. Like those in the *Eschez amoureux*, the details of this scheme are specific to one work, and do not seem to reflect any general tradition. It has been argued that chess had 'widespread traces of astronomical symbolism clinging to it' from its origins, but there is little in the Middle Ages to support such a view. The 'astronomical chess' which appears in the Castilian *Libro del Acedrex* of 1283 is actually a race game played with dice, using board and men entirely different from those of chess. The balance of probabilities is therefore that the Spanish writer stretched a familiar term to cover an unfamiliar game, while Richard de Fournival's allegory was his own invention. Analogies with warfare and fighting are obviously closer to the nature of chess, but they also tend to be unspecific, because other games too could be regarded as symbolic conflicts. Violent incidents like those in the *Olaf Saga* and in *Parzival* were juxtaposed with chess largely because chess had become a characteristic pursuit of each writer's audience. In earlier sagas such passages centred on the preceding game of *hnefatafl*. The convention of man playing chess against Fate or Death is similarly unspecific, and it is notable that, when Chaucer developed the theme in the *Book of the Duchess*, he imposed a meaning on chess which was contrary to its rules, by making the whole game depend on the loss of his queen. This suited his allegory, but the queen or *fers* was one of the weakest pieces in medieval chess. The same contradiction occurs in Gautier de Coincy's thirteenth-century *Miracles de la Nostre Dame*, where God plays chess against the Devil, and his queen (the virgin Mary) turns the game in his favour.

Nearly all the examples so far discussed therefore do one of two things: they refer to chess in general terms, or they read into it specific meanings which had little to do with the way in which it was played. Such allegorical ingenuity was not of course confined to chess. As early as the tenth century a form of *hnefatafl* attributed to the court of the English king Athelstan (924–940) was given a religious meaning as the 'Game of the Gospel', by interpreting the size of the board and the number of pieces to represent symbolic numbers in the bible. Later writers were quite prepared to find significance in packs of cards, or the pips on dice, if it suited their purpose. All these can be fairly described as literary allegories. They were introduced into the works in which they appear as stylistic devices, to heighten a story or draw attention to its implications. The writer in each case expressed himself indirectly, but he has devised a fairly clear-cut system of equivalents for the purpose, 'saying one thing to mean another' in a way his audience would be able to understand. The reader could discover the secondary meaning for himself by a process of retranslation. Sometimes the concealed message is so insubstantial that the whole device amounts only to a stylistic conceit; an opportunity to display skills of construction and parallel writing.

Yet even in this realm of literary artifice, the outlines of more serious issues can be perceived. A wider reading and interpretation of references to chess in medieval texts suggests that it was not imbued with hidden significance only when it was included in allegorical schemes. Sometimes at least, the game was thought to have a symbolic meaning already implanted in it, which merely had to be elucidated, much in the way that medieval scholars expected to derive truths about the universe from studying harmonic proportions in music. The prevalence of symbolism in medieval thought has been much debated and little can be said about it here, but it was extremely influential. Various philosophical schools accepted in one way or another, and tried to reconcile with Christianity, the view that the whole material world was only the reflection of immaterial forms and ideas which governed its outward appearance. The forms and ideas thus constituted a higher and more logical reality, only imperfectly and unpredictably translated to earth. It follows that almost any structural similarity between material things, however insignificant to the modern mind, might have been taken as evidence of an underlying association in the realm of ideas: a symbolic association. There were thus symbolic numbers and colours, symbolic animals and plants, all linked to various aspects of human affairs.[23]

In the case of chess, the meaning which became established in this way was the link between the different pieces and different social ranks, from king to commoner. These parallels were just as much the invention of medieval writers as the allegorical fancies described above, but through repetition, and perhaps through plausibility, they took on some of the force of symbolic equivalents. After all, they dated back to the first introduction of chess into the West, when the Arabic names of the pieces were progressively adopted and translated into western ones. The original oriental war game had been turned into a battle between two miniature feudal states, each with its hierarchy of king, queen, bishop (or judge), knight, rook (messenger or royal agent) and pawn (commoner or foot soldier) and this was reinforced by the representational designs of many chess sets. So when writers of the thirteenth and fourteenth centuries drew on this tradition, to write about society under the guise of writing about chess, the underlying links they set forth might have appeared to be well founded. The extraordinary popularity of some of these 'chess moralities' in the later Middle Ages helps to support such a view.

There was however one obvious problem. Since chess was a man-made diversion, any meaning concealed within it could hardly be inherent in nature like arithmetic or harmonic relationships; it must have been put there by the original inventor. In fact the vagueness prevalent in most medieval thought about the distant and non-Christian past meant that the difficulty never presented itself as a serious one. As interpretations of chess grew and developed, so did myths and legends about its origin; it has already been pointed out that Romance writers saw no incongruity in describing games of chess at the courts of Charlemagne and Arthur or the siege of Troy. Most medieval 'Troy Books', going back to the twelfth-century Benoît de Sainte More, attributed the invention of the game to the Trojans themselves, but Alexander Neckam preferred the Greek Ulysses and some later authors followed his lead. Others again, like Jean de Meun and Chaucer, picked on the Hellenistic ruler Attalus Asiaticus, who was usually credited in medieval tradition with the discovery of arithmetic. But the characteristic 'morality' account of the game's invention held that it was devised by a wise philosopher to teach an evil king how he should treat the different kinds of men he had to rule; an ideal basis for claiming that the whole game was charged with moral and political meaning from its origins. This may even be an echo of the Arabic legend that chess was created to educate a prince in the skills of warfare, and certainly the eastern story of 'the doubling of the squares' got through to the West and became a favourite among mathematical writers. Dante used it in the *Divine Comedy* to describe the innumerable numbers of angels he saw in Paradise.

It is therefore clear that some of these ideas had been linked with chess since soon after its reception into western Europe, but they only began to assume a coherent form when they were taken over by a number of clerical writers during the thirteenth century. The earliest of these was the author of a Latin sermon which Murray called the 'Innocent Morality', because it is ascribed in some manuscripts to Pope Innocent III (1198–1216). The papal attribution was rejected by Murray, and though later writers have been reluctant to commit themselves for or against it, it is likely on grounds of both style and content that the morality was written by a friar involved in preaching to laymen. The work first appears in manuscripts of the *Communiloquium*, a collection compiled later in the century by the Franciscan John of Wales, who taught at Oxford and Paris between 1260 and 1282, so John himself or one of his university colleagues may have been the true author. It is a short text, part of a general discussion about games and the theatre in the *Communiloquium*, but also capable of standing on its own as the basis of a real sermon, once adapted or expanded to suit the particular audience. The first few sentences set the scene of the comparison:

> The whole world is like a chess-board, of which one square is white and another black, following the dual state of life and death, praise and blame. The society (*familia*) of this chess-board are men of this world, who are all taken from a common bag, and placed in different parts of this world, and as individuals have different names. One is called king, another queen, a third rook, a fourth knight, a fifth *alphin*, a sixth pawn. However, the rule of this game is such that one man takes another, and when they have finished the game, just as they come out of one place and one bag, so they are put back in one place, without a distinction between the king and the poor pawn, as rich and poor are together.[24]

The writer then proceeds to particulars. King, queen, knight and pawn speak for themselves, the rooks are justices who travel around the whole land, their straight move representing just dealing; while the *alphins* are bishops who move and capture obliquely, because almost all prelates are corrupt and greedy. After developing these themes the author returns to the idea of conflict, the most important conflict of all, because at another level of meaning, the whole game is played against the devil. To be checked is to fall into sin, and to be mated is to be damned in hell, 'from which there is no redemption'.

It is hard to estimate the influence of this little treatise, because most of the ideas in it were probably circulating independently, but later translations into Italian and Icelandic give some clue to the breadth of its appeal. Between 1250 and 1475 at least eight new moralities of chess were written, and the genre as a whole seems to have become well established; it is likely that even more of them once existed and have not survived. In general, as these works were too short to be copied as separate texts, they had a better chance of being circulated when they were included in larger miscellanies, one of the most popular of which was the *Gesta Romanorum*. This was a collection of moralized stories first made in Latin soon after 1300, but later rewritten and expanded until the original hundred or so chapters had reached more than 180. From its origins the *Gesta* included a story based on chess and, in its later English translation of *c*. 1420–40, this brings out the social conservatism of the chess moralities very clearly.

Though all men may be equal in death (after the game), they are certainly not equal in life (during the game): 'And therefore let us not change of our estates, no more than the chessmen, when they be put away in the bag. Then there is no difference who be above or who be beneath, and so by the Spirit of Lowliness we may come to the joy of Heaven.'[25] The '*Innocent Morality*' too had urged common men to plod steadily onwards like pawns, not deviating in order to gain possessions or improve their situation, the better to reach salvation and their true reward. The bias is interesting, but hardly surprising, for it was inconceivable that literature of this kind could have appealed to the mass of the population. Nevertheless, these works did have a wide audience, and it was based on their adaptability. They could serve almost equally well as sermons or stories, sources of instruction or of entertainment, ranging between preacher's texts like the '*Innocent Morality*' and chapters in the *Gesta Romanorum* where only a perfunctory 'moral' was tacked on to the narrative.

But the most popular of all these medieval chess books, and the one which had the most influence on the game itself, has yet to be described. This was the 'Book of the customs of men and the duties of nobles' (*Liber de moribus hominum et officiis nobilium*) written by a Dominican friar Jacobus de Cessolis, around the year 1300. De Cessolis expanded the idea of the moralized chess, chess as a symbol of ranks and degrees in society, and wrote at much greater length, about 20,000 words in the original Latin text. Like the author of the 'Innocent Morality' he identified each chess piece with a particular status or profession, but he embellished these portraits with so many anecdotes and digressions that his book became a whole story collection in its own right. The *Liber de moribus* was primarily responsible for promoting the belief that chess was invented by a philosopher, here called Xerxes, to teach a tyrant, Evilmerodach King of Babylon, the error of his ways. The historical Evilmerodach was the son of Nebuchadnezzar (*c.* 560 BC) and makes a brief appearance in the Old Testament, though otherwise little is known about him. But the medieval friar shrugged off such limitations of historical evidence effortlessly. The *Liber de moribus* begins with a lurid example of Evilmerodach's wickedness, when he has his father's body cut up into three hundred pieces and fed to vultures, a scene which was exploited to the full by some later illustrators. After this, his repentance and return to virtue comes as something of an anticlimax. The message concealed in chess, which had such a beneficial effect on him, was that a king was just as dependent on the other ranks of society as they were on him. On his own he was as helpless as any of them would be in the same position, for all depend on one another and society functions only as a whole. De Cessolis drove home his point by giving a much more elaborate account of the third estate than earlier writers. Though he recognized that pawns in chess all have the same move, and have much in common, he characterized each of them separately to represent a different trade or profession, from labourers, smiths and masons to notaries, advocates and inn-keepers. Though the descriptive scheme was confined to secular society, 'bishops' being portrayed as judges and 'rooks' as royal messengers, it was still an extremely thorough one.

The *Liber de moribus* therefore drew on the notion, already prevalent, that chess was a symbolic representation of society and imparted to that notion much greater force and precision. The result was a work of extraordinary popularity during the later Middle Ages. A rather haphazard search by Antonius van der Linde in the mid-nineteenth century disclosed at least eighty manuscripts of the Latin text alone, and many more have been discovered since.[26] To these must be added the translations into vernacular languages. Two separate French versions were made between 1347 and 1350 by Jean Ferron and Jean de Vignay, followed by an abbreviated verse translation in the fifteenth century. There were translations into Italian and Dutch in the fourteenth century, Catalan and Swedish in the fifteenth, Spanish and Scots dialect in the sixteenth. Caxton put the book into English from the French texts of Ferron and de Vignay and published it twice, at Bruges in 1474/5 and at London in about 1483, as *The Game and Playe of the Chesse*. The first German verse translation was made early in the fourteenth century, and there were two more by 1337, in which year Kunrat von Ammenhausen completed his massively extended adaptation in over 19,000 lines. The next hundred years brought yet another metrical translation, as well as one in prose. Surviving manuscripts of these vernacular chess books have never been adequately surveyed, but the recent editor of the German prose version found over forty manuscripts of that text alone.[27] Figures like these class Jacobus de Cessolis' tract with the most popular works of medieval literature, for only those which had a wide and prolonged appeal survive in more than a hundred contemporary copies. Since the text takes for granted that its readers will already be familiar with the rules of chess, this provides evidence to confirm some of the conclusions already reached. Nor did the popularity of the book decline in the early years of printing. Between 1475 and 1505 there were twenty printed editions of it: six in Latin, five in German, three in Dutch and two each in English, French and Italian.

In this flurry of copying and translating the identity of the author was frequently obscured, and his name appears in peculiar forms which stray progressively further from the original: Cossolis, Cozolis, Sesselis, Tessalis, Thessalonia, Thessalonica . . . . Murray quite rightly rejected the older view that de Cessolis was a Frenchman, and showed from the internal evidence of his book that he must have come from northern Italy, but otherwise was unable to discover very much about him. But four documents of the early fourteenth century, three of them recently discovered in the register of a Genoese notary, throw a little light in the darkness.[28] They show that between 1317 and 1322 'brother Jacobus de Cessolis' was attached to the Dominican house there, that for at least part of that time he served as vicar to the local inquisitor, and that his name was derived from the small commune of Cessole near Asti, in the same region. It is still impossible to say with any precision when the *Liber de moribus* was written, except that it might have been at any time within the limits 1280 to 1320, after which the earliest translations that can be dated begin to appear. De Cessolis himself said in his prologue that the book was created in deference to the wishes of his fellow friars, who begged him to write down his sermons. But like its predecessors it flourished largely because of its adaptability; what began life as a *'sermon ad status'* (one concerned with the moral and religious duties of different ranks in society) then gained further popularity through its literary appeal. Modern critics sometimes class the chess moralities as 'estates literature', in the same genre as Chaucer's Prologue to the *Canterbury Tales*.[29] In some passages, like those in which he discusses social duties and natural law, de Cessolis' book even seems to pass over into political theory, though of an unsystematic and moralizing variety. Thomas Hoccleve acknowledged it as one of his three sources for the *Regement of Princes*, the advice book which he dedicated to the young Prince Henry (later Henry V) in 1412.[30]

The study of chess in medieval literature leads to the conclusion that for many players of the time the game must have appeared as a picture of the state in miniature, charged with symbolic meaning. It was an appropriate game for the upper classes, and their imitators, not only because they had time and money enough to play it, but also because it was ancient, prestigious and significant. This applied equally to the Kings of France and Dukes of Burgundy, whose libraries in the fifteenth century each contained seven copies of Jacobus de Cessolis' moralized chess book, as to that aspiring Norfolk gentleman John Paston, whose small collection of a dozen or so volumes in 1479 included the recently printed English translation, *The Game and Playe of the Chesse*.[31] Later on, men looked back to this characteristically medieval way of thinking, with repugnance, incomprehension, or perhaps even nostalgia. As an example of the latter one might quote the 'humanist' Sir Thomas Elyot, who wrote in his *Book named the Governor* of 1531:[32]

> The chess, of all games wherein is no bodily exercise is most to be commended; for therein is right subtle engine, whereby the wit is made more sharp and remembrance quickened. And it is the more commendable and also commodious if the players have read the moralization of the chess, and when they play do think upon it; which books be in English. But they be very scarce, because few men do seek in plays for virtue or wisdom.

The game of the Middle Ages

The technical history of chess in the Middle Ages presents many problems, and not much need be said about it here. Such evidence as there is, mostly derived from the problem manuscripts of *c.* 1250–1450, suggests that the general standard of play was not high, and this is perhaps to be expected of a game which enjoyed social rather than intellectual prestige. There must always have been differences between good and bad players, but no one of appropriate rank need have felt inhibited from playing through lack of study or practice. Few records even hint at the existence of organized competition or 'champion' players: the Florentine chronicler Giovanni Villani mentioned one such man who visited the city in 1266 and played blindfold games two at a time, but pointed out that he was *'un Saracino.'* The problem collections themselves were based on Muslim models, and though they evolved with changes in taste and fashion, they rarely showed any signs of technical advance on their eastern prototypes. Medieval chess was inherently resistant to opening analysis and the recording of games, except for selected excerpts which could be dressed up as problems, but no western writers wrestled with these difficulties as did al-Lajlaj in the tenth century.

As far as the rules of the game were concerned, there is rather more evidence of pressures for change in the West, though still no sign as late as 1450 of an imminent upheaval in the laws of play. Before 1200 alterations to the Moslem game seem to have been confined to external appearances: the black and white chequered board, which is mentioned as early as the 'Einsiedeln Verses', and the representational designs of the pieces. After 1200 pressures to speed up the game seem to have become stronger, and this led to a variety of experiments and local rules which diverged from each other in various ways. It became common, for instance, to allow pawns their modern 'privilege' of advancing two squares instead of one on their first move, and to give queens and kings an optional 'leap' of several squares on one occasion, to get them into play quicker. All of these appear in a number of widely dispersed sources, and were taken for granted by Jacobus de Cessolis. Another variation, used in northern Europe to accelerate the beginning of a game, was to set up the pieces differently, with the pawns already on the third rank and some of the pieces already deployed. This scheme seems to be described by Alexander Neckam, and used in the *Eschez amoureux*, but was less universally popular. The most controversial alteration of all was to use dice to determine which piece a player was able to move. There were oriental precedents for this, but it was probably re-invented independently in the West. The Castilian *Libro del Acedrex* of 1283 remarks on 'the weariness which players experienced from the long duration of the game when played right through' and mentions that for this reason 'dice have been brought into chess, so that it can be played more quickly'. But many other writers condemned this as contrary to the spirit of the game, and the exercise of skill which made it legal in the eyes of the church, including the author of the *Vetula*: 'this has only been done because few know how to play slowly, or for hope of gain.' Despite these variations, it is remarkable how consistent the rules of chess remained from one end of Christian Europe to the other. On the eve of the reform which was to change its nature, and ultimately its social appeal, chess, unlike cards or tables, was still recognizably a single game.

CHAPTER THREE

The New Chess and its Patrons c. 1475-1650

The transition from medieval to modern was a complex and gradual process, in almost every area of life. Few historians or readers of history now expect to find specific events which tipped the scales from one age to the next, still less do they put much faith in dates like 1485 or 1492, which for generations of school textbooks used to inaugurate a kind of official beginning of modern history. So it is ironic that the game of chess experienced the only major change in its internal structure in over a thousand years of documented history through a single and dramatic shift in its rules of play at just about this time, the late fifteenth century. Despite slight modifications and a series of experiments designed to speed it up, chess at the end of the Middle Ages was essentially the same game as that taken over from the Islamic world 500 years earlier. The sudden reform in the moves, of which there is certain evidence by the 1490s, created a new chess, identical in almost all respects with the game we play today; in the 500 years since that change took place there have again been only minor adjustments in the rules. First it is necessary to ask when and how the reform occurred before raising some broader issues: did a new game mean a new kind of appeal and social status compared with the pre-1500 period; was chess now evolving in a different direction in more than just its moves?

A new game

The modifications in the rules can be summarized fairly easily. Each pawn was now allowed an extended privilege move, but only if it were still on its initial square. Medieval players had been experimenting with this idea since the thirteenth century, so its appearance now was certainly the result of prolonged trials; its main effect was to speed up the early stages of a game without transforming the tactics of play as a whole. But the other two changes did have more sweeping effects.

The bishop's move was extended, so that it now had approximately the same value as a knight. Again there is a possible medieval precedent, though this time from a variant game rather than chess itself: the so-called 'courier' game known in several parts of Germany, and played on a board twelve squares by eight, with a number of new pieces in addition to the standard (medieval) men. Chief among these was the 'courier' which gave the game its name, and it had the same move as the 'reformed' bishop, which it may therefore have inspired. However, though 'courier' was mentioned by name as early as the beginning of the thirteenth century and was described in detail by Kunrat von Ammenhausen writing in 1337, there are no references to it outside Germany, while the new chess reached Germany comparatively late and as a foreign introduction. Because of this the influence cannot be proved, though it remains possible. But by far the most significant of the fifteenth-century changes which transformed medieval chess was the creation of a new queen move, for which there is no known medieval precedent. The medieval queen, despite the poetic conceits of Chaucer and others, was a rather weak piece, weaker even than the king, but the reformed queen combined in one piece the moves of rook and (modern) bishop, becoming at once the strongest unit on the board. This explains why in the earliest Spanish and French references the new chess was referred to as 'the queen's chess': *axedrez dela dama, eschés de la dame* or even more graphically *eschés de la dame enragée*. In Italian too, the game was soon referred to as *dela donna* or *ala rabiosa*: mad chess.

From the evidence of the modifications themselves it is therefore possible to regard the new chess as the culmination of a whole series of late medieval attempts to speed up the game. But it was also a specific new departure, containing at least one element for which there was no precedent. It must have been devised and perfected quite rapidly and probably within a single centre, before it began to spread round Europe. There are no records of the new bishop and queen moves being tried independently: everywhere they were introduced as part of a coherent new system, which soon began to acquire a theory of its own. Where then was this centre, and when was the game first created?

The first description of the new chess which can be accurately dated is in the *Repeticion de Amores: E arte de axedrez* of Luis de Lucena, which is also the first printed book on chess playing (as opposed to the moralized sermon of Jacobus de Cessolis) of which copies survive today. Lucena dedicated his book, which consisted of two unrelated works bound together, the 'Discourse on Love' and the 'Art of Chess', to Prince Juan the son and heir of Ferdinand and Isabella of Spain. This provides a valuable clue to dating, because Juan died young in 1497, only a few months after his marriage to Marguerite daughter of the Emperor

Maximilian. To this can be added the typographical evidence, which shows that the *Repeticion* was printed by Leonardus Hutz and Lope Sanz in Salamanca. Hutz and Sanz were typical itinerant masters of the early period of printing, and they only worked in Salamanca, which was not a major centre despite its university, in 1496 and 1497. The book can therefore be dated with some confidence, though little is known of Lucena himself.

He described himself as 'son of the most learned doctor and reverend protonotary don Juan Remirez de Lucena, ambassador and councillor of our lord kings' and a 'student at the illustrious university of the very noble city of Salamanca'; he was apparently a wealthy young man trying to follow his father in the pursuit of royal favour.[1] The *Arte de Axedrez* shows every sign of being a product of the transitional period. After the dedication and a general introduction, in which Lucena refers to the need 'to instruct those who know nothing about this game, so that my work is not without a preliminary foundation . . . to know the difference between the game which we now play, which is called "of the queen" and the game which used to be played', there are eleven specimen openings of the new chess, and a hundred and fifty problems, seventy-eight described as *del viejo* and seventy-two *dela dama*. Lucena himself made no claim to have discovered the new chess or its secrets; he was an unashamed compiler, who wrote that he intended to describe 'all the best games I have seen played by players in Rome and all Italy, France and Spain, and which I have been able to understand myself'.[2] It remains unclear, therefore, how long the transition had been under way before 1497, or where was the centre from which it was disseminated.

There are three more pieces of evidence which can be dated with rather less precision, to about 1500 or a little earlier, and provide a few additional clues. The most important of these is usually called the 'Göttingen Manuscript', though it probably came to Göttingen only in the eighteenth century. It is a short manuscript, of about thirty pages, and written in Latin. Like Lucena's book it contains a few specimen openings and some problems, in this case twelve openings and thirty problems, all of the new chess, with no mention of the medieval game. It must have been written or copied in France, because on a few occasions exclusively French terms are introduced into the Latin vocabulary, notably *stultus* ('fool') for bishop. The manuscript was also clearly compiled for a patron of high rank, who is addressed with enormous respect throughout, in terms which make it clear that the analysis was (hopefully) for his own use. Thus the first game begins: 'Your lordship plays the king's pawn to the fourth square from the king's place, and if the opponent does the same, play the king's knight to the third square of the king's bishop, and if he guards the pawn with the pawn of the king's bishop, take his pawn with the knight . . . .' The second game introduces the high-born initiate to another variation: 'Let us suppose, magnificent lord, that he does not guard his king's pawn with the pawn of the bishop but with that of the queen . . . .' Unfortunately neither the recipient nor the deferential instructor are named. In a series of articles[3] Dr F.C. Görschen has argued that, on grounds of Latin style and syntax, the original of the Göttingen manuscript must have been written by a Spanish or Portuguese speaker, and the few French terms introduced during subsequent copying. This seems extremely likely, though Görschen's further suggestion that the manuscript was compiled between 1471 and 1475 at the court of Alfonso V of Portugal and brought to France during that king's visit to Paris in the winter of 1474–5, passes over into speculation.

An Iberian origin for the Göttingen work is all the more plausible because its contents are very directly related to those of Lucena's book. Several of the twelve openings have parallels in Lucena's eleven, though in general they are more advanced than his, and every one of the thirty problems can be found among Lucena's selection. Furthermore, with one exception they are given in the same order in both sources, though in Lucena the Göttingen problems do not appear consecutively, but scattered through the whole work. It is hard to avoid the conclusion that the Göttingen author chose his problems from a larger collection which was either Lucena or something very close to it. Because of this H.J.R. Murray recognized the possibility that Lucena was the author of both works, in which case 'the Göttingen MS is Lucena's later, because more mature, work on chess'.[4] But it is equally likely that there were two separate compilers, who drew on common sources for their material, perhaps no more than a generalized knowledge in the case of the openings, but certainly a written collection for the problems. As it happens there is a possible candidate for this role, the *Jochs partits del scachs en nombre de 100* of Francesch Vicent, a Catalan book, printed in Valencia in 1495. Surviving copies were described in the nineteenth century by William Lewis, and rather more reliably by the Spanish scholar Mendez,[5] but none now remain. Probably the one seen by Mendez at Montserrat and destroyed by a fire in 1834 was the last, so we shall never know the place of this work in the origins of the new chess. Of course, if Vicent's book was the basis of the Göttingen problems, that manuscript could be no earlier than 1495, and the problem of dating the new game itself remains.

The other two early sources may be described more briefly. The first is a Catalan manuscript entitled *Scachs d'amor*, containing a poem which describes the courtship of Venus and Mars through an allegorical game of chess, rather resembling the technique of the medieval *Eschez amoureux*, though at less wearisome length. The game is played in the presence of Mercury, who acts as annotator, providing helpful explanations of the new chess rules for the reader, and the bogus nature of this classical mythologizing is neatly pointed by the revelation that each of these parts was 'played' by a contemporary: Francesco di Castellvi as Mars, Narciso Vinoles as Venus and the Abbot Fenollar as Mercury. The game between Castellvi and Vinoles is given in full, and may possibly be based on an actual encounter. The second source, a short French manuscript called *Le Jeu des Eschés de la dame moralisé*, reflects an attempt to create a morality literature around the rules of the new game. The allegory describes a game between the recipient of the work, evidently a high-born lady, and Lucifer. Each side has appropriately named pieces, as may be seen from the enemy's first move: 'He plays his pawn called Love of Self which is before his King of Pride . . . .' After three pages of sermon the lady gets in her first move, with her pawn called Love of God, and so on. The, presumably clerical, author manages to avoid any illegal moves, but the opponent's standard of play is so bad as to raise serious doubts about his diabolical status, and virtue triumphs almost by default. This, combined with the author's naive remarks about the new rules of play, suggest that the reformed chess had only just come to his notice when he used it as the basis of his little homily.

I have summarized the evidence in some detail because the technical revolution which brought about the new chess was the most important since the game first appeared. There are, however, no certain conclusions. After 1500 the reform spread rapidly all over Europe. Medieval chess does not appear in Spanish sources later than Lucena, except in the indirect form of Jacobus de Cessolis' morality which was published at Valladolid in 1549. The second extant printed chess book, the *Questo libro e da imparare giocare a scachi* of Damiano published in Rome in 1512, does not mention medieval chess, so the author must have seen little need to distinguish between the new game and the old. Chess-problem collectors were naturally more conservative, and reluctant to abandon the material which they had accumulated, though Lucena's book shows that there was already a tendency to remodel old problems to accord with the new game. Those which contained no queens or bishops naturally required no modifications at all. Nevertheless, problemists continued to copy specimens of the medieval game sporadically through the sixteenth century, though most of them referred in their works to the new chess as well, with the implication that that was the form used for actual play. A manuscript copied by Paolo Guarini at Rome in 1512 was the last Italian collection to make no mention of the reform. In France there was a printed pamphlet containing only medieval problems in the 1530s, the *Sensuit Ieux Partis des eschez*, but after that no more references to the old game at all. In England there is not much evidence to go on, but a late fifteenth-century problem manuscript was owned in 1529 by one Roger Hartwell, whose notes on it show that he was still engaged in solving its medieval problems. An elaborate chess conceit in a poem by Henry Howard Earl of Surrey (died 1547) contains the phrase 'check and guard', meaning a simultaneous attack on king and queen, and so implying that the new all-powerful queen was in use in his day. In Germany the final edition of Jacobus de Cessolis' morality, by Christian Egenolff at Frankfurt in 1536, contains a short note describing the new chess as a recent introduction from abroad, 'another way to play chess, called *current* ["rapid"] or *welsch* ["foreign"] chess'. *Welsch* is sometimes translated as 'Italian', but probably mistakenly; in that part of Germany it is more likely to have referred to France, if it meant anything more specific than foreign in general. There is thus hardly enough evidence to show how quickly the new game replaced the old in out-of-the-way centres or among the conservatively inclined, but such evidence as there is tends to suggest a very rapid change. England and Germany received the reform comparatively late, but apparently no later than the 1530s. By 1510 the new chess was well entrenched in Spain, Italy and probably France as well; by 1550 medieval chess seems to have confined to some parts of Germany, Scandinavia and Iceland. Nowhere else in Europe was it still found as an active game.

The question of origins must be left unresolved. The fact that there are no certain references to the new chess before the 1490s, combined with the existence of many medieval chess manuscripts of the mid-fifteenth century, some certainly as late as the 1460s, which make no mention of the impending change, suggests a target date between 1470 and 1490 for the innovation. This has been the general consensus among scholars, though it remains possible that the new game was devised earlier and 'lay dormant' for a while before it began to achieve popularity. As for the place of origin, it is only possible to echo Murray's remark that 'It is difficult to decide between the claims of Italy, France and Spain to have been the earliest home of the new chess'.[6] He himself inclined towards Italy, because Italy was the greatest centre of chess activity, as evidenced by the number of manuscripts of chess problems. But it is almost certain that the new game was devised by practical players rather than by problemists. While there is no conclusive proof, it is hard to ignore the fact that almost all the reliable early evidence is linked with Spain or Portugal. Even Damiano, though he published his book in Rome in 1512, said that he was a native of Odemira in Portugal, and gave the solutions to his problems in both Italian and Spanish. There was in fact a general tradition in early sixteenth-century Italy that Spaniards were good chess players. In Baldassare Castiglione's *Book of the Courtier* for instance, it is said that 'there are many Spaniards who excel at chess', and an implausible anecdote about a chess-playing monkey is set in Portugal.[7] Perhaps, after all, Lucena claimed to have travelled to 'Rome and the whole of Italy and

France' to learn something which he could have found equally well at home, and probably did.

If the invention of the new chess itself remains hidden in obscurity, one might reasonably hope for a more precise historical account of its subsequent spread and popularity. In fact there has been a great deal of vague speculation about this subject. It has been supposed by some writers that the new chess first became popular in Italy because of 'the Renaissance', and that it spread rapidly over Europe through 'the impact of the Renaissance on the medieval world' (how? when? which aspects of Renaissance culture?). Others have suggested that the powerful queen of the new chess reflected the emancipation of women at the end of the Middle Ages (which women? what sort of emancipation?). In this context it is ironic that the author of the earliest datable book about the new chess, Luis de Lucena, also wrote the *Repeticion de Amores*, described by its modern editor as 'the most extensive anti-feminist document of early Spanish literature'.[8] But it is art historians who have pushed this kind of impressionistic theorizing to the limit, in their studies of chess pieces as an art form. Thus Hans and Siegfried Wichmann say of the rule changes which brought about the new chess: 'The emancipation of the individual piece, which began to undermine the hierarchical concept of the game, might be regarded as a distant parallel to the development of man's power, which stood in a causal relationship to his increased urge towards individual independence.'[9] In fact, of course, the structure of the game remained hierarchical, and so in most respects did the structure of society. It is certainly a striking fact that the dominant piece in the new chess should be the queen, the only one with a female name, but no conceivable change in fifteenth-century history can explain it. The suggestion that the powerful chess queen was modelled on some dominant female personage of the period, whether Catherine Sforza or (far less plausibly) Joan of Arc, is no more than wishful thinking, unless some evidence to support it can be discovered.[10] But if such theories are disregarded, what effect did the change in the game of chess have on its social status?

Technical historians of chess tend not unnaturally to assume that a transformation in the rules of play led directly to alterations in the social appeal of the game and the way it was regarded. In the long run this was true, but through social as well as technical change, and it is not clear that the process had gone very far by 1600, or even 1700. Certainly, the new chess must have struck the casual player as a rather different undertaking from the medieval game. The increased striking power of the forces on both sides meant that the speed of attack and defence was quickened, while the consequences of a single weak move could be much greater. Christian Egenolff in the work already referred to, *Des Schachzabels grüntlich bedeutung* of 1536, wrote that in the new game 'it is necessary to pay more, and more diligent, attention, a skill which practice best gives and teaches'. Also, as the name *current* suggests, the opposed forces came into contact much quicker at the beginning of the game. The author of *Jeu des Eschés de la dame moralisé* was among the first of many who marvelled at the fact that an incautious opponent could now be mated in as few as four moves: 'after moving the pawn, the queen guarded by the bishop may mate the king in the fourth move, even on his own square.' This so-called Scholar's Mate seemed to sum up the enhanced power of the two new pieces, for beginners at least. The nature of the new chess thus made it possible, and perhaps even necessary, for players to protect themselves against such mishaps by a little prior analysis: a tendency already observable in the specimen openings of Lucena and the 'Göttingen Manuscript'. The medieval game was liable to be slow in beginning and long drawn out in its conclusion, especially between weak players. The margin of draw was considerable, and victory was usually achieved by the gradual process of taking all the opponent's pieces ('bare king'). Actual checkmates were rare, as witness the medieval custom that a checkmate entitled the winner to a double stake. For all this the new chess substituted a game much more rapid and incisive, one which lent itself easily to effortless displays of superiority, scarcely flattering to the high-born and thick-witted. The problem collectors of the later Middle Ages had already been moving the game away from casual experiment towards analysis and methodically recorded learning, but the advent of the new chess accelerated the process. Potentially at least, a choice was presented. Those who wished to excel at chess, or even play reasonably well, now had to study; those disinclined to study could turn to some other pursuit instead.

At first sight there seems to be a certain amount of evidence that the general appeal of chess was adversely affected in this way, through the change in the rules and the growth of technical knowledge. As early as the 1520s, in his *Book of the Courtier* (published 1527, but written mostly between 1516 and 1518), Baldassare Castiglione had one of his characters say that it is possible for chess

> to demand too much knowledge, so that anyone who wishes to become an outstanding player must, I think, give to it as much time and study as he would to learning some noble science or performing well something or other of importance; and yet for all his pains when all is said and done all he knows is a game. Therefore as far as chess is concerned we reach what is a very rare conclusion: that mediocrity is more to be praised than excellence.

When another character interjects that Spaniards play chess well without exhaustive study, he is told that 'they put in a great deal of study, but they conceal it'.[11] At the end of the century, in his advice book the *Basilikon Doron*, first published in 1598, James VI of Scotland wrote that:

As for the chess I think it over fond, because it is over wise and philosophic a folly. For where all such light plays are ordained to free men's heads for a time from the fashious thoughts on their affairs, it by the contrary filleth and troubleth men's heads with as many fashious toys of the play, as before it was filled with thoughts of his affairs.[12]

Finally Robert Burton in his *Anatomy of Melancholy* (1621), held that for some men there was

nothing better to distract their mind and alter their meditations . . . . But if it proceed from overmuch study, in such a case it may do more harm than good; it is a game too troublesome for some men's brains, too full of anxiety, all out as bad as study, and besides it is a testy choleric game, and very offensive to him that loses the mate.[13]

In addition, a greater variety of alternative indoor pursuits were gradually becoming available. Playing cards had been known in Europe since the fourteenth century, but as the range of card games increased they presented more of a challenge to chess, as well as to crude dicing and the older variants of 'tables' (backgammon). Other fashions, such as the popularity of domestic singing, dancing and music-making in sixteenth-century England, had a similar effect. In the wake of the Reformation, there was also the renewed attack on games and gaming by various puritan groups to be taken into account. There thus appears to be good cause to expect a decline in the popularity of chess after 1500, and several historians have claimed that such a decline actually took place, though their perspectives may have been distorted by an unrealistically high assessment of the game's universal appeal in the later Middle Ages. Murray subscribed to this interpretation of events, though he argued that 'the reform in the moves of chess towards the close of the fifteenth century delayed the triumph of cards for a time'.[14] But, in fact, such evidence as can be roughly quantified does not really lend support to these assumptions. If the technical chess literature preserved in late medieval manuscripts is compared with that in sixteenth- and seventeenth-century manuscripts and printed books, or if the casual references to the game in wills, inventories, letters and general literature are contrasted for the two periods, there is nothing to suggest a measureable decline in its popularity. Perhaps the extraordinary success of the moralized chess of Jacobus de Cessolis, described in the last chapter, provides the strongest evidence for an extremely widespread knowledge of chess in the later Middle Ages. Without such knowledge, however elementary, and some experience of the real game, the chess sermon would not have had the vogue that it did. But even here there is a parallel, in Marco Girolamo Vida's mock-heroic poem *Scacchia ludus*, which appeared in about forty printed editions between 1525 and 1616, and was translated into Italian, French, English and German. Thomas Middleton's play *A Game at Chess*

(1624) was essentially a piece of dramatized political propaganda, and that was the reason for its success, but it could hardly have been written in the form that it was, if the game itself had ceased to be a familiar feature of contemporary life by then.

Naturally, if this was so, it raises a further question: how could the popularity of chess be almost unaffected by such a major change in the rules and quality of the game as took place around the year 1500? A number of reasons might be suggested. The reform in the rules, while drastic in its eventual effects, was quickly learnt and did not require any change in the boards and pieces which were already in use. Christian Egenolff was able to reassure his readers in 1536 that *'current* chess is almost the same as orthodox chess, except that there is a difference in the moves of some of the pieces', which he then went on to describe. The new chess was evidently popular in its early years, otherwise it would not have supplanted the medieval game so easily, while the less committed players who were liable in the long run to be put off by its more technical nature, need only have been deterred when the general level of technical knowledge had risen uncomfortably high. Despite the advent of printing, and the appearance of some very talented and internationally famous players, this only happened very slowly. During the period down to 1650, there was only the most rudimentary knowledge of chess theory outside a few small and unrepresentative groups. For most men, only a little learning was required to keep up with the general standard of play, and that little was easily acquired, especially in an age of improved education among the nobility and gentry. Enterprising writers and printers met this trend half-way by producing books on chess like Arthur Saul's *Famous Game of Chesse-play* (1614), which contained only the absolute minimum of technical information and had much more to say about the etiquette and social advantages associated with the game. The popularity of books like this, while the works of the greatest player of that time, Gioachino Greco, were known only in manuscript, is highly indicative: chess was not yet restricted to an intellectual minority.

The new chess players

These generalizations may seem more acceptable in the light of a fuller survey of the chess literature of the period 1500 to 1650. Lucena's *Arte de Axedrez* of 1496/1497 was never reprinted and does not seem to have had a wide influence. Its lavish format and design may have been appropriate for a royal patron, but it was not calculated to enable the book to reach a wider market. The case was quite different with Damiano's *Questo libro e da imparare giocare a scachi*, printed at Rome in 1512. It was reprinted in 1518 and 1524, also at Rome, and then there were four more undated editions, which can be put in order by typographical evidence and the progressive dilapidation of the woodcuts in the text, before the next dated reissue, at Venice in 1564. This record of eight editions in just over fifty years is a striking one, though print runs were probably not large. It is unlikely that more than 200–300 copies of Lucena's book were produced, and more than 400–500 in any of the editions of Damiano. Nevertheless Damiano's book was, in contemporary terms, the first bestseller of the modern game. It was published at Paris in 1560, in a French translation by Claude Gruget, and this French version was then turned into English and published at London in 1562, with a reprint in 1569. The reasons for its success were largely commercial. Unlike Lucena's work, it was produced at a major cultural centre, and was not so dependent for its success on the influence of the dedicatee, who was Ioangeorgio Caesarino. It was printed in a small and economical format, very important at a time when hand-made paper was extremely expensive, and usually accounted for a third to a half of the total investment required to publish a book. Printers had to keep their presses running, and when large projects could not be found, they filled in time with compact books, which could be produced comparatively quickly from a few folded sheets. The mixture of type-faces in the different Damiano editions (roman and gothic) suggests that they were run off in just this way, using whatever spare type was available around the workshop. The biggest investment required was for the production of separate woodcuts for each of the seventy two problems and sixteen *trati sutili* ('studies') which made up the bulk of the text, even though these were smaller and rougher than the hundred and fifty-four used in Lucena. But once the wood blocks had been made they were handed on from printer to printer, and one set were re-used in five successive editions down to 1564, though they became blurred and were sometimes mended and patched. From the printer's point of view these blocks were the essence of the book, much more so than an accurate text, or the author's name, which was omitted from editions later than the third (1524).

Yet Damiano's selection of material also had something to do with the success of the work. It is striking, for instance, that the solutions to his problems appear in a dual-language form, both Italian and Spanish versions being given. His seventy-two problems were taken with only two exceptions from Lucena (or more likely from Lucena's original, since they appear here in a different order), but the introductory discussion and analysis seems to have been his own. Apart from general advice, the sixteen studies, and a final section on blindfold play, this consists of nine specimen opening variations, arranged in six chapters. Four of these 'games' are played level, and all of them were derived from Lucena, the 'Göttingen Manuscript,' or a related source, though in two cases Damiano clearly found improvements on the Göttingen analysis. But his other five examples were all played at various kinds of odds, with one player surrendering anything between a pawn and a knight. Damiano's emphasis on odds play is usually regretted by chess historians, who see it as a diversion from the main path of theoretical advance, but it probably contributed to the popularity of his book. The giving of odds by the stronger party, referred to in passing by Lucena but much more thoroughly worked out by Damiano, was yet another of the ways in which the impact of the new chess was softened for the casual or inexpert player. The habit persisted well into the nineteenth century and has become obsolete only in recent times, so its importance for the social history of chess has been very great.

In general Damiano held the field during the first half of the sixteenth century. Several distinguished figures were mentioned as the authors of books on chess, notably the mathematician Luca Pacioli (1455–*c.* 1509) who was a friend of Leonardo da Vinci, and Girolamo Cardano (1501–1576), the doctor and pseudo-scientist who developed the origins of probability theory out of his study and practice of gambling. But neither of these works can have had a very wide circulation, and neither appears to have been printed. In northern Europe there was not much demand for anything more sophisticated than Damiano even after 1550. The French and English editions of his book (1560 and 1562) actually omitted all the studies and problems, leaving a drastically truncated text which was much more of a 'courtesy' book than a serious manual of instruction. In Italy and Spain, however, there were at least some groups of more advanced players who began to find Damiano inadequate and out of date. The most famous of these men was Ruy Lopez of Segura, a Spanish priest who visited Rome in 1560, on ecclesiastical business connected with the recent election of Pope Pius IV. There he met the Roman chess players and encountered Damiano's book, without forming a favourable impression of either. He wrote in 1561 that Damiano's analyses were 'the sort of play which some players practice with those who do not know much about the game', though he added that 'a flamboyant player called "the Boy of Rome" played even with me' (that is without receiving odds). Convinced that he could do better himself, Lopez returned to Spain and published his *Libro de la invencion liberal y arte del juego del Axedrez* (Alcala 1561), a work in four books and no less than ninety-five chapters. One of the books was specifically devoted to pungent criticism of Damiano, and may have become known fairly rapidly in Italy. The whole work was eventually translated into Italian by Giovanni Tarsia, albeit inaccurately, and published at Venice in 1584. Lopez's book fails to convince the modern reader that its author was a strong player (though he may have been), but it certainly marked an advance in its method, by moving away from the typically medieval collection of problems towards more intensive analysis of the openings. By taking the starting position of the chess pieces as the point of departure, this also circumvented the technical difficulty of reproducing large numbers of diagrams, which was an important advantage.

The period between the publication of Lopez's book in 1561 and the mid-seventeenth century is sometimes described as the heroic age of chess. It was characterized by a number of players, all of them Italian in origin, who contributed greatly to the theory of the game and built up international reputations for themselves, but published hardly any of their ideas and did little to change the way in which chess was regarded in general. Even the stories of their own lives were so romanticized and embellished by contemporaries with literary ambitions that it is all but impossible to distinguish fact from fiction. Nonetheless, the stories of these shadowy figures and their epic contests with one another do reflect a new trend in the history of chess: the appearance of itinerant champions travelling from one court or centre to another in search of patronage and reward, like the most celebrated artists and musicians of the day. The new chess lent itself much more readily than the medieval game to such displays of competitive virtuosity, and in Italy and Spain at least some patrons thought it worth their while to maintain champion players, or reward their victories.

Before plunging into the confusion of events between 1560 and 1600, it is worth surveying the evidence on which any reconstruction must be based. Almost all of it is derived from Pietro Carrera and Alessandro Salvio, who both published books on chess in the early seventeenth century. Carrera (1573–1647) was a Sicilian historian and antiquarian rather than a serious chess player. His *Il Gioco degli Scacchi*, published at Militello in Sicily in 1617, was a very large book, but like his other works it was mostly a product of methodical compilation, and contained little in the way of original ideas. Salvio (*c.* 1570—*c.* 1640) had stronger claims to be a practical player and his more compact *Trattato dell'Inventione e arte liberale del gioco di scacchi* (Naples 1604) was mostly devoted to opening analysis and some early examples of recorded games attributed to contemporary players. But Salvio too had literary pretensions, which he betrayed in 1612 by publishing *La Scaccaide*, 'a tragedy drawn from the invention of the game of chess'. This work was for a long time thought to be lost, but it has now been rediscovered, though it is scarcely much read. Salvio must also have been a touchy man, because when he republished his *Trattato* in 1634 he added a whole new section attacking Carrera, on the flimsy pretext that the latter had criticized one of his moves. He also tried to outdo his rival's history, by replacing Carrera's comparatively straightforward account of the famous players of the late sixteenth century with a romantic and partisan biography of one of them, Giovanni Leonardo, nicknamed *Il Puttino* ('the boy'), which was the title Salvio gave to his book. Neither Salvio nor Carrera seem to have known Leonardo, who probably died between 1586 and 1590 at the age of forty-five, but they both claimed to have met his main rival Paolo Boi shortly before the latter's death in 1598, aged about seventy, and to have drawn information from him.

The essence of the story they told is as follows. Some time early in his career Leonardo met Ruy Lopez in Rome, and was defeated. This may have been as early as 1560, if it is the contest referred to by Lopez himself. Subsequently Leonardo played many games with Boi, and they appeared to be of equal strength. Both the Italian champions then resolved to go to Spain, where they had learnt (according to Carrera) that 'there were very famous players who were honoured and rewarded, not only by some of the nobles, but by the king himself, who took considerable pleasure in the game'. In 1574 and 1575 they each made the journey to Madrid and each of them defeated Lopez and was well rewarded by King Philip II, before going on to Portugal, where they played before King Sebastian. Carrera reproduces the text of a letter of recommendation dated August 22 1575, which Boi claimed had been issued to him by the King of Spain. Back in Italy again the two men continued to meet in the intervals of their various appointments, until Leonardo's death, after which Boi still travelled from post to post until he retired to his native Sicily towards the end of his life. But this bald narrative does not really do justice to the flavour of the story. The two writers outdid one another, or rather Salvio outdid Carrera, in the colourful details they could report: the tales of rich patrons and fabulous rewards, dangerous journeys, jealous rivals and heroic deeds. The result was something which could stand up to the most eventful of Renaissance memoirs, or the *novelle* of contemporary fiction. Both players were said to have been captured by pirates, but to have secured their liberty by playing chess with the chiefs of their captors. Boi also contrived to play chess among the Turks while riding on horseback, regardless of the fact that no Turk would have played European chess at this date, even on foot. Leonardo for his part was credited with a secret love affair in Genoa, which ended tragically in the lady's death. Finally, and inevitably, both men died at the hands of poisoners, through jealousy of their gifts.

The task of extracting historical truth from all this is not an easy one. That it is possible at all is largely because of the writings of Giulio Cesare Polerio, a younger contemporary who accompanied Leonardo to Madrid and remained there for several years afterwards. A number of manuscripts survive attributed to Polerio, some signed by him and others in the same hand, dateable to the period between about 1580 and 1600 or a little later. These provide contemporary evidence of at least the less lurid events described by Carrera and Salvio. Besides a partial translation of Lopez, they contain Polerio's own analyses, and those he had obtained from the collections of contemporaries, as well as a few possibly genuine recorded games, notably those played between the Italian and Spanish champions at Madrid in 1575. The oldest manuscript, which was in the process of compilation at the Spanish court in 1584, appears to have been Polerio's own 'common-place book' and acknowledges debts to several contemporary Spanish players as well as Leonardo. The others, apparently written in the 1590s, were fair copies made for patrons, though material was constantly being added and deleted, some of it in hands other than Polerio's own. Such collections were kept continually up to date, and none of the printed books which appeared between 1600 and 1650, not even Salvio's, would have rendered them redundant. Because of Polerio it is possible to build up a reasonably reliable picture of the Spanish and Italian chess of this period, which was naturally linked together by Spanish rule in Naples and Sicily. It seems certain that Leonardo and Boi did go to Madrid to try their strength against Lopez and others, though it is unlikely that they made a practice of losing the first few games in every match, the better to demonstrate their eventual superiority, as reported by Salvio. It also seems clear that there were a number of wealthy and generous patrons of chess, though their generosity cannot have been quite so great as in the stories. Philip II may or may not have given Lopez a gold chain with a gold chess rook on it and Boi a letter of recommendation; he certainly did not exempt Leonardo's birthplace of Cutro in Calabria from taxation, as Salvio asserts. But chess players do seem to have been maintained at the court in Madrid. The leading Italian patron in this period, down to his death in 1612, was Giacomo Buoncompagno Duke of Sora, the illegitimate son of Pope Gregory XIII. Again, the size of his gifts to chess players has probably been exaggerated, but the fact that he was a generous patron is well attested. Tarsia's Lopez was dedicated to him in 1584, and two of the Polerio manuscripts were still held by the Boncompagni family early in this century, as well as a number of related treatises.

Perhaps even more striking than the careers of the famous professional champions was the fact reported by Salvio in 1634 that keen amateur players were beginning to meet regularly in little groups, which they called 'academies', in some Italian centres. Salvio himself was a member of such a group, which met in Naples at the house of Alessandro Rovito, a successful judge and local administrator. Yet even in southern Italy such developments were exceptional, while further north there was much less sign of serious attempts to improve the standard of play, however much the game may have maintained its popularity as a genteel pursuit. Horatio Gianutio's *Libro nel quale si tratta della Maniera di giocar' a Scacchi*, published in Turin in 1597, was typical of the genre of 'polite' chess books, with a discussion of only a few openings, some of them played at odds. Meanwhile, the analysis in Polerio's manuscripts was considerably more advanced than anything in print, but it was known only to narrow circles of patrons and initiates, which was a serious bar to further advance. It is a striking fact that after an initial period when the theoretical ideas generated by the new chess found their way into print, there followed almost a century (1560–1650) when the most sophisticated work went back into manuscript again. Clearly this was not for technical reasons. The problems of printing chess books were considerable, but they did not increase after 1560, and there was nothing to prevent the appearance of Tarsia's Lopez in 1584, or new editions of Damiano in Bologna (1606) and Venice (1618), as well as the works of Salvio and Carrera. The usual explanation given for the avoidance of publication is that in the new atmosphere of competition leading players kept their ideas to themselves, for use in practical play. As it stands this argument is not very plausible: ideas could not be kept secret very easily and Polerio's notebooks suggest that new discoveries did become known, among the 'master' players at least. It is more convincing when translated into economic terms: in contemporary conditions a better return could be secured from a few rich patrons who thought they were buying something exclusive than from commercial publishers.

This also leads to the more general conclusions that there was not yet a large market for advanced works on chess. For many readers perhaps, one chess book was still as good as another. But a factor whose importance has been overestimated is the persistence of small differences in the rules of the game, concerning such matters as castling, between Spain, Italy and the rest of Europe. It is unrealistic to regard these variants as major barriers to the dissemination of new ideas, at all comparable to the social and economic factors. All evidence drawn from the later development of the game suggests that as soon as there was more interest in studying chess theory and freer circulation of the conclusions in print, the rule differences faded away. Such differences were symptoms and not causes of the situation that existed before 1650.

A survey of the career of Gioachino Greco, the last great player of the 'heroic age', serves only to strengthen these conclusions. Like many of his predecessors, Greco was born in southern Italy (in 1600 or a little earlier) but made his career in Rome, where he was a client of another member of the Boncompagni family, who was later Archbishop of Naples. Greco too published nothing in his own lifetime, but his earliest survivng manu-scripts, of 1619 and 1620, show that he was then very dependent on Lopez and what he had been able to pick up of unpublished works from the previous generation. They also show that he was an uneducated man, barely able to write grammatical Italian. As his career progressed Greco augmented his stock of inherited ideas and developed his own distinctive contribution; he also learnt to write better. But his real achievement was to bring the advanced Italian theory of his day to the rest of Europe, through his tours of France and England in the 1620s. In 1621 he was at the court of the Duke of Lorraine at Nancy, and then went on to Paris. In 1622 and 1623 he was in London, having been robbed on the road, according to another typical story, of the great sum he had made by his play hitherto. Returning to Paris in 1624, he is said to have gone on to Spain two or three years later, and then disappears from view. If later writers can be believed, he went to the West Indies and died there in the 1630s, but this is not certain. Throughout his brief career Greco copied, and sold, his manuscripts wherever he went, and they grew progressively longer, until they reached their fullest surviving form in those specimens written at Paris in 1624 and 1625.

In stark contrast to the more discursive books of the period, they made almost no concessions to the weak player. After a short introduction, sometimes dispensed with, each copy launches into page after page of opening lines and composed games, with only the most occasional explanatory comments. Greco usually procured decorated title pages appropriately worded for each of his customers, but the text itself was always in Italian and probably copied by the author himself. Naturally, this imposed strict limits on the number of copies that could be distributed, and only about twenty of these manuscripts now survive, including those made in Italy before 1621. Greco's influence on European chess was therefore very great in the long term, but severely restricted in his own lifetime. The seeds were sown in the 1620s, but only bore fruit after 1650 when his works were printed and widely distributed, in a more favourable social climate for the study of the game.

In the meantime French chess players had to rely on the Tarsia Lopez, which was translated into French and published in Paris in 1609, with reprints in 1615 (two versions) and 1636. The same work was rendered into German, though in rather a garbled form, in *Das Schach- oder König-Spiel*, published at Leipzig in 1616. The name of the author, 'Gustavus Selenus', was really the pseudonym of the scholarly Duke Augustus of Brunswick-Lüneburg, who also wrote on the occult sciences. In England even works of this degree of sophistication were not available. The only chess book printed in English in the first half of the seventeenth century was Arthur Saul's *Famous Game of Chesse-play* (1614), the classic example of a book designed to teach the aspirant to play decorously rather than well. Though Saul announced that 'by reading this small Book thou shalt profit more than by the playing a thousand Mates', he only managed to describe Scholar's Mate, Fool's Mate and one other opening in the course of his twenty-two chapters of rambling and discursive general advice. He was perhaps more concerned to emphasize that chess was 'An Exercise full of delight; fit for Princes, or any person of what quality, soever', the worthiest game ever devised, 'and so much esteemed of by the Nobility and Gentry of this our Kingdom, as also in all other Countries in Christendom'.[15] It is easy to regard Saul's book as merely comic, so little does it conform to the modern idea of a chess book, but it actually provides valuable evidence for the way in which the game was played by the majority of gentlemen amateurs all over Europe in the seventeenth century. Men who learnt how to play chess from books like this were not seeking something that was mentally challenging, so much as adopting a pastime that was traditional, dignified, and long established as appropriate to their rank. While enthusiasts struggled to decipher Greco's ill-written manuscripts, *The Famous Game of Chesse-play* was a commercial success. It was revised in 1618, and reprinted three more times after that.

The image of the game

Another way of testing general theories about the social status of chess in this period is to examine the image of the game in non-technical evidence: law, literature, correspondence, and the whole range of historical source material, some of which has already been referred to.

The sixteenth century was a period of cultural conflict: conflict not only between Protestants and Catholics, but also between censors and puritans on both sides of the religious divide and various forms of inherited culture over which they desired to exercise greater control. In this confused and intermittent struggle chess profited from being less exposed to attack than some other pursuits. Canon lawyers and Catholic writers in general usually followed the distinction made by the late medieval scholastics: that games of skill like chess were exempted from the general ban on gambling games, even for the clergy. In a manuscript *Disputatio* presented to the Emperor Maximilian I at Freiburg in 1498, Jacob Mennel undertook to prove this point 'from both canon and civil law'. Almost a century later the lawyer Thomas Actius took much the same view in his *De ludo scacchorum in legali methodo tractatus* (Pisa 1583). In Protestant Europe there were some rather more sweeping attacks on ungodly pursuits, but even there chess was frequently defended when other pastimes were decried. The game was especially congenial to those who were trying to define a middle way between libertarianism and control, seeking to wean men away from really objectionable pursuits by holding out the prospect of honest recreation instead. In 1581 Thomas Wilcox wrote in *A Glasse for Gamesters*: 'why, I pray you, should there not be as great recreation in the Game of the Chestes, the Philosopher's

Game, and such like, which in all men's judgements, are counted lawful, as in the Cards and Dice?'

Such opinions seem to have been common in clerical circles too. One of the specimens of rectitude exhibited in Samuel Clarke's *Lives of thirty-two English divines* (1677) was Paul Baines, who died in 1617. Baines went to some trouble to reform his wife's sister who 'used to play much at Cards, and such like Games', but as for himself, 'Little Recreation he used, but sometimes to play at Chesse'. Chess writers themselves enthusiastically adopted such attitudes. The translator of Gruget's Damiano in 1562 (usually thought to have been the printer James Rowbothum, but more likely William Ward who wrote the prefatory verses) claimed that 'this game or rather kingly pastime is not only void of all craft, guile, fraud, deceit, colour, swearing, staring, impatience, fretting, or falling out: but also it breedeth in plays a certain study, policy, wit, forecast, memory . . .'. This was contrasted with 'any art of dice play, of cogging, or setting dice, of falsehood in card play, or any other like sleights for the deceiving one another or for stirring men to anger as such games do often times'.[16] Criticisms like this did have some effect, as can be seen from the trouble taken by card manufacturers to adorn packs with maps and other useful information, the better to claim an honest educational value for their products.

It is not easy to define the cultural image of chess with any precision in the sixteenth and seventeenth centuries, but it is characteristic that the slow and halting growth of technical writing on the game was complemented by the persistence of very traditional literary embodiments of it. Some of the symbolic meanings which had been so strongly linked with medieval chess, and culminated in the extraordinary popularity of Jacobus de Cessolis' chess sermon, still clung to the game during the subsequent period. There was, after all, no reason why these long established notions should rapidly disappear around the year 1500. It has been argued above that the advent of the new chess did not alter the social status of the game, as a characteristic pursuit of the upper classes. This status reflected the fact that it was not just a common pastime among the nobility and gentry (and their imitators) but an appropriate one, because of its links with history and legend. Down to the end of the seventeenth century players and writers still knew almost nothing about the real origins of chess. They still saw it as an inheritance from the ancient past, and frequently used medieval myth to explain its invention. There were therefore no sudden changes in the way in which chess was regarded between 1500 and 1650. The meanings which men had tended to read into the game were not swept away, but only gradually modified by the changing intellectual climate of the period. What had once been a natural symbolic association, as between the different chess pieces and the ranks and degrees of society, slowly became instead a self-conscious literary device, adopted for reasons of style or exposition of material.

So it was that the moralized chess of de Cessolis continued to be popular into the age of printing, with a number of editions even after 1500. This is a striking testimony to the persistence of its general appeal, since by that time it was outdated in several different ways. The change in the rules of chess made nonsense of passages in which conclusions were drawn from the moves of the medieval pieces, though (at some cost to the coherence of the whole book) those particular passages could be rewritten or omitted entirely, as they were in the Spanish version published at Valladolid in 1549. Secondly, the text was typically medieval in that it contained large numbers of misattributions and garbled versions of classical stories, derived through numerous intermediaries and coloured by the accidents of manuscript transmission. In the fifteenth century this did not matter, even in Italy. Advanced classical learning was still restricted to small and unrepresentative groups, more so than many historians are prepared to concede, and reprints of Jacobus de Cessolis at Florence (1493) and elsewhere reflect this fact. But after 1500 the spread of classical education made it gradually less possible to tolerate such eccentricities of the text as 'the philosopher Xerxes' and the legends of the life of Alexander. In the third place there was the general shift in values referred to above. Sixteenth-century writers were perfectly prepared to employ chess as a literary allegory, but it no longer seemed apposite to link the game with the kind of moralizing found in the medieval text. So the Spanish edition of 1549, and one in Dutch published at Louvain in 1551, were the last printed versions of the work. Thereafter, as lamented by Sir Thomas Elyot in 1531, it gradually faded away, though Ruy Lopez and others turned to it for accounts of the game's origins. Arthur Saul still thought that chess had been invented by Xerxes, though at least he knew that Xerxes was a king and not a philosopher.[17]

Subsequent writers tended to use allegories of chess in a more secular way, and with one or two exceptions, they attained no great popularity. The only known attempt to construct a true 'morality' around the rules of the new chess, the *Jeu des Eschés de la dame moralisé* of *c.* 1500, found no imitators. Despite occasional references to Amazons, chess writers in general avoided drawing any symbolic conclusions from the reformed queen. When, in the second part of *Don Quixote* (published in 1614), Cervantes has Sancho Panza refer to the comparison of life with the game of chess 'where each piece has its particular importance', and his master replies 'every day you grow less simple and wiser', we need not suppose the author is being serious. Secular analogies of chess tended to return to its similarity with war. Sometime in the mid-sixteenth century Luigi Guicciardini, nephew of the Francesco Guicciardini who was a contemporary of Machiavelli, wrote a manuscript 'Comparison of the Game of Chess with the notable treatises of war' which he dedicated to Cosimo de Medici, Duke of Florence.[18] There were also a number of other ways in which writers could perceive social and political meanings in the game. Étienne Pasquier, in *Les Recherches de la France* (1560), developed a chess analogy at some length in order to support various conclusions, such as 'there is no danger in the state the king should fear so much as the revolt of his nobles'. In 1608 Guillaume du Peyrat, who described himself as 'Aumosnier ordinaire et servant' at the court of Henry IV of France, published *La Philosophie Royale du Jeu des eschets*, which was said to be 'pour Monseigneur le Daufin'. It was intended to teach the prince, then aged seven, a few useful lessons about the duties of a king, but in a congenial form. Jo. Barbier, who revised Arthur Saul's *Famous Game of Chesse-play* in 1618, saw a particularly happy parallel between individual advancement and pawn promotion, 'which rich reward of virtue conferred on the least, is a moral Emblem encouraging all in a Commonwealth, worthily to carry themselves, and to do their best devoire, for the honour of their King, good and safety of their country'.[19] Saul himself had already alluded to this in verse little more distinguished than his play:

And coming at the last in place,
where Knights and Lords did dwell,
Their King shall give to them like grace,
because they served him well.

Yet ere they can such honour have,
all storms they must abide,
And do their best the Kings to save,
What danger ere betide.

This was truly a tract for the times when the *Famous Game* was reissued in 1640. But on the other side, there was a Civil War pamphlet called *The Game at Chess: a metaphorical discourse showing the present Estate of this Kingdom*, published in 1643. In 1624 the playwright Thomas Middleton had drawn on the Saul–Barbier book, as well as many non-chess sources, to write his dramatized anti-Spanish polemic *A Game at Chess*, which played to packed houses for nine days running, an unprecedented achievement at the time. It was taken off only because of the protests of the Spanish ambassador, whose predecessor Gondomar was actually portrayed on stage as the Black Knight.

There remains the use of chess images for purely literary effects: conceits, figures of speech and allusions. Such references are too numerous for separate discussion, but one chess poem which must be mentioned, because of its extraordinary popularity, in the *Scacchia ludus* of Marco Girolamo Vida (*c.* 1485–1566). Before he became Bishop of Alba in 1533, Vida made his career in Rome, mostly by writing Latin verse. The *Scacchia ludus* is a mock-heroic poem, of 658 lines in its final form, which describes a mythological chess game between Apollo and Mercury, played in the presence of the other gods and culminating in the teaching of chess to mankind through the agency of the nymph Scacchis. Vida wrote and revised this poem almost as often as Castiglione rewrote his *Book of the Courtier* at about the same time. The recent researches of Mario Di Cesare have shown that there are four surviving drafts (rather than two as previously thought), and that the earliest of them was probably composed by 1510.[20] But when the poem found its way into print, first in a pirate version published at Lyons in 1525, and then in Vida's approved edition of his own works at Rome in 1527, its success was almost unqualified. Between 1525 and 1650 there were about forty editions of the Latin text, as well as translations into Italian (1544), French (1551), English (1597) and German (1606), the Italian and French versions each being reprinted several times. It was freely adapted into Polish by Jan Kochánowski in about 1555.[21] So great was the vogue of the poem that even Vida's attempts to invent 'classical' names for some of the chess pieces ('centaur' and 'archer' for bishop, or 'cyclops', 'elephant' and 'tower' for rook) came to be used by contemporary writers on the game, though the fact that 'tower' eventually became the term for the rook in most languages after 1800 was probably not his doing.

There were other poems written in the same genre as Vida's: notably the Catalan *Scachs d'amor* of about 1500 and the sixteenth-century *De ludo scachorum* of Francisco Caldogno, but none of them ever approached its success. The *Scacchia ludus* was a remarkable and isolated phenomenon. Simply through its popularity it appeared to come close to creating a kind of alternative mythology of chess, which might have replaced the declining medieval symbolism. As Johan Huizinga remarked about such changes in general: 'The Olympians and the nymphs get the better of the allegorical personages, who fade away in proportion as the poetic glory of Antiquity is more intensely felt.'[22] But in the end, the neo-classical imagery was too insubstantial and too tenuously linked with the game itself to influence the image of chess very much.

The general conclusion is therefore that the new chess of the Renaissance created the possibility of a new kind of game, one that was much more analytical and systematically competitive than medieval chess had been. But while it was now technically possible for this to occur, it was not yet socially possible; because nearly all chess players had no interest in promoting the study of the game and were under little pressure to learn more about it. They aimed only at the gentlemanly mediocrity advocated by Castiglione. More advanced chess theory could be supplied, but it was not on the whole demanded, except by small and unrepresentative groups of people. Because of this the achievements of individual players, even those of possible genius like Greco, were limited in their initial effect. Without a wider basis of support and freer circulation of ideas in printed books, chess moved only very slowly towards becoming a more intellectual game. Men like James I and Montaigne, who claimed that chess was too serious and absorbing to divert a gentleman's leisure hours, pointed the way towards an important change in the appeal of the game. But in their time, that change had hardly begun.

CHAPTER FOUR

The Game of the Intellectuals 1650-1800

In chess, as in music, the seventeenth century was a transitional period. There were new ideas and new attitudes, but it was hard to know which of them mattered most, or where they were leading. Only in retrospect, by 1700 or 1750, did contemporaries see more clearly which had been the important changes, the precedents for future advance. So it was in the eighteenth century that chess was finally seen to have broken away from its medieval inheritance. The rules of play had changed two centuries before, but only now was the game really regarded in a different light, taken up and pursued for new reasons and in a new way. Before and after 1700 the increasing difficulty and bookishness of chess diminished its traditional appeal, but simultaneously opened up new sources of support; from now on chess grew and flourished because of its intellectual and sporting qualities rather than its symbolic prestige. The process of change was a gradual one and the majority of chess players still played casually, but even so they were conscious of the changing image of their chosen diversion, perhaps indeed chose it for that reason. A symptom of this was the way in which, from the eighteenth century onwards, the most advanced technical writing about chess increasingly found its way into print and met with a ready market. The appearance of such books reflected growing communication between the few 'masters' at the top of the pyramid and the many players who made up its base, to the mutual benefit of both groups, so that the evidence of chess literature plays an important part in the study of the change.

The seventeenth century

It is partly for accidental reasons that the period between 1650 and 1700 has never been regarded as an outstanding one in chess history. During these years there were no outstanding players, no equivalents of Polerio and Greco, whose exploits were celebrated and whose ideas were passed on by later writers. But the existence of great players was not the only important factor. The predominantly Italian–Spanish chess culture of the Renaissance had failed to transform the medieval image of the game before 1650, despite the presence of such individual talents, because it was too shallow-rooted and narrowly based on aristocratic and courtly patronage. In particular, it had failed to create a wide interest in the increased possibilities of the game, so that in most of Europe the new chess was adopted without any corresponding desire to raise the standard of play. But the progress made by the game later on, both in its social appeal and in the way it was played, was not altogether without precedents in the earlier period. In Italy at least, some groups had begun to show more interest in the intellectual problems presented by chess, though much of their energy was diverted into studying the curiosities and antiquities of the game, as the works of Carrera and Salvio testify. And after 1650 there was further progress, despite the absence of great players, because the advances that had been made in chess theory since the time of Lopez began to find their way into print and become more widely known. Greco in particular almost dominated the chess of the period down to the mid-eighteenth century through the posthumous publication of his manu-scripts, which attained a popularity inconceivable in his own lifetime.

The process began, implausibly, in England, which hitherto had no chess literature more advanced than the abridged version of Damiano in 1562. In 1656 Francis Beale edited and published *The Royall Game of Chesse-Play . . . Illustrated with almost an hundred Gambetts. Being the study of Biochimo the famous Italian.* 'Biochimo the famous Italian', despite his suspiciously fairground ring, was none other than Greco (i.e. *Gioachino*), and the book was almost entirely based on Greco's manu-script legacy from the 1620s. The hundred gambits or specimen openings ('gambit' had hardly yet begun to take on its modern meaning of an opening involving a calculated sacrifice of material) certainly look as though they were translated directly from one of Greco's copies, though none of his surviving 'English' manuscripts of 1622–23 correspond precisely with the collection in the printed work. The editor Francis Beale was certainly conscious that his book represented a new departure. In his dedication to the Earl of Lindsey he referred to 'the necessity I have of desiring your Lordship's Protection for that I have attempted to publish, that which some Gentlemen have already in Manuscript, and peradven-ture to their displeasure . . . '. In some ways the motives behind the publication remain obscure. It must have been aimed at the same audience of aristocratic and pseudo-aristocratic amateurs as the earlier book by Saul and Barbier; in 1656 the printer even headed his errata list, 'Gentlemen, For few else will buy this Book, I intreat you to correct these Errors'. Beale therefore took the opportunity to augment Greco's games, which were given as in the manuscripts with almost no notes or explanation, by adding a much more elementary introduction taken largely from the Saul-Barbier *Famous Game of Chesse-play*, itself recently reprinted (in 1652). Presumably also in deference to the taste of his readers, he added a number of appropriate verses: two specially written dedicatory ones (by Eldred Revett and Richard Lovelace) and one longer poem, a sort of imitation of Vida dedicated to the lawyer John Budden, which had first appeared the previous year in *Musarum Deliciae*, by Sir John Mennis and James Smith. Like other works in the same genre, it contained numerous allusions to the symbolic meaning of the game, though these were now becoming increasingly self-conscious and unconvincing. As in Arthur Saul's doggerel, pawn promotion was equated with social promotion:

If bravely to the Armies head he move;
Such may his valour be, he may of right
Be an executor to Rook or Knight,
Whose Lands fall to the King (their Master dead)
With which this Pawn lives to be honoured.

It is a relief to turn from this sort of thing to the wholly unserious and graceful conceits of Richard Lovelace. The impression on the modern reader is bound to be paradoxical: not many of those who desired this kind of entertainment, and had to be told how to avoid 'Fool's Mate', were likely to derive much instruction from Greco's gambits, which made up most of the book. A clue may lie in the fact that the *Royall Game* was clearly intended as a gesture of political defiance. The title page, with its description of chess as 'Sometimes the Recreation of the late King, with many of the Nobility' and its portrait engraving of Charles I as a crowned monarch is sufficient proof of that, and a striking pointer to the fact that Cromwellian control of the press was no longer so great as it had been a few years earlier. Against this background the identities of those concerned in the book fall naturally into place. Lindsey was a notable royalist commander, and later one of the judges at the trial of the regicides. The printer Henry Herringman, later publisher of Dryden and bookseller to Samuel Pepys, seems to have had royalist sympathies, likewise the engraver Peter Stent. Beale himself was said by a contemporary writer to have served the king after leaving St John's College, Cambridge, in 1644. Perhaps a book on chess, while harmless in itself, seemed an ideal vehicle for a literary re-assertion of the royalist cause. The *Royall Game* therefore provides little evidence for a change in the traditional image of chess in England, or a willingness to treat the game more seriously from an intellectual point of view. It was a precocious work, which found no imitators. The next English chess book was yet another re-issue of Saul and Barbier (in 1672), while Greco's games did not appear again in English until *Chess Made Easy* of 1750.

The situation in France was quite different. The first printed edition of Greco's games, this time based on the more developed manuscripts of 1624 and 1625, was published in 1669 as *Le Jeu Des Eschets; Traduit de l'Italian de Gioachino Greco Calabrois*. After this there was a pause, during which the last Paris edition of Ruy Lopez appeared in 1674, but after Greco's 'Game of Chess' came out in a second edition in 1689 it rapidly established itself as the standard book on chess in the French language, and remained so until the mid-eighteenth century. There were new Paris editions in 1707, 1713 and 1714, while the treatise was also published at The Hague (1696), Leiden (1721) and Amsterdam (1728). Some of these copies must have found their way to England and elsewhere, but it was a common practice in the late seventeenth and early eighteenth centuries to print in Holland for the French market. The French government maintained a strict control over the number and operation of presses in Paris, for reasons of commercial regulation as well as censorship, but this policy only had the effect of attracting imports. The popularity of Greco's works meant that he acquired a new and enhanced posthumous reputation. In his *Dictionaire Historique et Critique*, first published in 1697, Pierre Bayle found space for two chess players among his biographical portraits: Paolo Boi *'le Siracusain'* and Gioachino Greco *'connu sous le nom du Calabrois'*, who 'was so excellent a player at chess, that it cannot be thought strange that I should give a short Article of him. All who excel in their profession to a certain degree deserve this distinction. He never had any equal to him at this game in any part of the world.'[1] Greco soon came to be generally known as 'the Calabrian', and even copies of his book were referred to as 'Calabrians'.

This wider dissemination of advanced technical literature simultaneously reflected and helped to create a situation in which France was replacing Italy as the natural centre of European chess, a contemporary trend paralleled in many other areas of culture. In Italy there is anecdotal evidence to suggest that groups of devotees were still meeting in several centres, much as Salvio's 'academy' had done in the 1630s, and that chess there was probably less exclusive than it was in France and England. All the social circumstances therefore appeared to favour the serious study of the game, but yet very little progress was made. It is true that there was no equivalent to the publishing boom of northern Europe, so that chess theory was less accessible to Italians; the works of Greco were hardly known in his native country and were not printed there until the nineteenth century. Such books as were available, in the north of Italy in particular, were of the 'courtesy book' genre, strong on general advice and literary anecdotes, but weak on specific analysis. This applies to the anonymous *Modo facile per intendere il vago e dilettevole Giuoco degli Scacchi* (Venice 1665), and to Francesco Piacenza's *I Campeggiamenti degli Scacchi* (Turin 1683). In the south Naples was still a more important centre, but even there little was achieved until the republication of Salvio's *Il Puttino* in 1723. As in the early seventeenth century, there was a tendency for interest in chess to be diverted into the study of its curiosities and antiquities, as evidenced in the posthumous publication of two confused books by Marco Severino: *La Filosofia, o vero il perche degli Scacchi* and *Dell' antica pettia* (Naples 1690). A similar enterprise in England produced the much more valuable historical work of Thomas Hyde, *De Ludis Orientalibus* (1694).

Elsewhere in Europe there was even less interest in studying chess, or in treating it seriously as intellectual competition. In Spain, which had been such an important centre of Renaissance chess, there were no printed books on the game after Ruy Lopez, until well into the nineteenth century. Once its narrow base of courtly patronage faded away after 1600, it seems there was no more interest in promoting skilled play or sponsoring leading players. Yet it cannot be shown that the game itself fell out of use in Spain, or even grew markedly less popular; it was simply confined to the role of an unstrenuous domestic pastime, in which role it maintained its appeal without interruption. This can be demonstrated from material evidence. Iberian chess sets of the seventeenth and eighteenth centuries are very distinctive, with figurines raised on 'pulpits' of carved acanthus leaves, and such sets are not uncommon by comparison with French or Italian sets of the same period. In Germany there was a similar hiatus, though a less drastic one, between Gustavus Selenus's *Das Schach- oder König-Spiel* of 1616 and the appearance of more modern works in the mid-eighteenth century. The parochial nature of German chess at this time is shown by the large number of variants in the rules, not just national or regional in nature, but varying from place to place, and so imposing barriers to anything beyond purely local competition. One place in Germany which turned its chess playing customs to good account was the village of Ströbeck in Saxony. Medieval chess was played there down to 1616, according to Gustavus Selenus, and so was the 'courier' variant of chess, which continued to be played long after that date, though it had apparently fallen out of use by 1825. Then at some stage in the nineteenth century the local population seem to have set out to attract chess-playing tourists, and a series of ever more wonderful legends (and possibly ever more peculiar forms of chess) was provided for the eager gentlemen who came to record them. Their success was extraordinary, and even van der Linde and Murray were tempted to adopt the absurd theory that the 'Ströbeck rules' were survivals from the Mongol invasions of eastern Europe in the thirteenth century![2] Beyond Germany, in Scandinavia and the Slav countries, the new chess was still in the process of establishing itself, so no very advanced study of the game was to be expected.

Yet the contrast between the situation in Italy or England, and the changes occurring in France, should not be exaggerated. Even the influence of Greco, and the wider dissemination of his works, could not of itself transform the limited social appeal of the game there. Small groups of serious chess players grew up in France, probably more than ever before and certainly better equipped with theoretical writings on the game, but they remained small groups and socially exclusive in nature. They were isolated from each other and from the larger numbers of people who played chess casually or domestically; their achievements went largely unrecorded. But at least they were developing an interest in the inherent qualities of the game, a desire to play it as well as possible, rather than with the casual indifference which earlier writers thought appropriate for a gentleman. This can be illustrated from one or two surviving pieces of evidence. In the closing years of the seventeenth century M. Asperling, a member of the French Garde Suisse, published his undated *Traitté du Jeu royal des Echets* at Lausanne. The author acknowledges debts to Greco and Lopez, but claimed that the greater part of the work was of his own devising. In fact Asperling's own analysis added little of value to his models, and he cannot have been a very strong player. The real value of the *Traitté* lies in its demonstration that even a weak player could now absorb and profit from the best chess theory of the previous period. More evidence can be derived from a manuscript written by a certain M. Caze sometime before 1706, in which year he presented it to the Earl of Sunderland.[3] The dedication is dated 'Amsterdam, le 1 Septembre, 1706', but elsewhere the author remarks 'I shall not conceal from your Lordship that it is nearly twenty years since this book was compiled'. The analysis was once again eclectic in nature, this time with references to Damiano, Lopez, Gianutio, Salvio, Carrera, Selenus, Greco, and two manuscripts, one from the Polerio group and the other a critique of Greco written by a contemporary, the mathematician Roberval. Caze added very little to these exemplars, but he did take an important step by including seventeen real games 'which were played in my presence by some of the best players in Paris', presumably in the 1680s when the manuscript was being put together. These show that the leading Paris exponents were now capable of taking inspiration from Greco's composed 'brilliancies', and trying to produce the same effects, however imperfectly, in their own games.

Also, Caze does look forward tentatively to a period when the best players would again have national and international reputations, like the Spanish and Italian masters of the Renaissance. Admittedly he was reluctant to reveal the names of the Paris amateurs of his acquaintance until twenty years had passed, and one of them (M. Nicolai) refused to have his games recorded at all, but at least one man was known to Caze, Sunderland and others as an internationally famous player in the early years of the eighteenth century. This was Alexander Cunningham, who gave his name to the 'Cunningham Gambit', first recorded by Caze, who also mentioned some games between Cunningham and Sunderland played in his presence shortly before 1706. Unfortunately there were two notable Alexander Cunninghams during this period, both learned and Whiggish Scotsmen who spent some time in Holland: one a classical scholar who died at the Hague in 1730, the other a diplomat and historian who died in London in 1737. It was probably the historian who was the famous chess player, since the classicist did not live abroad until he was ejected from his Edinburgh professorship in 1710, but the point is not important. Leibniz, who was mildly interested in chess, once wrote in some bafflement to ask which of the two 'Messieurs Synonymes' he had the honour to know, so it is not surprising that modern historians have the same problem. In another letter a few years later (in 1705) he wrote:

> The Earl of Sunderland has beaten all our chess players here; his supporters maintain that he is now superior to Mr. Cunningham, and that when passing through Holland recently he defeated him five times running. They also say that he has written a book on this game in Latin. Had I known this, I would have sought the honour of an audience to hear about it from him, for I approve strongly of rational games, not for their own sake, but because they serve to perfect the art of thinking.

Again, in 1707, Leibniz asked the same correspondent (Thomas Burnet): 'How does your compatriot Mr. Cunningham? Shall we see nothing of him? . . . If he would only publish his thoughts on the art of playing chess, he would oblige the public.'[4] This suggests that chess was now beginning to be taken seriously by at least some intellectual figures.

In the event, the chess-playing circles which flourished around the turn of the eighteenth century left very little as a legacy to later generations. Perhaps this was hardly surprising. It has already been pointed out that the influence of individuals tended to be limited, particularly when, like Cunningham and Sunderland, they may never have written books on chess, let alone had them published. But the enthusiasm of these groups, and their general intellectual interests, pointed the way towards a shift in the appeal of the game, which was soon to become more apparent.

Social change and popularity

The changes which took place in the status of chess during the eighteenth century were important, because they prepared the way for the emergence of the modern game as a sort of serious intellectual sport. Yet these changes are not easy to describe. In effect, what happened was that the social appeal which had sustained chess hitherto gradually weakened, but that at about the same time a new kind of social appeal grew up to replace it. It has been emphasized above that the typically medieval view of chess, as a leisurely and appropriately symbolic pastime which all men of gentle birth might be expected to play, though not too well, largely persisted into the sixteenth and seventeenth centuries. But this view now concealed an unresolved tension, because the rule changes disseminated after 1500 had made the game much more amenable to systematic analysis and serious competition. The more such analysis was written and published, the more chess began to have a special appeal for the intellectually inclined, so correspondingly the greater was the threat to its traditional standing with the unintellectual majority of the upper classes. In the eighteenth century this tension came out into the open. Earlier writers had complained that chess was becoming too serious for a gentlemanly diversion, but now there is more hard evidence that such men were actually abandoning it for other pursuits.

Alternatives to chess were not difficult to find in affluent society, and they steadily proliferated during this period. The relaxation of moral constraints on card playing, and the continual invention of new card games, was a particularly significant trend. Thus, though M. Caze's chess-playing circle in late seventeenth-century Paris included a number of 'aristocrats of service' – senior royal officials and lawyers – the real aristocracy at Versailles seem to have given the game little attention. In all his voluminous memoirs of life at court, the Duc de Saint-Simon never mentions chess once, though he alludes to a great variety of card games – *piquet, loo, ombre, hoc, brelan, lansquenet, bassette, papillon, petite prime . . .* – and speaks of the King and Mme de Maintenon playing 'the usual parlour-games' in their own apartments.[5] Such evidence as exists for the Restoration court in England suggests that chess was similarly little regarded there. Its members, when not dicing or card playing, perhaps followed the king's lead in preferring other forms of indoor sport. Outside the courts, the same process was at work in society generally. A clue to this can be found in the educational games treatises, which aimed to teach an aspirant gentleman everything he needed to know about sports and pastimes in order to achieve social success. These handbooks, which began in Paris with La Marinière's *Maison académique* of 1654, and in London with Charles Cotton's *Compleat Gamester* of 1674, went through numerous editions and had by contemporary standards a very wide circulation. They dealt mostly with active pursuits and cards, chess being regarded merely as one game among many, and that hardly the most important. Cotton began his chapter on chess with the remark that

Chess is a Royal game and more difficult to be understood than any other game whatever, and will take up sometimes in the playing so long a time that I have known two play a fortnight at times before the game hath been ended: and indeed I believe the tediousness of the game hath caused the practice thereof to be so little used; however since this pastime is so highly ingenious that there is none can parallel it, I shall here lay down some brief instructions tending to the knowledge thereof.[6]

Such men might still respect chess for its fame and 'ingenuity', but only too obviously they no longer played it. In France the situation was not quite so bad, because at least one of the families of treatises, the *Académie Universelle Des Jeux* (Paris 1730 and subsequent editions) included an independent section or volume on chess, consisting of Greco's games. The earlier Dutch editions of Greco's book had also formed part of such composite works, and they accounted for many of its reprints after 1730, though separate 'Calabrians' were also produced in both Paris and Holland.

In the eighteenth century these treatises were catering to a whole new social world, as the great households and humbler forms of domestic life were rapidly augmented by more informal types of social association: clubs and assembly rooms, cafés and coffee houses. Plays, concerts, journals and libraries were also part of this growth of sophisticated urban recreation, which drew country gentlemen to York or Norwich just as it drew the richer and more ambitious to the London 'Season'. The first coffee house opened in London in 1652, shortly after those of Paris, and by the early eighteenth century there were hundreds of them. They varied in style from lavish establishments to the 'penny universities', at which those of little means could broaden their horizons with conversation and a newspaper, but in theory they served the public as a whole. Such popularity was naturally counterbalanced by the desire of some people to maintain exclusiveness, so this was also a great age for the formation of social and political clubs with more or less restricted memberships. Once again the change was not without potential consequences for chess, as the main activity in most of these clubs was gambling. Straightforward gaming had always retained a certain appeal, but in the eighteenth century it was more thoroughly organized and more socially acceptable than ever before. Saint-Simon's memoirs make it clear that the ban on games of mere chance in Paris and at Versailles was only occasionally and arbitrarily enforced, while the stakes involved in games of all kinds grew steadily higher, particularly during the Regency period.

In England the curious assortment of statutes designed to restrict excessive gambling bore mostly on plebeian pursuits, through such measures as the duty on playing cards. A tirade of pamphlets by clerics and other public benefactors against the pernicious effects of gaming continued all through the century, but it had little effect on the actual behaviour of the rich and fashionable or of their imitators. Exclusive clubs like White's were almost wholly successful in promoting gambling as a regular feature of society life, despite the stories of high stakes and ruined men circulating in contemporary literature and correspondence. Books like Theophilus Lucas' *Memoirs of the Lives, intrigues and comical adventures of the most famous Gamesters and celebrated Sharpers* (1714) added a touch of romance to the lives of the professional gamblers, and emphasized that at least some of them were successful, though club proprietors generally emerged with the biggest gains. Even a hundred years later, in the early years of the nineteenth century, William Crockford, son of a London fishmonger, followed much the same path to success, serving lavish meals *gratis* to lure the aristocracy to his gaming tables and clearing a vast fortune from them, said to be over a million pounds.

No sharp-witted entrepreneur made his fortune out of chess in the same way. A stray surviving betting book from White's Club,[7] covering a period beginning in 1743, includes only two wagers on chess, though Lord Northumberland and Colonel Waldegrave were prepared to risk twenty guineas a game in 1752. The hundreds of entries in the rest of the book testify mainly to the number of ways in which an eighteenth-century gentleman could imperil his finances: there were bets on cards, bets on races, bets on trials of skill, bets on natural events, and simplest of all, bets on the outcome of other bets. If the primary intention was to gamble, chess must indeed have seemed an unnecessarily circuitous way of setting about it. It is therefore easy to see how the changing patterns of leisure and social life could imperil the previous status of chess as a natural and instinctive pursuit of the upper classes. Even its attraction as a domestic pastime was threatened by the development of more 'respectable' card games, in particular the vogue for whist which began in the 1730s. Contemporaries too were aware of this trend towards declining pópular-ity, and the fact that many men no longer chose to play the game at all. The Chevalier de Jaucourt, who wrote the article on chess for the *Encyclopédie* of Diderot and D'Alembert (in 1755), seems to have taken this view. Following Bayle he praised Boi and Greco as the leading players of the past, and then went on:

> Some fragments of the methods of play of these two champions have been collected and turned into a unified work called the Calabrian, [in reality almost entirely composed of Greco's work] which deals with the practice of this game. It could easily be augmented. But hardly anyone reads this book nowadays. Chess is generally out of fashion; other tastes, other ways of spending time, in a word other less excusable frivolities have succeeded it.[8]

Against this background of apparently unrelieved gloom, how was chess sustained as a reasonably popular activity at all? The answer lies mainly in the increasing prosperity which fuelled the growth of sophisticated and commercialized recreation, especially in England. Because of this, the range of available leisure activities constantly increased, but so too did the number of people who could afford to engage in them, who had time and money enough to adopt an affluent life style and imitate the taste of their betters. In other words, while chess now had a smaller share in the 'market' of genteel recreation, the size of the market as a whole was rapidly increasing. A decline in its popularity relative to other and newer games need not imply an absolute decline in the number of players. There is a certain amount of hard evidence to support this hypothesis. Eighteenth-century chess books never attained real popularity, comparable with the circulation of handbooks on the game in the decades after 1800, but the number of books written and editions produced in the second half of the century shows a clear advance on that in the first half. Contemporary commentators like Jaucourt were perhaps too influenced by short-term changes in fashion to assess this accurately; as it happened the 'Calabrian' came out in yet another Paris edition in 1757, only two years after his *Encyclopédie* article, and there were later editions after that.

In England the best guide to general popularity is provided by the immensely successful games treatises of Edmund Hoyle (1672–1769). Hoyle, whose handbooks were first produced in inexpensive separate parts before eventually being bound up together as the compendious *Hoyle's Games*, evidently aimed at a more middle-class market than the *Compleat Gamester* and its successors. He emphasized the ability to play games well as a social accomplishment, and dwelt little on the mystique of gambling. Beyond doubt he did well out of his books, so well that his main problem was the profusion of unauthorized editions, printed mostly in Dublin. The Dublin 'pirates' at this time maintained spies in the composing rooms of their London rivals, and were said to boast that they could print an accurate copy of any English book even before the original work was put on sale. In view of this popularity, it is interesting that chess was better represented in Hoyle's writings than in their predecessors of the late seventeenth and early eighteenth centuries. While his most successful work of all was his *Short Treatise on the Game of Whist* (1742, with ten editions by 1750), the sequel on piquet and chess (1744, five editions by 1750) was not far behind, and was supplemented in 1761 by *An Essay Towards making the Game of Chess Easily learned By those who know the Moves only, without the Assistance of a Master*. Though Murray is basically right to say that Hoyle's advice was reprinted unchanged from one edition to the next and was too general to be of much value to advanced players, it provided sensible guidance for beginners, and certainly constitutes evidence that though some people were giving up chess in the eighteenth century, others were discovering it for the first time.

Material evidence is also relevant here. Many more eighteenth-century chess sets survive than those from previous periods, and increasingly they were clearly distinguished into 'display' pieces and ones designed for practical play, the latter being far more numerous. But even the more ostentatious sets, in which every piece was a carved and painted figurine of wood or ivory, were produced in quantity to standard designs. Thriving craft workshops grew up to make them, particularly in Paris and Dieppe, and at least some of their output must have been intended for the English market. To the modern eye these products seem more like collectors' curios than something of real artistic merit, with perhaps a few exceptions like Flaxman's designs for Josiah Wedgewood, but contemporary demand was clearly considerable. The cheaper and plainer sets made of turned wood were correspondingly even more popular, and sometimes achieved a restrained elegance that is still extremely pleasing, and much more in keeping with practical use. On balance therefore, the evidence does not suggest any decline in the overall popularity of chess in the eighteenth century. But as the social appeal of the game was shifting, extending itself in some areas while being curtailed in others, it is hardly surprising that it sometimes appeared less popular, and may temporarily have been so, in some places at least. In his book *Chess* (Vol.2 1789), Richard Twiss quoted a 'Letter from Edinburgh' to the effect that 'There was formerly a Chess-club here, but of late in general every game has given way to Cards'. Yet in the early years of the nineteenth century the Edinburgh chess club was a flourishing concern once more.

But the extension of leisure opportunities in the eighteenth century did more for chess than merely to preserve its popularity in the face of increased competition. More informal social association and more organized recreation implied also a more frequent exercise of choice. The old rather rigid notion of accomplishments which every gentleman should possess, going back at least to the sixteenth century, and in a modified form into the late Middle Ages, was replaced by a wider range of interests and amusements, from which the affluent could select according to taste. No one could be expected to master them all. Those who chose to play chess now did so less because they felt it was expected of them, and more because they were genuinely interested in it.

These new chess players were in the main men of intellectual tastes, or those who wished to see themselves in that light. The inherited tension in the appeal of chess was thus resolved, because those who adopted it were now more prepared to treat it seriously. This provided a social base for the longstanding attempts made by small groups of enthusiasts to promote the study of the game. The way was now cleared, not only for sustained popularity, but for generally higher playing standards, and for the eventual development of modern competition and theoretical literature. It was the eighteenth century that brought to chess the specific adherence of intellectuals, and so gave it the high-brow, rather than high-status, image which has stayed with it ever since.

Having said this, it is necessary to introduce at once one or two qualifications. Within the whole range of genteel society, imitation of the aristocracy was still an extremely powerful motive, so it was important for chess and similar activities that at least some noblemen and leading figures should still appear to be devoted to them. This presented no real problem for chess. In fact, for a decade or so in the 1770s and 1780s it became extremely fashionable in Paris and London high society, but the fashion rested on no durable interests or institutions and melted away after a few years, leaving only the real devotees behind. Secondly it should be emphasized that, though chess was now widely respected as a thoughtful game, or even (as Leibniz had described it in 1705) as valuable mental training, almost no one took it so seriously as to rank it with the arts and sciences. Jaucourt was very weighty and judicious about this in his *Encyclopédie* article:

> Some people, struck by the fact that chance plays no part in this game, and that skill alone is victorious, regard chess players as endowed with superior abilities, but if this reasoning is right, why do we see so many ordinary men, and near imbeciles, who excel at it, just as some of the most gifted, of all kinds, have not been able to achieve mediocrity? Let us conclude that in this, as in other things, habit acquired in youth, constant and singleminded play, memory for combinations and the behaviour of the pieces, fortified by practice, in short what may be called the spirit of the game, is the source of the science of chess, and does not imply any other talents or merit in the player.[9]

Diderot, characteristically, put the same point rather more pithily in his famous dialogue '*Rameau's Nephew*':

> At Rey's [the Café de la Régence] the shrewd Légal, the crafty Philidor, and the dependable Mayot sally forth to battle. There the most amazing moves can be seen and the poorest conversation heard, for if you can be a man of wit and a great chess player like Légal, you can also be a great chess player and an ass like Foubert and Mayot.[10]

Nevertheless, there is no doubt that the image of chess, as perceived by players and non-players alike, did change in this period, with several interesting consequences. As the game was valued more for its own sake there was less interest in its hidden meanings, and the old world of symbolic interpretation finally faded away. The handbooks of the eighteenth century confined themselves strictly to the practical value of the different chess pieces. More gradually, knowledge of the game's real origins ousted the medieval foundation legends, which had hitherto held their own. As early as 1709, in his *Traité du jeu*, published at Amsterdam, Jean Barbeyrac made fun of the idea that chess, 'teaches the method of laying snares for others, and that moreover, as it is an image of war, it makes us hate peace and run to arms. Princes who want soldiers are ill-advised if they do not every where establish academies for Chess, which would in a short time enable them to raise a number of recruits yearly.' For in reality: 'They could scarcely on a Draught-board, or a Chess-board, have given more than a few general ideas, which a little experience teaches in a short time much more easily, and in an infinitely more distinct manner.'[11] It is true that in the eighteenth century the Prussian army used war games for training to an increasing extent, but they bore only a superficial resemblance to chess. Nor were the inherent moral qualities of the game much regarded by this time. In 1779 Benjamin Franklin wrote a short essay on *The Morals of Chess*, but the advantages which he attached to the game (foresight, circumspection, caution and perseverence) arose from its value as general mental training, rather than any specific analysis of its properties.

Another consequence of the tendency of chess to become more bookish and demanding in the eighteenth century was the occasional appearance of a reaction, which took the form of proposing changes in the rules of play. By this means perhaps, theory could periodically be disregarded and a fresh start made; there might in the end be many types of chess, as there were many card games. Sometimes too, it may have been thought that chess for three or four players would be more sociable and have some of the advantages of games like whist. One Filippo Marinelli advocated a form of three-handed chess of his own devising in *Il Giuoco degli Scacchi fra tre* (Naples 1722), and a number of later writers proposed chess *à quatre* for much the same reasons. Other variants were designed to remove supposed defects in the original game. In 1706, Caze had suggested, among other things, that the player with the white pieces should be compelled always to make the same initial move, so as to neutralize his unfair advantage in moving first. In London in the 1740s there was a temporary vogue for a form of enlarged chess played on a board of fourteen squares by ten. It was supposedly invented by the Duke of Rutland, who had devised several new pieces for it like the concubine (a familiar figure of the Hanoverian court), and it may have been played more out of deference to its progenitor than anything else. For the common feature of all of these proposals was their utter lack of success. Not only was 'orthodox' chess unimpaired, but with increasing competition and more writing on the game it moved in entirely the opposite direction, towards greater standardization and the progressive elimination of local differences in the rules. As early as 1749, in his *Analyze des Echecs*, André Philidor wrote loftily, though unhistorically, that 'This Game has in many parts of Germany been so disfigured as not to be known but by the Board and the Men . . . . In my opinion all these Deformities have been introduced by Wranglers, who have obliged their Adversaries to play according to their Whims.'[12] The careers of men like Philidor make an instructive contrast with those of Greco and the leading players of the previous age, reflecting just how much had changed in both chess and its social setting.

From Greco to Philidor

The process outlined above is a complex one, and hard to trace with any chronological precision. One can only say that, while changes were evidently under way in the first half of the eighteenth century, they become much more apparent after 1750 or so, when they coincided with the reappearance of leading players, whose ideas were at last a significant advance on those of Greco. The centre of European chess, already moving to France by 1700, was now extended to include England. In Italy there were a number of strong players, and even important books, but never the basis of social support required to sustain serious interest in the game on a large scale.

One sign of future developments was the fact that early in the century chess players in both Paris and London began to meet regularly at fixed venues to play and discuss the game. In Paris the leading chess resort was the Café de la Régence, in the Place du Palais-Royal; in London it was Slaughter's Coffee House in St Martin's Lane. The Café was evidently named after the Orléanist Regency of 1715–23, but it may not have acquired its chess reputation for another twenty or thirty years after that. Philidor later told Richard Twiss that when he began his career in the 1740s 'Chess was played in every Coffee-house in Paris', and in his *Confessions*, Jean-Jacques Rousseau spoke of making the acquaintance 'of M. de Légal, of M. Husson, of Philidor, and of all the great chess players of the time' at the Café Maugis in 1742.[13] Slaughter's Coffee House was established in 1692, and because of a vague remark by Twiss it has generally been supposed that a chess club began to meet there soon afterwards. The first definite proof is a reference in a manuscript of 1720 to 'Chess players at Slaughter's',[14] but this was early enough for men like Sunderland to have played there, all the more so because the group seems to have consisted of men who were Whigs as well as chess players. Within a few years they became quite well known. In his *Poems on Several Occasions* of 1729, mostly honest imitations of Pope, Joseph Thurston included some verses on chess, of which the concluding lines were:

Bravely they press to conquer, or to die;
Nor ever was it known a Pawn should fly:
Like sons of *Lilliput*, so small, so bold,
As we believe and *Gulliver* has told.

Their Laws, their Orders, and their Manners these;
The rest let *Slaughter's* tell you, if you please.'

Swift's *Gulliver's Travels* had been successfuly published a few years earlier, in 1726. Thurston's poem was not a fully-fledged political satire, though it contained topical jibes about the indolent king, the powerful queen, the selfish bishops, and so on. But a letter in *The Craftsman* of September 1733, described as 'a short Essay on the Game of Chess', was a more deliberate polemic, using its remarks about the game as a cover for a succession of cumbrous sallies aimed at contemporary figures or institutions. *The Craftsman* was a Tory paper, and during the long period of Whig dominance from 1714 to 1760 the Tories had little else to do but nurse their grievances and accuse their opponents of exploiting office, in a way they would have been only too eager to imitate given the opportunity. Thus of the bishop, we are told that 'this *prelatical Piece of Wood* is of very little Use in the Beginning of a Game; and He is by his Profession obliged never to move upon the Square'; a curious echo of the medieval moralities, though now in an entirely mock-serious vein. Within a week there was a separately printed reply in the Whig interest *A Letter to the Craftsman on the Game of Chess*, actually issued from Slaughter's, though as Murray remarks it shows no more real knowledge of chess than its rival. These literary efforts, particularly Thurston's, may have been inspired by the renewed popularity of Marco Girolamo Vida's Renaissance poem *Scacchia ludus*, which had a certain appeal to English neo-classical taste. The Latin text had been republished at Oxford in 1701 and 1723 (with Pope, Gay and Steele among the subscribers), and then in London in 1732 and 1740. This led in turn to six different English translations between 1736 and 1786, as well as another, not published until 1854, which may have been by Oliver Goldsmith.

But the group at Slaughter's were capable of something more serious, as was demonstrated in 1735 with the publication of Captain Joseph Bertin's *Noble Game of Chess*, 'Printed by H. Woodfall, for the Author: And sold only at Slaughter's-Coffee-House, in St. Martin's Lane'. Bertin was an army officer, said to be of French Huguenot origin, but little is known about him. His book was rather at the same stage of development as Caze's manuscript in 1706: that is, it shows a knowledge of Greco and some tentative attempts to make further progress which had not as yet got very far. Cunningham's Gambit again appears, though not by name. The author's caution was betrayed particularly in his opening analyses, which usually end with the unhelpful remark, 'And the Players may finish the Game'. Bertin's book was soon superseded, but it was of some consequence as the first original chess book of any size to be printed for a century.

The future lay increasingly in closer links between the two main centres of Paris and London. Already in 1706 Caze had proposed that a match by correspondence between teams representing each city should be commenced as soon as peace was restored, though the suggestion came to nothing. From the 1740s onwards more durable links were forged, at least for the exchange of ideas. Initially, the most important figure in this process was Philip Stamma, but after 1750 and for the rest of the century (until his death in 1795) it was André Philidor, the celebrated player of the age. Stamma's early life is obscure, and he first appeared as an important figure in the chess world when he published his *Essai sur le Jeu des Echecs* at Paris in 1737. This book had two striking features. The first was that most of it consisted of 'a hundred *parties* which must be regarded as equivalent to the secrets of this game'.[15] These *parties* were middle-game positions with brilliant sacrificial continuations, resembling the modern concept of a study, or a type of chess problem. Stamma himself believed that they taught valuable lessons for practical play, and claimed implausibly that they had all occurred in his own games. But by making such a collection at all, as no one else had done for about two hundred years, he prepared the way for the modern idea of the problem: a chess position composed primarily for its aesthetic rather than its practical value. For this reason the *Essai* was republished as an anthology down to 1800 and beyond, long after it had lost most of its value as a work of instruction. The second striking feature about Stamma's book was that it was conceived, at least in part, as an attack on Greco. Whereas his own positions could be resolved by forced play, Greco's brilliancies (or so he claimed) were possible only because of the attribution of weak moves to the defence. As for the King's Gambit opening, to which Greco devoted so much of his analysis, Stamma remarked bluntly, 'I regard this method as utterly useless and without foundation'. One or two modern commentators have denied his right to make these criticisms because of the equally glaring flaws in his own system, but this is to miss the point. Only when the longstanding dominance of Greco's ideas was destroyed, or at least openly questioned, would it be possible to evolve new methods of play. Stamma at least had the independence of mind to move in that direction, though he was perhaps not equipped to complete the task. But certainly one of his claims was taken too seriously at the time and has been since: the implication that in his chess writings he was drawing on some fund of oriental wisdom unknown to his contemporaries. Stamma constantly harped on the fact that he was a 'native of Aleppo in Syria', and emphasized not merely that chess had reached Europe from the Arabs, but that 'one may still see there very many accomplished players, and I dare say that there are scarcely any in Europe who may be compared with them'. Elsewhere he referred to 'the eastern method of play' which 'I am beginning to make known in the west, though I am a stranger here'. This was mostly sales talk. While it was possible that one or two of Stamma's *parties* were ultimately derived from Arabic or medieval problem collections, they were essentially his own work. There is no reason at all to suppose that European chess was even competently played in Syria at this date.

But it was natural that Stamma should use every opportunity to advance his own career. His *Essai* of 1737 was dedicated to Lord Harrington, whom he had met in Paris, and contained the scarcely veiled hint that 'In the situation to which fortune has reduced me, compassion will plead on my behalf'. Harrington was then Secretary of State for the Northern Department (i.e. principal foreign secretary) and in 1739 he responded by producing an office within his gift, the post of Interpreter of Oriental Languages to the British Government. The salary of eighty pounds a year was at least a modest competence, and Stamma must thereupon have transferred his activities to England. Once in London, he must have encountered the chess players at Slaughter's (Twiss hints as much) and it was probably they who encouraged him to reissue his book in English; it had already been reprinted in French at The Hague in 1741. In *The Noble Game of Chess* of 1745 Stamma not merely translated and revised his hundred problems, but also added seventy-four lines of opening analysis, in deference to the wishes of 'several people of Condition, Lovers of this noble Game, who have desired me to give an Addition to the former *Essay* and who have had the Goodness to encourage me in this present Edition'. It was probably the same sponsors who supported him in his disastrous match against Philidor, which took place in London in 1747. After his defeat he published no more on the game, and probably retired or died by 1755, in which year a successor was appointed to the post of Oriental Interpreter.[16] In one respect Stamma was certainly ahead of his time: his use of a concise form of algebraic notation in his books. But even here the influence of his rival prevailed, and Philidor's much more cumbrous descriptive notation continued to be more commonly used, in France until the nineteenth century and in England down to recent times.

Almost everything that Stamma had achieved, in forwarding the theory of the game and forging links between players in Paris and London, was carried much further by André Philidor in the course of a chess career that lasted over fifty years. Philidor's life is comparatively well documented, and this is mostly because of Richard Twiss, who included in his book *Chess* (Vol.I, 1787, Vol.II, 1789) a whole section of 'Anecdotes of Mr. Philidor. Communicated by Himself'.[17] Twiss's *Chess*, which has already been cited several times in this Chapter, is a vast rag-bag of bibliography and miscellaneous material, quite invaluable for the history of the game in the eighteenth century. His stories about Cunningham and his contemporaries are perhaps no more reliable than the oral tradition from which they were derived, but much more credence can be attached to the author's account of later events, which he was able to observe for himself. Francois-André Danican Philidor, according to both the 'Anecdotes' and later research, was born at Dreux near Paris in 1726, of a family of court musicians. The original family name was Danican, but they had gradually adopted the nickname of 'Philidor', which according to a story they believed themselves, had been bestowed on an early member of the dynasty by Louis XIII, because his oboe playing reminded the king of a previous royal favourite called Filidori. Some of his successors were composers, but the less talented ones spent their days playing a variety of instruments in the royal band, even the drums if they could manage nothing else. André's father, André Philidor 'L'aîné', had risen to the height of royal music librarian. Like J.S. Bach he also found time to beget about twenty children, partly by marrying a second wife over fifty years younger than himself in 1719, eleven years before his death. André was a child of this second marriage and so, when he completed his apprentice-ship as a chorister in the royal chapel of Versailles in 1740, not only his father but most of his elder brothers and cousins were already dead, and he was left to make his own career. The life of a music teacher and copyist in Paris at this time was not an easy one, as Jean-Jacques Rousseau testifies in his *Confessions*, and gradually Philidor took to chess, which he had already learnt as a child. By his own account in the 'Anecdotes', he 'applied so closely to the game that he neglected his scholars, and they consequently took another master'. His own master at chess was M. de Légal, born about 1700, who was then the strongest Parisian player.

By 1742 Rousseau already referred to the young Philidor as one of the leading masters and his reputation soon grew even further through his much-publicized feat of playing two games simultaneously without sight of the board. This does not seem very remarkable today, but it certainly impressed contemporaries. Over a decade later (in 1755) Jaucourt thought it worth recording in the *Encyclopédie*, mentioning that Philidor was eighteen years old at the time of his achievement, and describing it as 'one of the most extraordinary examples of the power of memory and imagination'. But Philidor was also pursuing his musical career. A motet of his was performed in 1743, and in 1745 he assisted Rousseau with his opera *Les Muses Galantes*, though Rousseau was subsequently disinclined to give him any credit for it. It was also a musical appointment which took Philidor to Holland in 1745, in company with an Italian called Lanza, whose daughter was a harpsichord virtuoso. The girl's death left him stranded, and he resorted to playing chess and draughts with English officers drawn there by the Austrian Succession War. In 1747, with their encouragement, he went on to England and was introduced to the circle at

Slaughter's by Sir Abraham Janssen, a baronet and gentleman of leisure whom Philidor later described as 'the best player he ever met with, after his master M. de Légal'.[18] Stakes were raised for a match between the young Frenchman and Philip Stamma, Philidor apparently having the confidence to agree to count all drawn games as losses to himself. He won by eight games to two, one of the two being a draw, and was now widely regarded as the first player of the day.

But Philidor's greatest contribution to eighteenth-century chess was yet to come. In 1748 he returned to Holland and wrote there the first version of his book on the game. By visiting the English army camp at Eindhoven he managed to secure a subscription from the infamous Duke of Cumberland for fifty copies, which naturally inspired many junior officers to follow their commander's lead. The book was therefore published with every appearance of success as *L'Analyze des Echecs*, at London in 1749, with reprints in 1752 at London and 1754 at Leipzig. There was also an English edition, *Chess Analysed* (London 1750), and a German edition, *Die Kunst im Schachspiel ein Meister zu werden* (Strasbourg 1754). Philidor himself went to Germany in 1751 and played before Frederick the Great at Potsdam, before making his way back to Holland and England. Only in 1754 did he return to Paris, with the intention of resuming his musical career. The *Analyze* was thus immediately popular, especially in England. It seems to have met a demand and also to have helped to create one, so much so that in 1750 a rival London publisher brought out a new edition of Greco as *Chess Made Easy*, in an attempt to capture part of the newly revealed market. Evidently Philidor's reputation and the influence of his patrons helped to launch his book, but its continued success must be put down to its inherent qualities. Philidor was not content merely with criticizing earlier works like those of Greco, or with suggesting piecemeal improvements in their lines of play; he set out to demonstrate a whole new approach to the study of the game. As Jean Biou has pointed out,[19] even the use of the word '*analyse*', with its contemporary aura of scientific and mathematical enquiry, proclaimed the novelty of his method.

The problem hitherto had been to bridge the gap between very general advice, of the kind offered by Hoyle, and very specific analysis like that in Greco, consisting of strings of suggested moves without any explanations, or clues as to the principles from which they were derived. The beginner might profit from such hints as 'Never crowd your game by too many men in one place', the seventh of Bertin's nineteen 'Rules to be observed in playing the Game of Chess' (another one was 'To free your game, take off some of your adversary's men, if possible for nothing'!), but once he had got beyond this stage he was faced with a jump into the unknown. Whereas the really talented could perhaps overcome this by treating

Greco's games as points of departure for their own ideas, the average player could only learn them off by heart, and was then helpless when faced with a divergent move, even if it were weak. The books of Bertin and Stamma were open to the same criticism. Philidor was well aware of these shortcomings in the works of his predecessors, as may be seen from his Preface of 1749:

> . . . they have given us, notwithstanding their Prolixity, but very imperfect Rules, and such as can never make a good Player; they have opened several Games, and left us to end them as well as we could, by which means the player is as puzzled, as if he had been left to begin the game without any Instructions at all.

Nor was he diffident in promoting his own ideas:

> I have seen several Players, who had learnt the Calabrois and other Authors by heart; and who, when they had played the first four or five moves, did no longer know what they were about: But I may boldly say, that whoever once knows how to put in practice the Rules I have laid down, will never be in that case.[20]

Philidor's 'Rules' put great emphasis on pawn play, and the use of the pawns to control the centre of the board. But the essential thing about them was that they were not stated in isolation, but embodied in illustrative games specially composed for the purpose. In each case the winner triumphed by playing according to Philidor's principles, so that the reader had every chance to grasp what those principles were, and to employ them in his own play. Though the *Analyze* of 1749 contained only nine games, all were furnished with sub-variations to illustrate deviations from the main line and explanatory notes to many of the moves; all of them culminated in clear-cut and unambiguous results. Murray quite rightly identified 'the lucidity, the assurance and the brevity of the book' as reasons for its success, and described it as written 'with all the confidence of youth'.[21]

Philidor had therefore written a new kind of chess book, admirably calculated to appeal to men who knew a little about the game, but were prepared to study intelligently to learn more. There is a certain amount of evidence that it was received in this way. Of course some people were incorrigible and never grasped the new approach. Among these was Rousseau, who described in his *Confessions* how he first became interested in the game in about 1733:

> I bought a chess board, I bought a Calabrian; I shut myself up in my room and spent days and nights endeavouring to learn all the games by heart, forcing them into my head, and playing by myself endlessly and without relaxation. After two or three months of this fine occupation and these inconceivable efforts, I went to the cafe, thin, sallow and almost stupefied. To try myself out, I played against M. Bagueret again; he beat me once, twice, twenty times.

So many combinations were mixed up in my head and my brain was so dull that I seemed to have nothing but a cloud before my eyes. Every time I have tried to practise by studying games with Philidor's book or Stamma's the same thing has happened to me: I have completely worn myself out and found my play weaker than before.[22]

This image of the hapless philosopher might be contrasted with a helpful note appended to a later edition of Philidor's book, the *Analyse du Jeu des Echecs* of 1821.

The best way of studying profitably . . . is to play through the games on a chessboard one after the other, to examine each move well in detail and to discover its purpose; ask how you yourself might play in such or such a situation, then compare your move with that of the author, and seek out the reason why the latter might be preferable in the event. It is by this kind of practice that you will make progress, and after several months of this kind of study, you will know more than you could learn by wasting whole years playing this game without instruction and without principles.'[23]

This was much closer to the author's intention of teaching concepts rather than moves, and a measure of his influence over the intervening period.

After 1755 Philidor stayed in Paris for the next fifteen years. Though there were several reprints of the *Analyze* in English and German, Frenchmen at least were satisfied that Paris was still the capital of the chess world, as Denis Diderot asserted in *Le Neveu de Rameau*, which he probably wrote in 1761: 'If it is too cold or wet I take shelter in the Café de la Régence and amuse myself watching people playing chess. Paris is the place in the world, and the Café de la Régence the place in Paris where this game is played best.' Yet Philidor spent most of this period of his life pursuing his first vocation, as a musician. Disappointed in hopes of obtaining a post at court, he turned to the Paris stage, and produced fifteen *opéras-comiques* between *Le Diable à quatre* in 1756 and *La Nouvelle école des femmes* in 1770, including one based on Fielding's novel *Tom Jones*. He was married in 1760 to a leading singer, Elisabeth Richer, and started a family with every appearance of prosperity. It was therefore a change of direction when he again went to England in 1771, with the intention of bringing out a new edition of his *Analyze*. Perhaps the popularity of his music had declined slightly, and Philidor was now turning back to his youthful source of income, but this is far from certain. It is just as likely that he had never lost his interest in chess, and now wished to publish his latest ideas, partly to answer criticisms of the original work. At all events, Philidor arrived in London in 1771 with a letter of introduction from Diderot to the musicologist Charles Burney, who had himself been in Paris the previous year to collect material for his *General History of Music*. This is confirmed by an entry in the diary of his daughter, the novelist Fanny Burney:

The famous Philidor, so much celebrated for his surprising skill at the game of Chess, is just come to England. He brought my father a letter of recommendation from the celebrated M. Diderot. He is going to have a new edition, with considerable amendments and additions, of a book upon Chess, which he wrote formerly in England. A plan of his work M. Diderot has drawn up for him, but he had got it most vilely translated. My father had the patience, from the good-natured benevolence of his heart, to translate it for him himself. M. Philidor is a well-bred, obliging, and very sociable man; he is also a very good musician.[24]

But at this time new developments were taking place in London chess. In 1770 a number of players had formed a chess club at the Salopian Coffee House, Charing Cross, and in 1774 there was a new one at Parsloe's Subscription Room, 'next door to the Thatched-House' in St James's Street. As Twiss described it in 1787:

The number of Members is limited to a hundred, as in the Chess-club at Paris: and the Members of the one are admitted into the other, without being ballotted for. The terms of the subscription are three guineas. Soon after the institution, several zealous Members made a subscription among themselves, in order to defray Mr. Philidor's expenses, and enable him to attend them during the winter [i.e. the London Season].

It is not clear whether this last remark refers to the foundation of 1770 or 1774, but probably the latter. Certainly, from 1775 onwards Philidor regularly spent a few months of every year in London, and in the succeeding decade he wrote only one new opera, though a choral work, the *Carmen Seculare*, was given in London with some success in 1779. His chess reputation was now at its height. The revised version of the *Analyze*, almost doubled in length, came out in 1777 at London, in both English and French editions, and was dedicated to the members of the chess club, all of whom subscribed for copies. A handsome engraved portrait of the author was included in many copies. The whole subscription list, with its 280 names (compared with 127 in 1749) was one of the most impressive of its kind in the eighteenth century. Apart from a sprinkling of intellectual celebrities, headed by Diderot, Marmontel, Suard, Voltaire and Gibbon, it contained a great roll call of noblemen and politicians: including Calonne, Choiseul and Talleyrand in France; Rockingham, North, Shelburne, Fox, Townshend and many others in England. There were no less than thirteen dukes. Chess had suddenly become fashionable, and the whole fashionable world scrambled to join the London club. Murray alluded to it as 'the last rally of the English nobility to claim chess as the game most typical of their order',[25] but this is to misstate their motives. It was the exclusiveness of the club which concerned these men, not that of the game, and in any case the fashions which dictated their behaviour rarely lasted very long. The foundation of the parallel Paris club in 1783, under the patronage of the Comte de Provence (later Louis XVIII), perhaps prolonged the trend for a while by increasing the social advantages of membership, but in the late 1780s it was clear that decline was setting in. The outbreak of the French Revolution, and subsequent severing of links with Paris, came as the final blow.

Naturally this affected Philidor's own career severely. Surviving letters which he wrote from London to his wife in Paris show that he was becoming increasingly dependent on his earnings from chess, which he remitted home whenever possible. Besides his honorarium from the club, he was free to make additional income out of giving lessons, and from 1782 he also put on public displays of blindfold chess, to which non-members of the club were admitted for the sum of five shillings. In a letter of that year Diderot urged him not to play in this way, and to abandon these 'dangerous experiments' for the sake of preserving his reason, but Philidor was probably not unduly worried.[26] He assured his wife that 'this does not fatigue me as much as some people seem to believe. Therefore do not be worried about my health', but naturally did nothing to discourage the enthusiasm of the English press, who reported his feats with the same wonderment as Jaucourt in 1755. But he may have been more affected by Diderot's other argument, that it was undignified for a great musician to turn himself into a showman, and that 'the reputation of the Calabrian will never equal that of Pergolesi'. Philidor himself wrote: 'It is ridiculous that the composer of *Ernelinde* should be obliged to play chess for half of the year in England in order to keep his numerous family alive.' Though he was always treated as a gentleman, and formed genuine friendships with some of his London patrons, like the Saxon ambassador Count Brühl, he certainly did not wish to regard himself as a mere professional chess player; it was not yet a respectable calling. All this was compounded by the decline of the London club. A third edition of the *Analyze* was published in 1790, but this time in English alone, and with only sixty-six subscribers. In 1793, when Philidor again made his usual journey to England, he found himself trapped there by the outbreak of war, and then by the fact that he had been accidently placed on the list of proscribed *émigrés*. It took two years for his family in Paris to clear his name and before he could return home he died, in August 1795.

But the end of the temporary vogue for chess in high society does at least make it easier to identify those who really had an enduring interest in it: the subscribers of 1790, or those whose recorded games survive from these years, whether played against Philidor or each other. These 'typical' keen chess players in London were not great noblemen, or for that matter great philosophers, but they were commonly gentlemen of intellectual tastes. A high proportion of them had written and published books, on subjects ranging from ancient history to science and technology. Count Brühl, besides being a diplomat, built his own astronomical observatory and wrote on chronometry. George Atwood, who recorded some of Philidor's offhand games at the end of his life, was a mathematician and Fellow of the Royal Society, who also wrote on the construction of arches and the stability of ships. Henry Jennings (who later called himself Nowell) was a celebrated collector and author of miscellaneous works. Francis Maseres was a lawyer described by Jeremy Bentham as a 'public-spirited constitutionalist', who also produced over twenty books on history, mathematics and other subjects. General Conway wrote essays and patented a new kind of furnace in the intervals of his military and political career. Even Dr Bowdler wrote on medicine and was a Fellow of the Royal Society and the Society of Antiquaries, as well as editing the infamous *Family Shakespeare* in his later years. These six are the only individuals who can be identified with any confidence among the dozen or so known opponents of Philidor during the last decade of his life, whose names are preserved by chance in two contemporary manuscript notebooks.[27] To them might be added the chronicler of the chess club, Richard Twiss, who was also an intellectual of a kind. Though his travel books were much parodied and his researches into making paper out of straw of dubious worth, he contrived to be elected a Fellow of the Royal Society.

It is because of the support of men like this that the desertion of the fashionable world did not disrupt the appeal of chess in late eighteenth-century London and Paris for very long. Already in the 1790s cheaper unsubscribed editions of the *Analyze* were being published, and circulated amongst a larger and less exclusive audience. Philidor's career was made possible by the changing social appeal of the game in his day, but by his own influence and especially through the success of his book he brought out all the implications of the change. Chess was generally better played in 1800 than in 1750, and more than anyone else André Philidor was responsible for the improvement.

The eighteenth-century achievement

Another effect of Philidor's career was to reinforce the status of London and Paris as the two leading centres of the chess world, and the starting points for nineteenth-century developments. A brief survey of eighteenth-century chess elsewhere in Europe serves only to confirm this. In Spain there were still no printed books on the game, or evidence of any desire to study it seriously. In Germany the confusion of local rules was only gradually being overcome, and it is indicative that this happened largely through the process of importing modern chess ideas from France. Philidor went to Potsdam and played before Frederick the Great in 1751, much as Voltaire went there to teach him to write French verse. It is beside the point that neither of them was entirely successful in their objectives. Once published in a German edition in 1754, the *Analyze* was reprinted five times in that language between 1764 and 1797 (there were also three editions in Dutch and one in Danish), and Philidor's book thus blotted out the few insignificant works on chess written in German since Gustavus Selenus's *Das Schach- oder König-Spiel* of 1616. The first German chess book of any independent importance only appeared with Johann All-gaier's *Neue theoretisch-praktische Anweisung zum Schachspiel*, published at Vienna in 1795. In Russia and eastern Europe the situation was much the same, except that the whole process of foreign influence and native reaction did not really get under way until the early nineteenth century. In colonial America there was not even a tradition of primitive chess, and players of any kind were few and far between. One of them, Benjamin Franklin, wrote to his London bookseller in 1752:

> Honest David Martin, Rector of our Academy, my principal Antagonist at Chess, is dead, and the few remaining Players here are very indifferent, so that I have now no need of Stamma's Pamphlet, and am glad you did not send it.[28]

Only in Italy in the eighteenth century were there chess players whose abilities and achievements were comparable with those of Philidor. As in Germany, the persistence of local rules showed that there was still little organized competition and only a limited market for theoretical literature, but after 1750 chance brought together three very talented individuals in one centre, the northern town of Modena. The first of them, Ercole del Rio, published his book *Sopra il giuoco degli Scacchi* there anonymously in 1750 and little is known about his life except that he seems to have been a lawyer. In form his treatise was mid-way between those of Philidor and Stamma. Like Stamma he included a good number of openings and a collection of problems, but like Philidor he added explanatory comments to some of the moves, though they were fewer and more laconic than those in the *Analyze*. Del Rio's work was supplemented by his friend and opponent Giambattista Lolli (1698–1769) in the vast and compendious *Osservazioni teorico-practiche sopra il giuoco degli scacchi*, published at the nearby city of Bologna in 1763. Lolli procured some additions from del Rio, but also added extensive notes and commentaries of his own, in an attempt to have the best of both worlds: the widest range *and* the most detailed discussion possible. The problem with this was that the book swelled to a considerable size; it was a folio of 632 pages, and according to Twiss ridiculed by contemporaries for its bulk. The third of the 'Modenese Masters', Domenico Ponziani (1719–1796), was reader in law at the university in Modena, and later became a priest and canon of the cathedral there. His *Il giuoco incomparabile degli scacchi* (Modena 1769) was an attempt to survey and build on the ideas of his predecessors, but in a rather more compact form. In the main he was successful in this and had the greatest influence of the Italian chess writers of this period; *Il giuoco incomparabile* was reprinted at Venice in 1773, and then brought out by the author in a revised second edition at Modena in 1782. Judged from one point of view, the quality of these books emphasizes that despite everything chess theory was still comparatively limited in the eighteenth century; a few gifted men in one small town could absorb it and add to it almost entirely by their own efforts without difficulty. But this would be an oversimplification. Despite reprints before and after 1800, Ponziani's conclusions were not widely known even in Italy itself; while from the 1790s the absence of organized clubs and mass publishing meant that Italian chess was left further and further behind in comparison with the advances made in France and England. There were to be no Italian chess writers of any note in the nineteenth century. Whatever conclusions the modern critic might reach about the merits of these books, the basis of social support in the north ensured that Philidor's *Analyze* would have a greater and more enduring influence.

But what were their relative merits? Unlike French and English contemporaries the Modenese authors had no scruples in judging and criticizing Philidor's work. This appeared most plainly in the 'Letter of Information about Sig. Philidor's Book' which del Rio contributed to Lolli's *Osservazioni* in 1763. He found things to praise in the first edition of the *Analyze*, in particular the famous study of the endgame with rook and bishop against rook, but little of merit in the openings because they failed to prove the correctness of Philidor's general 'rules', so that 'to tell the truth, he could have spoken less rashly and with more profundity'. This of course begs an important question, whether Philidor's games represented an attempt to discover the best possible moves, as del Rio assumed, or a coherent and perhaps simplified system specifically written for the purpose of teaching. There is a certain amount of evidence that the latter was the case; for instance at one point in the *Analyze* there appears the note 'I let your Game be lost only, to show the strength of two bishops against the rooks', when the position should really have been drawn. Modern commentators have tried to show links between Philidor's actual games recorded near the end of his life, and his earlier theoretical principles, in particular his remarks on the importance of the pawns: 'My chief Intention is to recommend myself to the Public, by a novelty no one has thought of, or perhaps ever understood well; I mean how to play the Pawns: They are the very life of this Game: They alone form the Attack and Defence; on their good or bad Situation depends the Gain or loss of each Party.'[29] From a teaching point of view this was admirable, because the pawns formed the most static element in the game, and therefore the easiest to generalize about. And although Philidor may have believed in the correctness of his 'rules', he put them into practice with appropriate flexibility in real play, and would probably have done so all the more if he had faced stronger opponents. In fact he was never constrained by defeat to rethink his ideas very seriously; in the 1777 second edition of the *Analyze* he merely extended the book and modified one or two of the most dogmatic assertions of 1749 by adopting less aggressive wording. It is striking that the only rival chess book published in England or France during the period of Philidor's dominance, the *Traité théorique et pratique du jeu des échecs, par une société d'amateurs* (Paris 1775 and 1786), was written by four men: Verdoni, Léger, Carlier and Bernard, who according to Twiss 'are not able to cope with Mr. de Legalle or Mr. Philidor, without receiving a pawn and the move'. Their criticism of 'the greatest player in Europe', as they called him, was therefore appropriately deferential.

Nothing here provides much support for H.J.R. Murray's view that the chess of this period was sharply divided into Italian and French 'schools', each of them with historical roots going back to the origins of modern chess. Murray wrote that 'Philidor belonged essentially to the school of Lopez, which, as a result of the many French editions of Lopez's work in the seventeenth century, had become the school of the majority of French players', so that 'It was natural that the earliest criticism of the *Analyze* should come from Italy, because the Italian players had never accepted the Lopez principles'.[30] There is much to question in this view of distinct national traditions. The concept of a school of play is itself inherently ambiguous, particularly when it is implied that players derived their ideas only from predecessors in their own tradition. The criterion which Murray used to distinguish between French and Italian chess – an emphasis on positional pawn play or tactical piece play – is a drastic oversimplification. The evidence suggests rather that 'schools of play' did not retain distinct identities for long periods; the leading players of each generation tried to improve on all the earlier work known to them whatever its origin, and in the process they naturally learned from it. Thus Greco and Salvio, though Italians, were heavily influenced by the work of Lopez after it was published at Venice in 1584. It is clear that Greco had succeeded Lopez as the dominant influence on French chess long before Philidor's day, nor is there anything in the *Analyze* to suggest that in reacting against Greco he was looking back to earlier writers. His theory was, as he himself described it, a 'novelty'. Philidor, Stamma and del Rio were in many ways part of the same movement. They all began to see the inadequacy of earlier books, particularly those of Greco, and set out to produce something better. In the process their ideas diverged, but they still had much in common. It is a crowning irony that in the field of music, where for a time there really were distinct Italian and French styles, Philidor's reputation was based on his openness to Italian influence. He was, in Diderot's words, 'the originator of Italian music in France'.

One notorious product of eighteenth-century chess which managed to cross national frontiers without losing any of its appeal was the so-called Automaton Chess Player, invented by Wolfgang von Kempelen (1734–1804), a Hungarian civil servant, in about 1769. The device consisted of a life-size mechanical figure seated by a chest, on which was placed a chessboard. Any audience present and those who wished to challenge the 'Turk', for the figure was also turbanned and equipped with a long pipe, were shown in stages the interior of the chest, which bulged with mysterious wheels and pieces of machinery. Then the game began, the Turk moving the pieces with its left hand to the accompaniment of appropriate mechanical noises, and being occasionally rewound by the exhibitor. It was first shown before the Austrian court in 1770, but its real fame began in 1783 when Kempelen decided to make a tour with it around Europe; he started in Paris with great success, then went on to London, Leipzig, Dresden, Amsterdam and probably other places as well. This continued until 1785, when Kempelen returned to his administrative career and the 'Turk' was packed away, only to emerge again after its inventor's death in 1804. Spectators were invited to guess how the device worked, and it is intriguing that in this period they mostly assumed some process of thought transference from the exhibitor to the mechanism, while in the nineteenth century credulity more frequently took the form of a belief in the artificial intelligence of the machine itself. Actually, of course, it was worked by a concealed operator, as even some contemporaries divined, and the inventor's skill lay mostly in constructing the chest in which he was hidden. But no one at the time was really sure how the trick was done. In Paris the 'Turk' played Philidor, and naturally lost to him, but in London it was for a season a rival draw to his own blindfold displays, being shown at the same admission charge of five shillings. Everywhere it went, it was pursued by publicity handouts and tracts variously designed to explain and denounce it; everywhere it made money. It was an appropriate chess contribution to the century of Cagliostro and Mesmer.

This is perhaps an unfair note on which to end an account of eighteenth-century chess, which is mostly an account of progress. The Paris and London chess clubs were in abeyance for a few years after Philidor's death in 1795, but the lapse was merely temporary. Though chess had become the diversion of an intellectual, or pseudo-intellectual minority, its social appeal was wider than ever before, and the general standard of play higher. Further advance was not long delayed.

CHAPTER FIVE

The Beginnings of Popularity 1800-1914

Chess in nineteenth-century Europe continued to develop very much along the lines laid down between 1750 and 1800. It remained a game for educated men, or those who saw themselves as such, but education was now more widespread than ever before. It remained a genteel game, but gentlemen were now increasingly numerous. Partly because of these social developments chess became gradually more popular, and its popularity took various forms, some of which also promoted a higher standard of play. Chess clubs separated themselves from gentlemen's clubs, coffee houses and subscription rooms, and matches between clubs were common from the 1820s onwards. Like the aristocratic Chess Club of the eighteenth century, the new organizations served as channels for raising money and promoting interest in the game. Books on chess were available in greater numbers and at lower prices than ever before. Matches between the leading English and French players in the 1830s and '40s gave way, after 1851, to international tournaments, drawing celebrated players from as far away as Russia and America. The interest aroused by these competitions led to the proliferation of chess magazines, and the appearance of chess columns in periodicals and newspapers. Naturally too, they led to a movement for the final codification of the rules of the game along standardized lines. And in turn, all these developments attracted more beginners to take it up.

Naturally, the process was not without its limitations. The transition from a café or a coffee house at which boards were available to a specialized chess club was not an easy one. In the early part of the century clubs continually sprang up, flourished for a few years, and then disappeared in a welter of recriminations and unpaid subscriptions. It might be pleasant to have one's cigars wrapped in printed chess problems, as they were at Huttmann's Coffee House, when it sheltered the Westminster Club in the 1830s, but the cigar itself was the main thing, as far as most of the customers were concerned. Chess magazines were almost equally transient.

125

The social image of the game was also calculated to repel a large part of the population: those not of genteel status, and to a lesser extent women and the young. Properly constituted chess clubs only appeared among students at the universities after the 1870s, and the standard of play stayed very low down to 1914. The general promotion of chess in schools would have appeared a quixotic project. It might also be said that in the nineteenth century, as in the eighteenth, chess did not gain in popularity relative to other pursuits. All leisure pursuits profited in varying degrees from general changes: the fact that if there was not necessarily more free time, there was at least more money and thought to be spent on it, more expert instruction on how to use it, and more eagerness to employ it profitably. Some of these general changes, it is true, were particularly helpful. The improvements in printing which made available cheap and mass-produced handbooks was one development which particularly assisted a theoretical game like chess.

Books and players

At first sight there was little sign of incipient popularity around the year 1800. Among the really wealthy and fashionable, chess was perhaps too dependent on the 'French connection' to survive the Revolution and European war. The aristocratic support of the Chess Club at Parsloe's was already falling off before Philidor's death in 1795, and never really recovered. Verdoni, one of the joint authors of the *Traité des amateurs* of 1775, was induced to settle in London, but he never had Philidor's name or reputation, and the post of resident professional seems to have been left unfilled when he in turn died in 1804. Parsloe's was no longer the centre of attention and its members sponsored no more displays or publications. The demise of Philidor's friend Count Brühl in 1809 was probably a final blow to its fortunes. Nor, in these years, was the loss made good by activity elsewhere. The *Picture of London* said of Parsloe's in 1803 that it was 'Famed for elegant dinners, and a chess club. N.B. The only one in England'. Directories still listed the chess club in 1814 and 1819, but then it is heard of no more, and later writers thought that it finally disbanded around 1825. In Paris the Revolution naturally proved even more of an obstacle to the organization of chess, although some of its leaders including Robespierre himself were reputed to be players. But by the late 1790s the determined adherents of the game were again meeting regularly at the Café de la Régence, led by Bernard and Carlier. Napoleon Bonaparte himself may have played there, though the games sometimes attributed to him are notorious forgeries, copied inevitably from Greco, still the most obvious source of brilliant and showy games.

In fact, the lull in organized chess activity around the turn of the century was a deceptive one, and the pessimistic thoughts voiced by Richard Twiss's Edinburgh correspondent of the 1780s, that chess was everywhere giving way to other games, proved not to be realized. The best proof of this is the continued publication of chess books in both London and Paris. In Paris there were new editions of Philidor's *Analyze* in 1803 and 1812, while Montigny's *Stratagèmes des échecs*, a problem collection based mainly on the works of Stamma and Lolli, appeared in 1802. London saw an even greater profusion of chess books, though most of them were modelled on Philidor, whose name was still the best guarantee of a sale. They began with straightforward reprints, like *Chess Analysed* of 1791, which was taken wholly from the 1750 English first edition, then progressed gradually towards more mixed compilations, which were usually announced as containing 'The whole Analysis of Chess by Mr. A.D. Philidor' but had some new material as well. Any additions were naturally represented as improvements and one of the first American Philidors, *The Elements of Chess* (Boston, 1805), was not the only version to claim 'explanatory notes, new modelled; and arranged upon an original Plan'. In London the series began with *Chess Made Easy* in 1797, then ran through Peter Pratt's *Theory of Chess* of 1799 and *Studies of Chess* in 1803, with five more editions by 1825; the Rev. Thomas Pruen's *Introduction to the history and study of chess* of 1804, and an anonymous *Easy Introduction to the Game of Chess* in 1806, which had four more editions by 1820. This was an impressive tally, to which some more genuinely original works were to be added after 1808. The authors, or editors, very much resembled the keen chess players of the late eighteenth century. They too were miscellaneous writers and self-professed intellectuals, with a wide range of interests. Peter Pratt, for instance, translated a life of Alexander the Great and wrote a history of Japan. The Rev. Pruen was the author of a treatise on Jenner's method of inoculation. Their works were not yet cheap enough to be truly popular, but they were more numerous than ever before, and clearly aimed at what was thought to be a growing market amongst unskilled players, who had to be conducted in easy stages from elementary maxims to the distilled wisdom of Philidor. The age of mechanized printing was only just beginning, but there were some signs of technical advance too, in particular the reappearance of printed diagrams, which could now be produced with movable type.

There is therefore ample evidence that the general support of chess was sustained, or even enhanced, in the old centres of Paris and London by the end of the Revolutionary period. The same was true of Italy, and of those parts of central Europe where chess had grown in popularity through French influence. There were, for instance, new editions of Ponziani's *Il giuoco incomparabile degli scacchi* in 1801 and 1812. Both Berlin and Vienna had chess clubs, though they were reputed to be very weak, because they were too exclusive to admit the strongest players. The leading Paris player, Alexandre Deschapelles, went to Berlin after the Battle of Jena in 1806 and returned boasting that he had been able to give a rook odds to all the Germans, though not everyone believed him. In Vienna there was at least one strong player, Johann Allgaier, who saw through the press three more editions of his *Neue theoretisch-praktische Anweisung* of 1795 before his death in 1823. In Holland there was sufficient demand for several new Dutch editions of Philidor after 1800.

Perhaps the greatest relative advance in chess activity took place in the United States of America. Benjamin Franklin wrote his essay on *The Morals of Chess* as early as 1779, but he wrote it in France and it was probably first published in London before it appeared in the *Columbian Magazine* in 1786. Earlier, Franklin had the greatest difficulty in finding opponents in America and certainly had to procure his chess books from Europe. But after 1800 the 'Philidorian' handbooks began to appear in an American guise; first *Chess Made Easy* (Philadelphia 1802), then *The Elements of Chess* (Boston 1805), based on London editions of 1797 and 1799 respectively. To some extent they were modified for American readers. Where Peter Pratt in 1799 had eccentrically suggested changing the names of some of the pieces – notably queen, rook and pawn to minister, peer and commoner – the Bostonian editor went one better and proposed a set consisting of governor, general, colonels, majors, captains and pioneers. Neither of these suggestions was well received, but chess was more securely established in the clubs and drawing rooms of the American East Coast. Six more such books were published between 1817 and 1830, as well as one French edition which claimed to have been printed at Philadelphia but in fact seems to have emanated from Brussels, presumably with a view to the American market. Russian chess literature began in the 1820s, with I. Butrimov's '*On the Game of Chess*' (St Petersburg 1821), and A.D. Petrov's '*The Game of Chess*' (St Petersburg 1824), the second of which was yet another version of Philidor. Spanish speaking areas were perhaps the last to be caught up in this general movement. The first Spanish Philidor edition appeared in 1832 in Mexico. Also, once the Spanish and Latin Americans had got Philidor, they seemed extraordinarily disinclined to abandon his book for anything more recent. Whereas the last important English edition of the *Analyze* was George Walker's in 1832, there were more than twenty editions in Spanish between 1832 and 1930.

Exact figures for the print runs and sales of such books are naturally not available, but in general they increased rather than decreased at this time, in England at least. Subscription lists were not so commonly required to induce a publisher to invest his money in a book, if there was a promising market for it. The demand for chess sets also seems to have been

(a)

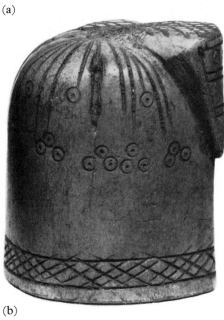

(b)

1 (a) *Left*, Rukh. *Centre*, Shah.
Two early Islamic chess pieces,
Egyptian 8th–9th century. *Right*,
Bishop. (b) Knight. (c) Rook.
Three early-medieval western
pieces, probably 11th century

(c)

(a)

(b)

2 (a) King, bishop, knight.
(b) Seven knights. From the
'Lewis' collection of chessmen,
c. 1150–1170

(a)

3 (a) Bishop. 14th or early
15th century, probably from
south Germany (b) Rook.
14th or early 15th century,
German or Scandinavian

(b)

(a)

4 (a) The philosopher invents the game of chess. (b)
He teaches it to the king. Two woodcuts from
William Caxton's *Game and Playe of the Chesse*,
1482/3

(b)

(a)

5 (a) A 14th-century ivory mirror back. (b) Illustration from *Libro di giuocho di scacchi*, Florence 1493

(b)

6 Title page of Thomas
Middleton's satirical play, *A Game
at Chess*, 1624

The high and Mighty Monarch CHARLES by
the grace of GOD King of Great Brittaine
France and Ireland

P. Stent excudit

THE
ROYALL GAME
OF
CHESSE-PLAY.

SOMETIMES
The Recreation of the late
KING, with many of the
NOBILITY.

Illustrated
VVith almost an hundred
GAMBETTS.

BEING
The study of *BIOCHIMO*
the famous *Italian.*

LONDON,
Printed for *Henry Herringman*, and are to be
sold at his shop at the sign of the Anchor,
in the lower walk of the New
Exchange, 1656.

7   Title page of *The Royall Game
of Chesse-Play,* 1656

Aux François étonnés de sa Mâle Harmonie,
Il montra dans son art des prodiges nouveaux
Dans ses délassemens admirant son Génie,
On voit qu'en ses jeux même il n'a point de Rivaux.
Par M. Davesne

F. Bartolozzi delin. et sculp. 1777.

8 Engraved portrait of Philidor,
from his *Analyse du jeu des échecs*,
1777

9 Paul Morphy's name used to
advertize cigars, 1859

GAME of CHESS.

(a)

10 (a) Caricature by George Cruikshank, 1835 (b) The first Oxford and Cambridge chess match, 1873. From the *Illustrated London News*

OXFORD AND CAMBRIDGE CHESS MATCH.

(b)

(a)

11 (a) Stage setting for the world championship match between Fischer and Spassky, Reykjavik 1972. (b) A more typical international tournament at the Chess Olympiad, Lucerne 1982 – the game between Korchnoi and Kasparov

(b)

12 Title page of Lucena's
Repeticion de Amores: E arte de
axedrez, Salamanca 1496/7

The blacke syde.

q.K	q.g.xn. q.b		K	k.B			k.R
d	d	d	d				d
		k.xn.	p		d		
O	p	p		P			
P	P			Q		p	P
q.R	q.xn.	q. B		K	k.B	k.xn.	k.R

The whyte syde.

Thou shalte remoue thy Kinge to the seconde house of thy kinges bishoppe, then he shalbe forced to saue his Knight in the second house of his king. And thou shalte geue him checke with thy Queene, in the fourthe house of hys kynges Rooke.

13 Chess notation. From *The Pleasaunt and wittie Playe of the Cheasts renewed,* 1562

Gambett. lxix.

WHite kings pawn two houses
  Black the same
White kings bishops pawn two houses
  Black queens pawn two houses
White kings pawn take the queens pawn
  Black queen takes the pawn
White queens knight to her bishops third house
  Black queen to her kings third house
White kings knight to his bishops 3 d. house
  Black kings pawn takes the pawn and checks
    with the queen
White king to his bishops second house
  Black kings bishop checks at the fourth house
    of the queens bishop
White queens pawn two houses
  Black Kings bishop to the queens 3 d. house
White kings bishop checks at the contrary
    kings knights fourth house
  Black king to his queen or bishops house
White kings rook to his kings house
  Black queen to her kings bishops 4th. house
White rook gives mate.

H 2   Gam-

14 Chess notation. From *The*
Royall Game of Chesse-Play, 1656

Another defence of the three **Pawns** GAMBET *at the fourteenth move.*

GAME III.

WHITE, the king's pawn, two moves.

Black, the same, two moves.

W the king's bishop's pawn, two moves.

B the king's pawn takes it.

W the king's knight in his king's bishop's third square.

B the king's bishop in his king's second square.

W the king's bishop in his queen's bishop's fourth square.

B the king's bishop gives a check in the white king's rook's fourth square.

W the king's knight's pawn covers.

B the pawn takes it.

W the king castles.

B the pawn takes the white pawn, and gives a check.

W the king in his rook's place.

B the king's bishop in his third square. ¹⁴ *Move.*

W

15 Chess notation. From Bertin's
Noble Game of Chess, 1735

32. Pawns-Clofe Game.

White.			Black.		
p	e	4	p	e	5
p	d	4	p	d	4
d	d	4	b	c	6
d	d	1	f	c	5
f	c	4	p	d	6
b	c	3	b	e	5
f	b	3	c	g	4
g	e	2	d	h	4
Caftle.			p	g	5
c	e	3	Caftle.		
d	d	2	b	f	3
p	f	3	c	f	3

* ✚

Knights Gambett.

White.			Black.		
p	e	4	p	e	5
p	f	4	p	f	4
g	f	3	p	d	6
p	d	4	p	g	5
f	c	4	f	g	7
Caftle.			b	c	6
p	c	3	d	f	6
p	e	5	p	e	5
p	e	5	d	g	6
h	e	1	g	e	7
p	b	4	p	a	6
p	a	4	Caftle.		

*

F

16 Chess notation. From
Stamma's *Noble Game of Chess*,
1745

maintained, to judge from the numbers of surviving specimens in collections. Pseudo-oriental chessmen were imported to Europe from India in increasing quantities, while ivory-carving workshops at home turned to topical designs like the Napoleonic chess set. George III headed the other side, with Nelson and Wellington as bishops. Such curiosities will always appeal to collectors, but as the popularity of the game increased a higher and higher proportion of the market must have been taken up by comparatively inexpensive sets intended for practical use, like the French '*directoire*' designs. A certain amount of anecdotal evidence, from literature and correspondence, helps to confirm the impressions given by the study of printed books. Even Kempelen's automaton chess player had a new lease of life at this time. It was bought by Johann Maelzel after the inventor's death in 1804, and toured Europe successfully with its new owner between 1805 and 1808, going even to Paris. In 1809 or 1810 the machine was bought by Napoleon's stepson Eugène de Beauharnais for the very large sum of 30,000 francs, simply in order to learn the secret of its operation. Clearly, the device still had the power to fascinate.

Even in this period of apparent turmoil and dislocation there is therefore much evidence of interest in chess, and the new willingness to study it which had characterized the age of Philidor. Knowledge of the game and the conclusions of the eighteenth-century theoreticians were more widely disseminated now, both socially and geographically, than before 1800. Given the existence of this underlying basis of support, as well as more effective means of spreading new ideas and conducting theoretical debates in print, it could not be very long before organized high-level chess reasserted itself. Events were to show that the old centres of Paris and London were still best placed for further advance. In the first quarter of the century they developed largely in isolation, but after 1834 the quickening pace of international competition drew in players from all over Europe. It is arguable that the change proceeded more rapidly in London than in Paris, and certainly it is better documented there.

The revival began as early as 1807, with the foundation of the London Chess Club, which met at Tom's Coffee House in Cornhill. It was very much a City club, gathering, in the words of the later writer F.M. Edge, 'under the shadows of the Bank and Royal Exchange, and but a step from Lombard Street'.[1] The regular members and backers therefore included a good number of financiers and professional men, whose regular support gave the London club a continuous existence from 1807 down to 1870, while attempts to start similar clubs further west, in more fashionable districts, repeatedly came to grief. In this respect the London Club followed the lead of the book publishers, achieving in effect a great degree of emancipation from volatile upper class patronage, the 'Season', and everything that had gone with it in Philidor's day. Aristocrats and public figures were always welcome in these clubs, if only as figureheads and chairmen of organizing committees, but leading players and writers were no longer so dependent on their support. The leading player and writer at London in these early days was J.H. Sarratt, a schoolmaster who obviously saw no advantage in changing his profession without achieving promotion, and so regularly styled himself 'Professor of Chess'. Sarratt was very much a man of the new age, who taught chess as a social or intellectual accomplishment. William Tuckwell, an Oxford surgeon who founded the Brazen Nose Club in 1810, was stated by a friend to have received lessons from 'the great J.H. Sarratt, whose fee was a guinea a lesson'. The modern critic is bound to wonder whether the professor gave good value for his guineas, for though Sarratt was thought by contemporaries to be a strong player, there is not much evidence of it in his surviving games or published works. His *Treatise on the Game of Chess* of 1808 was hardly an advance on the books of the other 'post-Philidorians', and even Peter Pratt, who was regarded by everyone as a poor player, was able to reply to Sarratt's criticism in 1810 and score a few palpable hits in the process.

Sarratt's main claim to fame from a technical point of view was the emphasis he placed on sources of chess ideas other than Philidor, whose name had such a strong hold in England. He began the process of making available in English the whole inherited literature of chess, by publishing two volumes of translations before his death in 1821: *Damiano, Ruy Lopez and Salvio* (1813) and *Gianutio and G. Selenus* (1817). The translations were muddled and inaccurate, but they initiated a trend. William Lewis published new editions of Stamma in 1818, Greco in 1819, and Carrera in 1821; J.S. Bingham produced a translation of Ponziani in 1820; and John Cochrane's *Treatise on the Game of Chess* in 1822 consisted mostly of del Rio and the *Traité des amateurs*. Sarratt's contribution was a useful one, but he hardly broke much new ground. Other contemporaries too were aware of the eighteenth-century Italians' criticisms of Philidor and the need to modify some sections of the *Analyze* in deference to them. While Sarratt stood out by openly siding with the Italians, it is a mistake to think that the difference between French and Italian styles of play was all-important. At times too, his enthusiasm led him to make some very silly statements, as in his suggestion that the games of Lopez and Salvio had never been surpassed by later players. This might be charitably disregarded as promotional writing; Sarratt was above all a professional.

The same was true of his pupil and successor William Lewis (1787–1870), who saw Sarratt's last work, the *New Treatise on the Game of Chess*, through the press after his death. As a city clerk, he was a natural recruit to the London Club and able to perceive the professional advantages of the game. In 1818, when Johann Maelzel once more took to the road with the chess automaton, which he had just repurchased from Eugéne de Beauharnais, Lewis accepted the job of operator for a season. His first published work, in 1817, was *Oriental Chess or specimens of Hindoostanee excellence in that celebrated game*, containing many problems from a book published in Bombay in 1814, Shastri's *Essays on Chess adapted to the European Mode of Play*. This began a series of intermittent but intriguing contacts between England and native players in the original homeland of chess. Lewis described himself merely as a 'teacher' rather than a 'professor' of chess, but his attitude to the game was much the same as Sarratt's. In the 1820s he took out a patent for the manufacture of a new kind of piano, but he ran himself into financial difficulties and soon turned back to chess once more for his income. Nor were Sarratt and Lewis alone in this. Philidor editions and handbooks by a variety of authors continued to be published. There was even a *Practical Chess Grammar* (1817) by W.S. Kenny, one of the dedicated text-book writers of the time, whose pedagogic genius ranged from scientific discoveries to ancient history and phrase books in French and Italian. Even the most calculating purveyor of genteel self-improvement could find chess worth teaching, and a market for his books.

Despite all this there were as yet few connections between London and other counties. Many of the books printed on London presses must have found their way to country customers, but it is hard to find evidence of organized activity in provincial towns early in the century. Certainly chess clubs were founded, and for a year (1813–14) the *Liverpool Mercury* possessed the earliest known regular chess column as well, but the clubs seemed to have no secure or permanent existence. They came and went with the enthusiasm of small groups of people. It was therefore a major advance when the London Club embarked on the first of a series of formal correspondence matches, against Edinburgh in 1824, each side forming a committee to decide on its moves. The new development was all the more striking when Edinburgh, led by the bailie James Donaldson, emerged as the winners in 1828, by two wins to one with two draws. Lewis published the games, despite the result.

Contacts with Paris were also in their infancy in this period. In 1807 the *Gentleman's magazine* reported a match in Paris between Deschapelles and Carlier, promoted by Francis Henry Egerton later Earl of Bridgewater. Egerton was a notorious eccentric remembered chiefly for leaving a large sum in his will for the best essay on 'The Goodness of God as manifested in the Creation', which led to the writing of the so-called *Bridgewater Treatises*. He lived in Paris as much as he could and seems to have had no connection with chess in London. In 1821 Lewis went to Paris with John Cochrane, then a young man reading for the Bar, and the two of them played a series of informal matches with Deschapelles and his leading pupil Louis de Labourdonnais, at a variety of odds and without much success. Relations then lapsed for a while as the Paris players could not organize themselves to accept a challenge to a match by correspondence, made by the London club in 1824. The strength of the leading Paris players could not be doubted, but chess there was almost entirely café chess. There was a great emphasis on the giving of odds, on rapid informal play and on sheer showmanship. The scene was appropriately presided over by Deschapelles, with his war wound and endless fund of Munchausen-like anecdotes, including the story that he became a world-class chess player in two days' study of the game. After 1821 he largely gave up chess in favour of whist, at which he claimed to make over 30,000 francs a year. Typically, though he lived until 1847, he never wrote anything about the game for publication.

Clubs and matches

In 1830 there was still only one real chess club in London, following the failure of a number of attempts to found new ones in the 1820s. Elsewhere in Europe too, such clubs were only just beginning to struggle into existence. It is therefore hard to explain the rapid advance of the next two decades towards institutionalized competitive chess. There was change, or advance, in all three of the main aspects already discussed: basic popularity, organization at a higher level, and the theory and practice of the game, and naturally all three were linked together. One can point to the accumulation of preconditions – social change, the growth of publishing, more efficient transport – which helped to break down local and national barriers, but the mainspring of change around 1830 is still elusive. Given that the number of potential recruits to a whole range of leisure pursuits was increasing, there was perhaps a large element of chance in the process of growth of any one of them, though the nature of individual games tended to define the limits of their social appeal.

Certainly, well publicized competition between leading players helped to spur on the foundation of more genuine chess clubs, which were meant primarily to compete with each other rather than to consume 'elegant dinners'. The patriotic feelings roused by the London and Edinburgh match were an early sign of this, but the real turning point was the match between Labourdonnais and Alexander Mac Donnell, which took place in London in 1834. Mac Donnell (1798–1835), who was Secretary to the Committee of West India Merchants in London, had come to the fore when Lewis gradually withdrew from competitive play after 1830, while Labourdonnais had now supplanted Deschapelles as the first player in Paris and travelled to London with the express intention of extending his reputation. Both sides found backers and they played solidly through the summer and autumn, five matches and part of a sixth; though later writers tended to regard the whole affair as one enormous contest. This is still the largest number of games ever played successively in match conditions. Labourdonnais certainly won, and though there are slight differences between contemporary reports of the score, it is most likely that he did so by forty-five wins to twenty-seven, with thirteen draws. The match conditions were very different from modern ones. The two contestants, neither of whom knew a word of the other's language, were placed in the midst of a 'concourse of amateurs'. Labourdonnais was described by one English observer as a 'large slovenly Frenchman' who spent most of his time spitting and cursing, if not actually singing and laughing, while Mac Donnell, dour and determined, drove his opponent to distraction by thinking for up to an hour and a half over a single move. Compared with some later matches, however, this was a chivalrous encounter. Mac Donnell admitted himself fairly beaten, though he won some famous games, and described his opponent as 'the most finished player of the age'.

The interest aroused by the great match was extraordinary. Joseph Méry even wrote a poem about one of the games called *Une Revanche de Waterloo*, which was published in 1836, whereupon the Rev. D'Arblay, Fanny Burney's son, replied with another entitled *Caissa Rediviva*, extolling Mac Donnell's play. The match also proved the making of the new Westminster Chess Club, in whose rooms it took place. It had been coaxed into existence in 1831 by George Walker, but after 1834 grew to have over 300 members. Between 1834 and 1836 the Westminster players embarked on a new correspondence match with Paris, where a private club for serious devotees of the game had at last been organized. They lost both the games and their £50 stake, but Walker was not deterred from publishing the games in a pamphlet and indignantly blamed members of the London team for not upholding the club's honour more keenly: 'Every sort of excuse was tendered for absence but the true one; which was, that they had no stomach for the fight!'[2]

While some Englishmen yearned for revenge, Deschapelles was provoked by his countryman's success to challenge any Englishman to a match at odds in 1836, a typical piece of bravado which came to nothing. His message was taken to London by one of the younger French players, Pierre de Saint-Amant, whose report, later published in Paris, is an interesting commentary on the relative status of the two capitals. While London had nothing resembling the Café de la Régence or its very best players, he was struck by the much wider vogue for the game, which in England had become 'national and popular'.[3] The nearest approach to the Régence was probably Ries' Cigar Divan in the Strand, founded in 1828, which had a great reputation as an informal chess centre by the late 1830s. A guidebook of 1855 mentions the Divan, 'where the leading chess publications are accessible to visitors and where as many as twenty chess boards may often be seen at the same time'.[4]

Naturally some of this activity found its way into print, and aroused even wider interest. Nearly all the 1834 match games were recorded by Mac Donnell's Boswell, William Greenwood Walker, and in 1835 Lewis published fifty of them in his *Selection of Games at Chess*. Following Mac Donnell's early death in 1835 Greenwood Walker brought out his own tribute, *A selection of games at Chess by the late Alexander M'Donnell*. (1836). This trend of publishing contemporary games, begun by Lewis' *Fifty Games at Chess, which have actually been played* of 1832, was a recent one, as the title suggests, but extremely important. Systematic recording and printing of the best contemporary games was much more use to players than reprints of Greco or Damiano. The public enthusiasm generated by the great match was thus turned into study and instruction. Between them, Lewis and George Walker carried this process much further. Lewis had by 1830 extricated himself from his speculations in pianos, and beginning with the *Series of Progressive Lessons on the Game of Chess* (1831) wrote over the next fifteen years a whole series of instructional handbooks, which at last constituted an advance on Philidor's method of teaching. H.J.R. Murray argued that Lewis was the first to fuse together the tenets of Philidor and Italian chess to produce a 'new school, which we may term the Lewis or English school'. It 'governed the practice of all English and German players down to the time of Wilhelm Steinitz' and 'reached the highest point in the play of Paul Morphy'.[5] On reflection, it does not seem likely that a whole generation of players, many of them (like Staunton) much stronger than Lewis, should have been 'governed' in this way, and recent studies of their games have clearly shown that they were not. Nor can Lewis be truly credited with a heroic synthesis of different chess traditions, for Murray's whole picture of sharply delineated national schools of play in the eighteenth century does not correspond with reality. Lewis was certainly eclectic and well read, but his main influence was as a teacher, and of more lasting significance among weaker players. The evidence of his games and books suggests that he himself was a competent player but not much more; and after 1830 he preserved his reputation by playing very little.

George Walker (1803–1879) was never a full chess professional and never claimed to be a first-rate player, though he once remarked, 'I fancy I might have reached the steps to the throne by giving over my business, and sending the hat round once a year'. His business was initially in publishing, though he later became a stockbroker, and it was as an organizer and entrepreneur that he contributed most to the game. He repeatedly tried to found new chess clubs in London until he was eventually successful. He began the first popular chess column in 1835, in

Bell's Life in London, and continued to edit it down to 1873. He attempted to start a specialist chess magazine, the *Philidorian*, in 1838, though it came to grief after a few months. Above all he brought into being the first really popular chess literature anywhere in Europe, by indulging in a price-cutting war with William Lewis which led to a feud between the two men for ten years. In 1832 Walker brought out his *New treatise on chess* at the then unheard-of price of three shillings and sixpence, with an improved second edition at five shillings, still a fraction of the usual charge. Lewis matched him with *Chess for beginners* (1835) at the same price, but Walker replied with *Chess made Easy* (1836) at three and sixpence. Lewis finally made his point with the half-crown *Chess-board companion* in 1838, and Walker conceded, remarking that 'if I carried on the war with Chess for the Masses, at a single shilling, my competitor would rejoin with a sixpenny Chess for the Millions'. The obvious point to be made is that the public were the real beneficiaries in all this. The *Chess-board companion* alone went rapidly through nine editions.

As Saint-Amant had implied in 1836, Paris and other centres could not emulate this popular appeal. Labourdonnais did write a rather sketchy book in 1833, and edited a new chess magazine, *Le Palamède*, from 1836, but as he grew ill the monthly issues ceased to appear and lapsed altogether in 1839. In desperate straits, he accepted an offer to come to London and play at the Divan for two guineas a week, but he died soon after his arrival in 1840, the indefatigable George Walker raising a subscription for his widow. Saint-Amant was now generally regarded as the leading player, and revived the *Palamède* in 1842. In Germany in the 1830s, a group of young players subsequently known after the constellation, as the 'Pleiades', formed a new and less exclusive Berlin chess club, firmly devoted to the advancement of the game. One of them, L.E. Bledow, translated Lewis' *Selection of Games* in 1835 and brought to Germany too an eagerness to emulate the achievements of Labourdonnais and Mac Donnell. The whole group of six or seven was only together for a few years, but they seem to have stimulated each other's play and researches much like del Rio, Lolli and Ponziani did in the eighteenth century. It was still possible for a small group of talented men to advance chess theory, so long as they had access to the rather greater amount of technical literature now available, and a few contacts with visiting masters. Their enduring achievement was the *Handbuch des Schachspiels* of 1843, begun by the army officer Paul von Bilguer and completed after his early death by another of the company, the diplomat Baron Tassilo von der Lasa. 'Bilguer's Handbook' may have owed something to the works of Allgaier and Lewis, but it was really the first encyclopaedic treatment of the chess openings on modern lines. Brought up to date in successive editions, it remained the bible of German players, and many others, at least down to 1914. The achievements of the 'Pleiades' may perhaps have been exaggerated by contemporary legend and the subsequent reputation of the *Handbuch*; nor is there really enough evidence for a critic to evaluate their own opinions of each other's play. It was still a time when great reputations could be founded on offhand games, and only one of the group, Bernhard Horwitz, submitted himself to the sterner tests of formal matches and international tournaments conducted in public. But they certainly prepared the way for the emergence of stronger players and the rise of Germany as a third force in European chess.

The Mediterranean countries as a whole saw no similar activity. There is no reason to suppose that chess grew less popular as a domestic pastime, but there was little formal organization and no strong players able to improve on the inherited theory of the eighteenth century. In Italy in particular variant local rules were a problem, and there was no equivalent of the *Handbuch*, which cleared up some eccentric conventions in Germany. Eastern Europe had rather more signs of change. A group of Hungarians playing as representatives of Pesth caused a minor sensation in the years 1839–42 by beating Paris in another of the now well-established matches by correspondence, though one of them, Joseph Szen, had practised his game by visits to London, Paris and Berlin in the late 1830s. In Russia A.D. Petrov was equalled in reputation by I. Shumov and C.F. Jaenisch, author of the *Analyse nouvelle* (1842–43), a work still much under the influence of Philidor.

Such developments were an important pointer to the future, but more than anything else the 1840s was the decade when London finally succeeded Paris as the admitted capital of the chess world. This was mostly the work of one man, Howard Staunton, whose achievement has only recently begun to be recognized. Staunton was born in 1810. His early life was obscure, but there seems no evidence for the rumour that he was the illegitimate son of the fifth Earl of Carlisle. At first he was an actor, playing according to his own account with Edmund Kean, and only took up chess at the late age of twenty-six. He learnt the game mostly at the Divan, and by 1841 had became secretary of the Westminster Chess Club and launched the *Chess Player's Chronicle*, a magazine which he edited and presided over down to 1854. His chief opponent at this time was John Cochrane, who had gone to India around 1825 in pursuit of his legal career, but returned on leave in 1841. Staunton improved through practice and by February 1843 he won a match against his companion very easily, by fourteen games to four. In March 1843 he suffered an irritating reverse, losing a short six-game match to Saint-Amant, who was regularly in London because of his business as a wine merchant. This match was probably informal, and it was played for a stake of a single guinea, but Staunton was sufficiently confident to seek a full revenge, and he issued a challenge. It was agreed that there should be a match in Paris for £100, the winner being the first to take eleven games. This was in effect a re-enactment of the great Mac Donnell–Labourdonnais contest of 1834 and attracted much attention. In the words of a contemporary, Charles Tomlinson: 'In the chess clubs of the country the greatest excitement prevailed, and the games, as and when received, were played over and over.'[6] Staunton's victory by eleven games to six with four draws left little doubt of his superiority, though the match was followed by an acrimonious debate, in which Saint-Amant claimed that the score between them was now one match each and nothing was proved without a further trial. The new weapon of the press was brought into play, enabling the principals and their supporters to snipe at one another from behind their emplacements in the *Palamède* and the *Chess Player's Chronicle*.

Nevertheless, Staunton's victory was decisive, and it had various consequences. Inevitably, it brought his own combative personality to the fore in English, and even European, chess. Staunton went through life in a series of quarrels and controversies caused mostly by his own deviousness and vitriolic writing. Even before the Saint-Amant match he was capable of answering a correspondent who had asked whether George Walker's *New treatise on chess* was approved by the London Chess Club committee: 'The only sanction given to Walker's puerilities by the Committee is to laugh at them. His books on Chess are no authority except among the lowest class of players.'[7] Staunton also had a hand in the collapse of the once flourishing Westminster Chess Club by 1843, though Walker contrived to fill the gap with his new St George's Club. In view of all this it is hardly surprising that the two men were estranged; it is only remarkable that they were reconciled so quickly. Even after Staunton had sold the *Chess Player's Chronicle*, he kept a chess column in the *Illustrated London News* from 1845 to his death in 1874, in which he was liable at almost any time to start an argument with almost anybody. But in other respects Staunton's achievement was a considerable one. He wrote valuable books, particularly *The Chess-Player's Handbook* of 1847, which replaced Lewis's *Lessons* and became the standard reference book for English club players down to the end of the century, with twenty-one reprints by 1935. He worked hard for the promotion of chess, and the causes he adopted, like a national chess association and an internationally agreed code of rules, were extremely sensible ones. At dinners and functions up and down the country, he lent his name and prestige to local enterprises. That prestige was very great; a speaker at the Yorkshire Chess Association dinner in 1845 was only reflecting the general view when he announced that 'we have the satisfaction of knowing that the Chess Champion is an Englishman'. Another earnest of this was the appearance of the 'Staunton Chessmen'. This new design for an elegant and functional chess set was made by Nathaniel Cook at an unknown date, but by the time a patent was secured in 1849 Staunton had agreed to let his name be used to promote the new pieces, and even wrote a small *Chess Player's Textbook* (1849) to be given away free to future purchasers. Nearly all modern sets intended for practical play are derived from the 'Staunton pattern'. But of all Staunton's personal contributions to chess the greatest were the distinctive ideas he developed in his games, and his organization of the first ever international chess tournament in 1851 – of which more below.

In the meantime his victory in 1843 had more general consequences for English and European chess. The leading foreign masters flocked to London to study and play the game. The journalist F.M. Edge wrote rather romantically in 1859: 'About 1820, the Holy Alliance (of Sovereigns against the people) began playing its pranks: proscribed fugitives, martyrs to liberty – *soi disant* and otherwise – came over to England in shoals, and amongst them were to be found thorough adepts in the mysteries of chess. These refugees rekindled the fire in Britain.'[8] Edge was not really the most reliable authority on the earlier history of the game and only one chess player of note, Adam Zytogorski, a Pole who came to London after the 1830 Revolution, really had claims to be a political exile. Many more foreign masters came to England in the wake of Staunton's success, simply to pursue their careers. In 1845 they included the German Bernhard Horwitz, one of the 'Pleiades', and the younger Daniel Harrwitz, as well as Lionel Kieseritzky, who came from Livonia. The aspirants made little impact on Staunton, to whom Horwitz and Harrwitz both lost matches in 1846, but they found it worth their while to stay in London, Harrwitz from 1848 to 1856 and Horwitz permanently. Kieseritzky did not get a match against Staunton and went on to Paris. But these men were just the advance guard of a whole wave of immigrants. Johann Löwenthal, another genuine refugee, fled from Hungary to America after 1848, but settled in London in 1851. His countryman Ernst Falkbeer arrived in 1855 and the greatest of all these players, the Bohemian Wilhelm Steinitz, came to London for the international tournament in 1862 and made his home there afterwards. The little colony of foreign players occasionally aroused native irritation. Staunton wrote testily in 1858:

> that preposterous custom of engaging an ignorant foreigner to edit Chess in an English newspaper makes us ridiculous wherever the game is known . . . . Indeed the practice if not checked would shortly have given to some half-dozen refugees a complete monopoly of English periodical Chess. You have no conception of the exertion these fellows have been making to get the Chess in their hands.[9]

But most English chessplayers were flattered to see their country at the centre of world activity, and aware of its advantages. Before the onset of regular international tournaments, and with long-distance travel still slow and expensive in most of Europe, the concentration of leading players in London, and to a lesser extent Paris, created a kind of forcing house for the development of the game. In their way, the matches of 1834 and 1843 had altered the organization of chess and its public image as much as Philidor's successful career two generations earlier.

Tournaments and competition

Between 1850 and 1875 chess emerged with a new clarity as a middle-class game, albeit one for a minority with more or less intellectual tastes, still predominantly male and middle-aged. Once again the process was most rapid in England, for a variety of reasons. The inherited tradition of the game reacted with new conditions stemming from wealth and economic development to generate change. It was admittedly change of a relative kind. Aristocratic participation became steadily more token in nature, like that of the duke who was found to head the Committee of Management for the 1851 international tournament. At the same time the game began to spread to the newer middle classes of the Midlands and the North, who were less inclined than their predecessors to follow aristocratic pursuits uncritically. Men who had grown rich on the doctrine of work, and based their religion on it, did not take easily to sophisticated use of leisure, even though the stable prosperity of the decades after 1850 made it more and more available to them and their families. That such men were unsure how to enjoy themselves, or whether they ought to, is apparent from their attempts to work out theories of 'legitimate' recreation, some of them painfully utilitarian. The purpose of leisure activities, according to W.H. Miller, was simply to 'bring back body and mind fitted again for the business of life . . . with the least expense possible of time, strength and money'.[10] Even for more cheerful writers, the central doctrine was that true recreation was not mere diversion or amusement, but another kind of work, performed for the good of body and soul. William Gladstone was a fine example, spending his holidays felling trees on his estate or joining forces with Lord Lyttelton, sometime president of the British Chess Association, to engage in such mind-cleansing pursuits as translating Tennyson's *Lotos-Eaters* into Greek.

Naturally it is hard to establish how many families followed such principles to the full, beyond the careful avoidance of activities that were obviously frivolous or disreputable, and so socially damning. Nevertheless, the proponents of chess were ready to meet these values head on. Clergymen bulked large in the ranks of English amateur players during the nineteenth century, though they sometimes played under pseudonyms. As Staunton wrote in his introduction to *The Chess Tournament* (1852):

Chess was not designed to be a waste of time or an excuse for indolence; it is not a pursuit to be lounged over for want of better employment, or, like a game of chance, to be made the means of low gambling. Chess was intended to be the recreation of men of genius and practical energies; men who are fully alive to the responsibilities of their social existence; men who, even in their amusements, are desirous of bracing and invigorating to the utmost their intellectual powers.

Again, few chess players were likely to be as self-righteous about the game as Staunton, but at the least they need feel no uneasiness in playing it, which was important. Chess could meet the demands of the moralist in one way, by being played at home and so strengthening the domestic circle, but equally well it could provide a valid reason for association. A slightly later French observer, A. Esquiros, remarked on the 'tendency of the English to form groups through the attractions of certain pleasures . . . . In France men like to meet for the sake of meeting; the Englishman is perhaps less sociable: he requires an object, a community of tastes, a peculiar tie, which draws him nearer his fellowmen.'[11]

Contemporaries certainly observed these changes and recorded their impressions. F.M. Edge, who became Paul Morphy's secretary during his triumphant tour of Europe in 1858–59 and wrote a book about his achievements, was less a moralist than a Victorian radical who enjoyed poking fun at the aristocracy, but his criticisms of metropolitan life were of a common type:

We have thousands of men, composing the British aristocracy, at a loss to get rid of their time; sauntering down to their clubs at mid-day; listlessly turning over the leaves of magazines and reviews, until their dinner-hour arrives. Why, in the name of common sense, do not these men learn something of chess, and thus provide themselves with a pastime which not merely quickens Time's chariot-wheels, but quickens the intellect?[12]

Naturally, it is easy to talk about the rise of middle-class culture, and hard to find more than anecdotal evidence for it, so it is worth examining the organization of British chess at this time in rather more detail.

It is a striking fact that the British Chess Association, the first national body to promote the game to be found in England, or anywhere else, had its origins not in London but in the Yorkshire Chess Association, which first met in 1841 under the presidency of a local Member of Parliament. Staunton and the leading foreign masters were induced to attend some of its meetings, but it was a local initiative which led in 1852 to the expansion of the organization into a 'Northern and Midland Counties Chess Association', whose territory was to extend from Birmingham to Newcastle. Finally in 1855, and at the suggestion of the president, who came from Liverpool, the Association became a national one and had its first 'national figure', Lord Lyttelton, as president. The strength of the game in the larger industrial towns seems to have been considerable. The first ever international tournament was held in London in 1851, but the second, in 1857, was in Manchester. Before the second London tournament of 1862 there were three more provincial ones, in Birmingham, Cambridge and Bristol, and of these only the Cambridge event was a failure through lack of local support.

There was always give and take between London and the provinces in these matters. After 1843 chess players were drawn to the capital from English country towns as well as from Germany and Eastern Europe. Elijah Williams gave up his job in Bristol, inspired by Staunton's example, to seek his fortune as a player in London. But the process also worked in reverse, as those who had lived in the city or visited it, moved elsewhere and set up chess clubs on the metropolitan model, as did Captain Kennedy in Brighton in 1840. After 1850 or so chess clubs become too numerous to keep track of, and it would take a massive search through local records to get anywhere near the total, which continued to grow in the second half of the century. The same is true of chess columns in provincial newspapers, which were first listed by A.C. White in 1907 and then amounted to 387 in Britain and Ireland.[13]

It might be thought that the contrast implied here, between England and the rest of Europe or America, is somewhat overdrawn. If the time scale is extended this is true; while there were more chess tournaments in Britain than anywhere else in the 1850s and 60s, there were more in Germany during the rest of the century. But the important thing is that these developments, which formed a common pattern, took place in England first. A number of reasons for this have already been discussed, and one more might be apparent by this stage. Organized chess was primarily an urban, or suburban, phenomenon, while Britain was a great deal more urbanized than any other country in the mid-nineteenth century, and served by the most advanced transport system. Augustus Mongredien, an impeccable free-trade economist, man of letters and keen chess amateur, took advantage of this to hold the presidencies of the London and Liverpool chess clubs for many years in plurality, and to make his presence felt in both. As early as 1845, the year before the formation of the commercial Electric Telegraph Company, Staunton arranged a telegraph game between himself and Captain Kennedy in Gosport, and a home team in London. Once the games were finished Staunton and Kennedy rather comically caught the last train back to town, but they had made their point. By the 1880s there were telegraph matches with India.

The contrast between England and France was a sharp one, despite the many resemblances earlier in the century. Even before 1850, France had failed to develop a large market for instructional books and any signs of chess clubs like those across the channel; after 1850 there was nothing to correspond with the great network of provincial organizations and journalism which sprang up all over England. Even in Paris the chess clubs led a precarious existence. Edge reported that in 1858: 'the Paris Cercle des Echecs, which met in rooms over the Café de la Régence, found that the influence of the arena down stairs was too great for them, and they broke up their meetings, and are now to be found *en masse* in the public café.'[14] One or two outstanding players could not make the game generally popular unless their efforts coincided with helpful social and economic conditions, and lack of general popularity in the end made it harder to sustain the outstanding players. French chess entered on a long cycle of slow decline.

But Germany, and to a lesser extent Holland and America, followed the same pattern as England had before them; clubs proliferated and the game began to appeal to a much wider section of society. English chess players were aware of German competition as soon as English industrialists, if not before. By the 1880s, when the British Chess Association was going through a patch of gentlemanly inactivity, the German Schachbund, founded in 1887, seemed as purposeful as the new Germany itself, holding large tournaments every two years with great efficiency, and supported in turn by the German clubs. The *Deutsche Schachzeitung*, founded in 1846, appeared thereafter without intermissions, unlike the *Chess Player's Chronicle* which folded in 1862, though London was never without a chess magazine of some kind.

When considering the effects of these changes on high-level chess and the theory of the game, it is again necessary to take account of individual achievements and the consequences of a few great events. The greatest event of all, perhaps, was the first international tournament in 1851. From the beginning it was Staunton's project, designed to coincide with Prince Albert's Exhibition in the same year, and like everything Staunton did it was attended with controversy. The Committee of Management set up in 1850 under the leadership of the Duke of Marlborough seemed representative enough, but its members came mostly from Staunton's own club, the St George's, which was to stage the event. This led the rival London Club to boycott the proceedings, and with the aid of George Walker's column in *Bell's Life,* to try to undermine the whole enterprise. But there was considerable support from elsewhere: from the provincial clubs; from France, where a co-operative committee collected subscriptions at the Café de la Régence; and from India, where John Cochrane was again established. He was able to send a hundred pounds from the Calcutta Chess Club as well as twenty in his own name, a very substantial contribution, which reflected his success in promoting European chess in India. Only a few years before, Cochrane had discovered a native player, 'Moheschunder Bonnerjee,' who he claimed showed remarkable talent for the modern game and who became a 'paid attaché' of the Calcutta club, some of his games even being published in London. In 1851 the Committee of Management needed all the money they could raise, for they had to provide prizes on a scale which would match Staunton's ambitious *Prospectus*, and travelling was expensive. No contestants were expected from India, but Löwenthal was induced to return from America, Jaenisch came from Russia, Szen from Hungary, Anderssen from Germany, and Kieseritzky from Paris. Entry fees were charged, but these were waived to attract some foreign players, while others were promised that their expenses would be refunded if they failed to win a prize. In the event Jaenisch was left out because he could not manage to arrive until the tournament was over, a reflection of contemporary conditions of travel in Eastern Europe. The English contingent was almost complete, lacking only the historian Henry Buckle, who was usually reckoned second only to Staunton himself.

In the event Staunton's dedication to the realization of his scheme led to his own downfall. He himself had probably drawn up the details of this new form of competition, which he described in his *Prospectus* as 'A series of grand individual matches' and a 'General Mêlée'. The sixteen competitors simply played matches with each other on a knock-out basis, drawing for new opponents after the conclusion of each round. There was no seeding system, so some of the most fancied players were eliminated after only one match of three games. This led the Committee to decree that the remaining matches should be of seven games each, but nevertheless Staunton lost his semi-final against the German schoolmaster Adolf Anderssen, by four games to one. Anderssen went on to win the final from Marmaduke Wyvill, who was Member of Parliament for Richmond and very much an amateur, but had an easier draw; and Staunton's discomfiture was completed when he lost the play-off for third prize to his former protégé Elijah Williams. In the opinion of many, this made Anderssen the new unofficial 'chess champion' and Staunton certainly seems to have felt that his dominance was threatened, because he at once challenged his rival to a full match on the scale of 1843: a stake of £100 and the best of twenty-one games. Anderssen postponed the engagement because he had already been away from home for over two months, and the match never took place, as Staunton gradually withdrew from competitive play to work on his edition of Shakespeare, which he completed in 1860. The matter remained unresolved, though no one was very surprised about it; there was as yet no concept of a formal world championship, or of the means by which one might be awarded.

Staunton himself always explained his failure in 1851 by saying that he was too busy organizing the tournament to do himself justice, but he had also thought himself to have a chronically weak heart since an illness in

1844, which had prevented his planned return match with Saint-Amant. It is difficult to evaluate claims of this kind, which were made by or about quite a number of chess players in the nineteenth century, just as Philidor had been warned by Diderot that blindfold chess would ruin his health. Physicians tended to have views about nervous illness which led them to exaggerate greatly the strain caused by playing chess, and it is hard to know how much substance lay behind their various diagnoses. All the same it is worth noting a point made by R.N. Coles,[15] that except for the young amateur H.E. Bird, the finalists Anderssen and Wyvill were the only players below forty in the London tournament.

Modern critics, like most unbiased contemporaries, accept that Anderssen was a worthy winner of the first international chess tournament, and he was certainly among the two or three strongest players in the world for the next twenty years. But from a historical point of view, it really did matter less who won or lost than how they played the game in 1851. This was because the international tournament, once it became securely established, transformed competitive chess beyond recognition. Previously the only test of strength except that of offhand games had been the extended match between two individuals. Prolonged negotiations were often necessary to 'make the match', each player had to find his own sponsors or stake-money, and the strongest players were often reluctant to risk their reputations by playing level. They might, like Deschapelles, or even Staunton when he played Harrwitz in 1846, insist on giving odds as a mark of status. Match terms have always proved hard to determine, even in modern times with the Fédération Internationale des Échecs to hold the ring. The tournament broke through many of these barriers and created something more like free trade in international competition. Organizers of such contests were themselves responsible for raising a prize fund, they drew up common rules and conditions to apply to all competitors, and they sent out invitations or requested entries from anyone who wanted to play. It is easy to see why tournaments were a comparatively late innovation in nineteenth-century chess. As compared with matches, they demanded more administration and more financial support from the clubs and other bodies who ran them. The appropriate institutions had to be evolved first.

But for players the tournaments at once offered a wider range of competition, and before very long a better chance of making a living from the game. It cleared the way for the appearance of more professional players, though Staunton himself lamented this prospect in his book *The Chess Tournament* of 1852:

> Chess never was, and while society exists, never can be a profession. It may to a great extent strengthen the mind of the professional man, but it must never become the object of his life. It is because its true character has been lost sight

of by the zealous or the mercenary, that victory at any cost has become a more important object than the advancement of the science.

Staunton wilfully disregarded the fact that 'the science' was advanced much more by free competition than by high-mindedness. Once the 'tournament circuit' was fully established, it provided a whole new stratum of top-level chess, restricted to professionals and those who could play up to professional standards. The clubs and the amateurs supported this new phenomenon, and the way into it for the individual still lay in success at the club level, but club chess itself was gradually relegated to second class status. The change was not an immediate one, for as late as 1872–74 Steinitz conducted the London side in an old fashioned club correspondence match with Vienna, for the sizeable stake of a hundred pounds, but in the end it was irresistible. 'Society', in Staunton's genteel meaning of the term, did cease to exist, or at any rate to apply to leading chess players.

But before this could happen tournaments had to be more frequent, and their operation had to be more carefully regulated. The number of tournaments held and the size of the prizes was an important consideration. Amateur and professional status had never been rigidly separated in chess. Men like Staunton did not hesitate to collect their stake money after winning matches, or to sell their books and magazines, but they would have denied that the game was their main source of income. In the 1840s a professional player like Harrwitz had to take a retainer from the London club; economically he was therefore in much the same position as Moheschunder Bonnerjee in Calcutta. Prize money gave the professional more dignity and independence. Regulation too was important, for fair competition. The London event of 1851, as we have seen, was a sort of uneasy compromise between tournament and match play. The first American congress, held at New York in 1857, followed the same system. Only after this did the true tournament evolve, in which each contestant played one or more games against every other contestant, and the winner was he with the highest total, even if he happened to have lost to the man who was placed second or third. This principle was first employed in an international event at the second London tournament, of 1862. Then there was the problem of draws, which did not matter much in a two-way match, but could be of great importance in an all-play-all tournament. In 1862 drawn games were simply replayed until one player won, but this 'timeless' arrangement was a dangerous precedent for tournament organizers. After Dundee in 1867 it became almost a universal practice to score draws as half a point, as it still is, though reforms in the system are occasionally proposed.

That left the most vexing question of all, the regulation of time. How long should a player be allowed to think over his moves? In the early nineteenth century the great majority of games between leading players were offhand games, nearly all of which must have been played very rapidly, like Philidor's recorded games, but once large stakes and reputations were involved, conditions could easily swing to the opposite extreme. In the last game of the 1843 Staunton and Saint-Amant match a mere twenty-nine moves were played in the first eight hours, and only then was there an hour's adjournment and a new session. Seven or eight hours play at a stretch became quite common. In 1851 Staunton considered that he had suffered from the exceptionally slow play of Elijah Williams, and said so in his tournament book: 'When games are prolonged to twelve, thirteen and twenty hours each, and single moves occupy two hours and a half, the effect upon an invalid can well be imagined.' Henry Buckle, who played largely for amusement, is supposed to have taken pains to avoid such opponents, remarking with Johnsonian vigour that 'the slowness of genius is hard to bear, but the slowness of mediocrity is intolerable'. A formal time limit was the only possible solution, and a series of experiments began. Staunton had suggested a maximum of twenty minutes for any move in 1844, and this was tried out in a match between Harrwitz and Löwenthal in 1853, but it was not really satisfactory. A key move might demand more than twenty minutes' thought, yet twenty minutes for every move would still exceed anyone's endurance. The solution discovered in 1861 and used in the London 1862 tournament, was to set an overall limit of two hours for every twenty-four moves, each player's moves being separately timed with sand-glasses. All that remained was the perfection of a mechanical chess clock, combining two clocks with a mechanism to stop one and start the other when a move was made. Such a clock was devised by Thomas Wilson of Manchester, and first used in the London tournament of 1883.

Another requirement of the new tournament age was a more comprehensive code of rules, to cover small but potentially decisive details in such matters as pawn promotion. Again Staunton was first in the field. He had intended the 1851 congress to include a 'Constituent Assembly for remodelling the laws of chess' which would 'be elected by the great body of players present at the Tournament'. This proposal came to nothing but Staunton continued working in the 1850s to persuade the new British Chess Association to adopt the plan, and published a draft code in his *Chess Praxis* of 1860, which was discussed at London in 1862. The process of harmonization begun in the eighteenth century was thus accelerated by tournament play, though it could not be brought to a final conclusion until the appearance of an international chess authority in the 1920s. One final effect of tournaments was to put an end to the practice of odds giving in high-level chess. Technical standards improved so that even the best players could not afford to give their opponents a pawn start, much less a knight or a rook. Also, a great difference between the strongest and weakest players in a tournament mattered less than the same disparity in a match with no one else involved. A few tournaments with handicaps were tried in the early days, as at London in 1866, but the practice was soon abandoned.

Before going on to the end of the century and the full flourishing of the new competitive system, it is impossible to avoid mentioning someone who was in many ways the last and greatest of the gentlemen amateurs. Chess in America had made considerable progress since its first faltering steps before 1800, but the number of American clubs, and the standard of play in them, still lagged considerably behind that in Europe, and especially England. This, however, did not rule out the appearance of single players of outstanding talent, and in the 1850s there was such a player. Paul Morphy, who was born of a rich New Orleans family in 1837, learnt chess early and in 1850 won an offhand game from Löwenthal during the Hungarian's stay in America. In 1857, at the age of twenty, he won the First American Chess Congress in New York, and in 1858 the New Orleans chess club challenged Staunton to come to America to play the young champion. Staunton predictably replied that it would be more appropriate for the aspirant to come to Europe, where he would meet 'many champions whose names must be as household words to him, ready to test and do honour to his prowess'.[16]

Overcoming the opposition of his family Morphy set out, and landed at Liverpool in July 1858. He then proceeded to storm his way through European chess, winning matches against Löwenthal in London, then Harrwitz and Anderssen in Paris, while astonishing spectators with his virtuosity at offhand games and blindfold displays, in which he played up to eight games at a time. His only real disappointment was his failure to meet Staunton, whom he probably still regarded as the world's most famous player. After three months' prevarication Staunton finally declined a match in October 1858, pleading the prior claims of Shakespeare. Morphy could only appeal to Lord Lyttelton, whom he addressed as 'the Maecenas of English Chess', to confirm that the cancellation was caused by no fault on his own part, which Lyttelton did, in conciliatory terms. There is no doubt that if the two had met in 1858 Morphy would have won, but there was to be no further opportunity, because after returning home in 1859 he showed an increasing reluctance to take part in serious chess competition. He would play only in games at odds, only in informal surroundings, latterly only with his close friends, notably Charles Maurian. He declined challenges to play new matches from the Austrian Ignatz Kolisch and the Russian Alexander Petrov, even when he was again in Paris, from December 1862 to January 1864 and in 1867. The American Civil War, the decline in the fortunes of his family and his failure to establish a legal career in New Orleans, all combined to drive Morphy into introspective seclusion. After 1875 he developed paranoid delusions. He died in 1884.

Morphy's meteoric career led him to be fêted on both sides of the Atlantic. A bust of him was unveiled in Paris, and a series of dinners and presentations greeted his return to America. Unfortunately his premature retirement makes it difficult to assess his importance in chess history. Many of his views about chess playing were diametrically opposed to the way in which the game was to grow and develop. Throughout his life nothing offended Morphy more than any suggestion that chess was a profession or that he wished to profit from playing it. He even declared himself opposed to the long-established practice of staking money on one's own matches, and wrote to Staunton, 'my earnest desire is never to play for any stake but honor'. On these terms he would have run out of worthy opponents if he had continued to play chess for the rest of his life, as his own combination of large talent and large means was an uncommon one. In terms of social history, Morphy was a throwback. His contribution to chess theory and practice is another matter. Morphy was above all a great competitor, a player who wore down his opponents by the sheer accuracy of his moves, and simply made less mistakes than they did. Like Labourdonnais in 1834, he was 'the most finished player of the age'. His secretary and biographer F.M. Edge announced in 1859, though probably without consulting his principal, that 'Morphy can give Pawn and Move to every living player'. But unlike Staunton and Steinitz he was not a great theorizer about the game, and wrote very little.

The New York *Chess Monthly*, to which Morphy himself had been contributing games as co-editor since early in 1858, reported in 1859 that 'Hundreds of people now play chess who, a half-year ago, were utterly ignorant of the moves'. Chess also invaded the popular press, and Morphy again was the greatest prize; Robert Bonner the publisher of the New York *Ledger* offered him 3,000 dollars in advance for a weekly chess column in May 1859. 'The chess columns of the United States', wrote D.W. Fiske a month or two later, 'now form a formidable brigade. From as far East as Boston to as far West as San Francisco, from southernmost Texas to northernmost Minnesota'.

But by the end of 1860 Morphy had withdrawn from all his journalistic engagements, and without his magnetic attraction, plans for new books and tournaments came to nothing. A New York newspaper article of July 1861 summed up the whole phenomenon:

The Chess-mania which seized upon the whole nation when Morphy's brilliant star first rose on the horizon, was violent and exaggerated; and as his star rushed up into the zenith of its world-wide renown, and then with equal rapidity withdrew itself from the public gaze in the obscurity of private life, from which there seems small prospect of its re-appearance, the fever died away with it, and it is not to be wondered at that Chess Clubs and Chess Columns, that owed their existence to the excitement of the day, should dwindle away and disappear.[17]

Within a few years of Morphy's retirement American chess was largely where it was before his appearance. The second, third and fourth American chess congresses were not held until 1871, 1874 and 1876, and they were won by players who were Europeans or had learned most of their chess in Europe. In the meantime, the future lay elsewhere.

Championships and professionals

By the 1870s, the interlocking system of clubs and tournaments, which brought together patronage and competition on a new and unprecedented scale, had reached a kind of maturity, and it continued to develop on the same lines down to 1914. This was a great age of organization and regulation in all competitive games: in England for instance the Football Association was founded in 1863, the Amateur Athletic Club in 1866 and the cricket county championship began in 1873. In chess too, more matches and tournaments were sponsored in countries like England and Germany, where there were more players and the game had a wider appeal, as measured by club activity, book sales and so on. Where the game was less generally popular, there had to be greater reliance on large contributions from a few wealthy patrons. At Paris 1867, a tournament planned to coincide with another Great Exhibition, the first prize was a Sèvres vase worth 5,000 francs presented by the Emperor Napoleon III. At Vienna in 1873 the first prize was presented by the Emperor of Austria. Yet the best supported tournament of the whole period was that of London in 1883, which was floated on a fund of 1,600 pounds drawn from a wide variety of sources, including the Maharajahs of Vizayanagaram and Travancore and the Viceroy of India, but also clubs and individuals all over England.

By comparison, patronage in Russia was largely centred in wealthy circles in Moscow and St Petersburg, and their chess clubs. Modern writers like Arpad Elo, who emphasize the growth of Russian chess by listing the increasing numbers of master players born within the Russian Empire (including Russian Poland) in the nineteenth century, overlook the fact that many of them migrated to western-orientated centres like Vienna to learn and practice the game, even before 1914.[18] Soviet writers have often emphasized the dependence of Russian chess on a few rich sponsors before the Revolution, but they do not usually point out that this was much truer of Russia than of the more developed countries in western Europe. In Germany there were even tentative moves towards a working class chess movement before 1914. Working men's chess clubs were set up, and in 1912 sixteen of them meeting at Nuremberg decided to form a union and began publishing the *Arbeiter-Schachzeitung*, or 'Worker's Chess Magazine'. An article in one of the early issues points out that with 'the reduction of the working day from one of eleven or twelve hours to one of eight or nine, and the enforced observance of Sunday as a day of rest'[19] there was no reason why chess should not become more popular. Like later Soviet ideologists, the writer emphasized the educational value of the game, and announced a drive to secure the affiliation of the many clubs still outside the union. This was a striking, though perhaps isolated, exception to the generally bourgeois appeal of the game. Much more typical of the years 1900 to 1914 was a rash of tournaments held at fashionable resorts: Monte Carlo (1901, 1902, 1903, 1904), Ostend (1905, 1906, 1907), Karlsbad (1907, 1911), San Sebastian (1911, 1912) and Abbazia (1912). Wherever there was a casino, it seemed, there could also be a chess tournament.

Throughout these years the game became more lucrative and professionalized, though only a few leading players could afford to have no other sources of income. The life of the professional chess master was far from easy. When asked by a well-wisher at Vienna in 1898 why he did not retire from competition, as he had won fame enough, Steinitz is supposed to have replied that he could spare the fame but not the prize money. He was then over sixty years old, but he wrote himself in an autobiographical fragment that he had never managed to save enough to keep his family in comfort, 'though I was chess champion for twenty-eight years!'[20]. At almost exactly the same time, 1899, in London Sir George Newnes was setting up a national testimonial fund for J.H. Blackburne, who was born in 1841, five years after Steinitz, and had been for twenty-five years the leading British chess professional. Sir George believed that there was 'a general feeling that the time had come when a substantial sum should be given to or invested for him' against his declining years, and £400 was forthcoming, though that sum would hardly have covered very many years and Blackburne lived until 1924.

Young players also had their problems. Harry Pillsbury (1872–1906), the American who came close to Morphy's youthful achievements by crossing the Atlantic to win the great Hastings tournament of 1895, used his powers of memory to earn money by giving displays reminiscent of variety theatre. He would play games of chess simultaneously without sight of the board (his record was twenty-two), while also conducting a hand of whist and memorizing lists of words shown to him briefly by members of the audience. The *New York Times* attributed his death in 1906 to 'an illness contracted through over-exertion of his memory cells', though the real cause seems to have been syphilis. Between 1898 and 1904 Pillsbury also found work as the operator of 'Ajeeb, the Oriental Wonder', a chess automaton constructed as an imitation of Kempelen's original machine, which itself had been exhibited in America by Maelzel between 1826 and his death in 1837. And at this time Pillsbury was widely considered as a candidate for the world championship.

Besides the practical difficulties of converting public interest into a regular income, the professionals faced the entrenched opposition of traditionalists who objected to the whole apparatus of guaranteed fees, appearance money, and payment of expenses to competitors. After the match between Steinitz and Blackburne held at the West End Chess Club in 1876, a writer in the *Chess Player's Chronicle* took violent exception to the half-guinea admission charge and wrote that 'the thoroughly mercenary spirit in which this latest exhibition of professionalism was conducted throughout, has heartily disgusted all true chess-players'. As late as 1890 Leopold Hoffer wrote in the *Chess Monthly* that the proposed terms for a match between Steinitz and Gunsberg, by which the loser would take one third of the stakes, were 'contrary to the English ideas of sport'. This was an example of convert zeal, as Hoffer himself was born in Hungary and had settled in England only in 1870, but it was a common enough attitude. Matches and tournaments, particularly tournaments, were vital to anyone who wished to make a living out of chess, because they offered not merely prize money but also reputation, which could be turned to good account in journalism and other engagements.

But the many 'amateur' players were still quite capable of scooping the pool. If anyone could have lived off his winnings in the years 1888–94 it was Siegbert Tarrasch (1862–1934) who took five consecutive first prizes, but Tarrasch was a doctor of medicine and the very image of German bourgeois respectability. Jacques Mieses, himself a chess professional though never a player of world class, wrote sensibly in 1914 that:

> From the strictly sporting point of view a professional is one who accepts fees for his engagements; and on this basis every chess master must *ipso facto* be a professional, as he plays for a money prize. We should distinguish only two types of master, the one who devoted himself exclusively to chess, and the one who has some other calling as well.[21]

Mieses defended the fees of the professional player, on the grounds that they had increased no more than those of men in other walks of life. The world chess champion was just as entitled to value his services at a high price as Caruso in the opera-house.

In fact the size of prizes and the number of tournaments did increase in the years 1900–14, and that is one reason why so many influential young players appeared during that period, though most of them only developed their strength fully after 1918. One only has to consider a roll-call of famous masters, all of them born in the 1880s, who first played tournament chess in the decade 1901–10: Akiba Rubinstein (1882–1961),

Rudolf Spielmann (1884–1942), Aaron Nimzowitsch (1886–1935), Savielly Tartakower (1887–1956), Efim Bogolyubov (1889–1952) and Richard Réti (1889–1929). The ideas of these men were largely responsible for the 'great leap forward' of chess theory in the 1920s, but all of them were professional players, in the exclusive sense, before 1914. To them one could add the names of J.R. Capablanca (1888–1942), who was given a largely honorary diplomatic post by the Cuban government because of his chess reputation, and Alexander Alekhine (1892–1946), who despite family money and legal studies was also close to being a full time player.

Even in the late nineteenth century the term 'chess master' came into much more frequent use to describe a player of accepted status. 'Grandmaster' gained currency after the tournament at St Petersburg in 1895–96 to which only the world's five leading players – Steinitz, Pillsbury, Tarrasch, Emanuel Lasker and the Russian Mikhail Tchigorin – were invited. This experiment of a 'super-tournament' was occasionally repeated, as at Ostend 1907, where the six strongest players met in a separate contest, or at San Sebastian 1911, where entry was restricted to those who had won at least two prizes in other tournaments. A recognizable hierarchy was emerging. It only remained to have a coherent system of national championships leading up to the summit of the world championship itself. In the event, national championships, when they became common after 1900, were almost always decided by regular tournaments with the winner holding the title only until the next event, while the world championship evolved in the opposite direction, towards match play. Within reasonable limits, the acknowledged world champion could decide whose challenge he wished to accept, and negotiate terms to suit himself. It is hard to say just why this distinction arose between the different kinds of championships. As we have seen, an informal idea of the champion was already current before 1850: Staunton was usually regarded as the leading player after 1843, and Anderssen after 1851, except for Morphy's brief career in 1858 and 1859. But none of these players made precise claims to a title, and the claims of their supporters rested only on a preponderance of public opinion.

The world championship proper was the creation of Wilhelm Steinitz (1836–1900). Born in Prague, Steinitz made his early career in Vienna, but settled in London, which was still the natural capital of the chess world, after playing in the tournament of 1862. In 1866 Steinitz met Anderssen in a match in London, both players being backed entirely by stakes subscribed in England. Steinitz won by eight games to six, and this was the basis of his later claims to have been 'chess champion for twenty-eight years', though contemporaries were not so sure. Now over fifty (he was born in 1818), Anderssen won the Baden tournament of 1870 and defeated Steinitz in both their individual games, though Steinitz finally established his superiority in the Vienna tournament of 1873. For the next decade or so his main rival was Johannes Zukertort (1842–1888), a German-educated doctor, who also claimed to be an accomplished soldier, linguist and pianist; his manifold talents contrasting strongly with the single-minded Steinitz, whose chronic illnesses and irascible temper were strongly reminiscent of Staunton. Steinitz had some supporters in London, but he was generally unpopular, and according to contemporary legend it was a cabal of plotters at the Westminster Chess Club who induced Zukertort to settle in London in 1872, specifically to upset him. At first the new arrival had little success, but when in 1883 he convincingly won the great London tournament, Steinitz challenged him to a match rather than the other way round, so recognizing that the title of champion was still at the mercy of public opinion.

The final reckoning took place in 1886, in America, to which Steinitz had emigrated after the 1883 tournament. This time there was no ambiguity: the match was announced as being 'for the chess championship of the world', the stakes of $2000 were the highest ever known, and Steinitz won by ten games to five with five draws. Zukertort died two years later, his death being yet another widely attributed to the mental strain of playing chess, but Steinitz went steadily on, despite suffering severely from the more tangible symptoms of arthritis. Though the next few years were those of Tarrasch's great run of tournament victories, no one suggested that anyone except Steinitz was the world champion. He won matches against Mikhail Tchigorin (1889 and 1892) and Isidor Gunsberg (1890–1891) before at last losing to Emanuel Lasker in 1894, in a match in which the stakes were double those of 1886. Lasker held the title down to 1921, and besides defending it in matches he was sufficiently successful in tournament play for there to be no more real doubts about the form which the world championship had assumed.

Emanuel Lasker (1868–1941) was a German, though his outlook was always cosmopolitan. He obtained a doctorate in mathematics in 1902, and wrote books on philosophy with dogged persistence, but he was only really successful at chess, though he sometimes hardly played the game for years at a time. Lasker was in many ways a distant figure in the increasingly active world chess scene after 1900; between 1901 and 1914 he played in only three tournaments. Yet despite this, and despite the fact that he was already reasonably financially secure, Lasker braved all criticism from the anti-professionals and from potential challengers for his title, by insisting on high fees for all his appearances. He had witnessed Steinitz's declining years at first hand and he wished never to be in a similar position himself. It is possible that in the long run this attitude helped to raise the economic status of chess players as a whole, despite the hostile reception from some contemporaries.

It is outside the scope of this book to describe the characters and careers of all the leading players who contributed new ideas to chess theory before 1914, but one general question is worth asking here. Did the increased professionalism of chess lead not merely to improved standards, but to a different style of play, one characterized by 'professional' caution and pragmatism rather than risk and enterprise? This is exactly how many commentators saw the so-called 'Modern School' created by Steinitz, which did emphasize the avoidance of static weaknesses and injudicious play, such as launching attacks without certain preconditions. The germ of these ideas may have been present in Steinitz' play earlier on, but he began to shape them into a coherent theory in the 1870s, and coined certain key phrases like 'the accumulation of small advantages', which were widely quoted as the essence of his method. Steinitz himself was quite prepared to be judged on these 'principles', and claimed in 1899 that he had been 'champion of the world for twenty-eight years' because he was 'twenty years ahead of my time'. But critics tended to look back nostalgically to the more open play of Anderssen and Morphy, and supported the claims of Zukertort, Tchigorin, or any other modern player who seemed to be following the old ideas. Some patrons tried to revive daring play artificially by the power of the purse, sponsoring tournaments like Vienna 1903 or Abbazia 1912, in which the King's Gambit had to be played in every game. As late as 1913 H.J.R. Murray wrote that 'The Modern School is dull and unenterprising in comparison with the school which it has displaced, but it keeps the draw in hand, and is supposed to *pay better* in matches and tournaments' [my italics], while he praised Pillsbury for having 'the courage to adopt the older methods in a tournament'.[22] Yet Zukertort, Tchigorin and Pillsbury were just as much professional players as Steinitz. Perhaps both contemporaries and later writers have made too much out of this divergence of styles, and the distinction between 'romantic' and 'realist' does not amount to anything more than the subjective assessment of individual temperaments.

It has already been pointed out that the notion of 'schools of play' in chess can be ambiguous and misleading. In practice each player took the ideas of his predecessors as his starting point, and tried to create new ideas with which he could beat his opponents, who were naturally engaged in the same activity themselves. In the late nineteenth century this process of change became too rapid for the formation of monolithic schools, even had they been possible earlier. Many players claimed to follow Steinitz' theories, including even Emanuel Lasker, but they soon found themselves reordering and revising them in the light of experience and their own abilities. If a player allowed his theoretical assumptions to harden into dogmas, as they tended to do when written up as textbooks, he weakened his ability to conceive new ideas and to compete at the highest level.

Because of this, it seems, Tarrasch became a great teacher but a less successful player. Even this is only one side of the story. A subtle and adaptable general outlook might be desirable for competitive success, but sheer accuracy of technique and calculation was just as important. Modern critics have recognized that Staunton anticipated an extra-ordinary range of modern ideas in his games, but he rarely succeeded in executing them with much technical fluency. By contrast, some of Morphy's judgements about chess, such as his condemnation of 'close games', particularly the Sicilian Defence, because the era of their popularity 'afforded but comparatively few specimens of brilliant play',[23] can almost be categorized as superficial, but there is no doubt that Morphy had the greater talent for practical play. Inevitably, it was only a matter of time until a later player, perhaps Morphy himself if he had not retired so prematurely, combined his technical accuracy with deeper strategic thinking. By this process the standard of play was steadily raised.

It is therefore impossible to explain the development of chess style by reference to social or institutional change. Murray was mistaken when he wrote that 'The Modern School is the direct result of the modern Tournament system'.[24] There was no single 'professional' or 'tourna-ment' style; but a wide range of individual solutions to the problems posed by the new type of competition. It was natural to imitate the methods of the most successful players, but impossible to reproduce them. Yet the changes in the social basis of chess sketched above – the rise of clubs, mass publishing and the organization of tournaments and championships – created the conditions necessary for stronger play and a greater variety of styles. It is hard to avoid using words like 'growth' and 'progress' to describe the history of chess in this period, and especially so in the years leading up to 1914, as more and more young players came to the fore and organized chess spread to all parts of the 'civilized' world.

In May 1914 the St Petersburg tournament finished with a narrow and exciting victory for Emanuel Lasker, just ahead of Capablanca, who had now emerged as his most likely challenger. In July another great tournament began at Mannheim in Germany. It was still in progress when Germany declared war on Russia on 1 August and the tournament was abandoned. Prizes were distributed on the basis of positions after eleven completed rounds, and the winner was Alexander Alekhine. But on the next day, Alekhine and the other Russian competitors were interned as enemy aliens, to the accompaniment of typical reports in the British press that 'they were brutally ill-treated by the German soldiers, who from sheer savagery assaulted them with the butt ends of their rifles'.[25] True or not, such horror stories left most chess players still sharing the general opinion that the war was only an interruption to their activities and things would soon go on as before. Capablanca gave an interview to a correspondent of the *Glasgow Herald* while sailing to Buenos Aires to keep a chess playing engagement, and spoke of the general interest in his forthcoming match with Lasker, who was himself reported to be predicting a speedy German victory. No one appreciated how long the interruption was to last, and how much the situation would have changed when normal activities were eventually resumed.

CHAPTER SIX
The Sedentary Sport 1914-1980

The changes brought about in Europe by the Great War of 1914–18 affected almost every organized social activity, including games and sports. In the long run, the most important development in chess during the 1920s and '30s was the growth of a mass chess movement in Soviet Russia. By contrast, the inter-war years in the West seem a period of haphazard development, with no systematic promotion of the game and the leading masters working as individuals, very little assisted by national organizations. Yet such organizations were nevertheless growing up, and so was the International Chess Federation (Fédération Internationale des Échecs, usually known as FIDE) founded in 1924. These things may be classed with the more spectacular developments in Russia, because they too pointed the way to a new age of increased regulation and nationalistic rivalries, an age which came into being after 1945. Soviet domination notwithstanding, chess thus resembles many other sports in its general post-war history. But chess remains a highly individualistic game, so that tensions between individuals and the new regulatory bodies are never far from the surface; the careers of Robert Fischer and Viktor Korchnoi are only exceptional manifestations of a general problem, which continues to this day, though it naturally varies from country to country. Parallels may be sought in the twentieth-century regulation of other sports, arts or sciences.

Chess outside Russia

In the immediate aftermath of the Great War of 1914–18 supporters of the game were concerned to repair the damage done to the system of competition and the livelihood of the players. Naturally there were casualties, though many of the leading players either owed no allegiance to the main combatant countries or were too old for active service. Late in the war general conditions were particularly bad in Germany and Central

157

Europe, where the cessation of hostilities was followed by food shortages and economic crisis. This bore heavily on the many professional chess masters living in that region, as tournaments were few and opportunities to make a living out of the game shrank almost to nothing. Karl Schlechter, a respected figure and a man who had drawn a world championship match with Lasker in 1910, died in Budapest during 1918, apparently from malnutrition. The competitors in the first All-Russian Chess Olympiad, held in Moscow in 1920, stopped playing half way through and refused to complete the tournament unless they were given more rations and prize money (surprisingly, their demands were met). The disruption of nationalities, barriers to free travel and the impoverishment of groups and institutions which had once provided patronage meant that recovery was delayed. Not until the early 1920s were tournaments again organized over most of Europe, as in the pre-war years.

When chess did re-emerge from the shadows of the war, it was hardly possible to restore it as it had existed before 1914. The number of tournaments remained fairly consistent, at about ten to fifteen a year, but their size and scale did not. Great events involving up to twenty players and lasting six weeks or more, which had once been relatively common, were now almost unknown. Of about sixty international tournaments held in the five years 1920–24, only two had more than sixteen competitors, and over twenty had less than ten.[1] The fashionable resorts, if they were still fashionable, were not so accommodating; royal and aristocratic patronage was no longer forthcoming. The result of this was not an upheaval or a drastic change in organization, but a general scaling-down of activities in most of the chess world. Patronage was still essential for organized competition, at both national and international level, but the rarity of individual sponsorship on the grand scale meant that clubs and organizers now had to turn to more broadly based subscriptions, of the kind already familiar in England. Thus the Great Victory Chess Congress (only subjects of the allied and neutral powers were invited) held at Hastings in 1919 was supported in part by the Hastings Chess Club, but primarily by an appeal to players all over the country. As Philip Sergeant recorded, 'the response to this was so good that ultimately, in spite of a gross cost of more than £888 for the congress, a surplus of over £93 was carried to the general fund of the Federation'.[2]

The British Chess Federation, founded in 1904 from the remnants of the nineteenth-century Association and one or two rival groups, played an increasingly important part by providing administrative and financial continuity in between great events and special appeals. Available funds were channelled towards common objectives rather than dissipated, as they had been on occasion in the nineteenth century, by the mutual jealousies of the independent clubs, and when the Federation organized another important international tournament, at London in 1922, they were able to meet a good part of the cost of over £1000 from their own accumulated resources. This was the way the German Schachbund had worked since the 1870s and 1880s, providing a voluntary link between the chess clubs, to which most serious players belonged, and the rarefied heights of international competition, while also appealing to national loyalties. It was the model eventually imitated by most of the emergent national associations, except those in which government direction supervened.

From a geographical point of view the distribution of the game's appeal in the early 1920s was not drastically different from what it had been before 1914, though many national frontiers and allegiances had moved. There was a shift of emphasis away from Russia, which was largely cut off from international competition until the Moscow tournament of 1925, while Soviet attempts to promote chess more widely were as yet in their infancy. But in America, where competition was not interrupted by the war, chess seemed at last to be more generally popular. Capablanca and others made successful tours across the country to the west coast, giving lectures and displays. Organized chess also took a firmer hold in the one-time colonial territories of Canada, Australia and South Africa, in South America, and even in India, where the European game was beginning to make inroads into the dominance of the old oriental one. But despite all this, the centre of world chess still remained in Europe, judged either by the total number of players or by the national allegiances of the accredited masters. The revival of clubs and tournament play after 1918 was here only the first step. By the early 1920s national chess associations had been set up in most of the countries newly created or remodelled through the Versailles treaties, and some of these, like Hungary and Czechoslovakia, have been among the world's leading chess nations ever since. In some, it is true, there were political difficulties. Two chess associations were founded in Czechoslovakia in 1921; one (the larger) run by Czechs and the other by Germans. In Germany itself the old Schachbund was enfeebled by internal divisions, and able to organize only small-scale tournaments and competitions. Meanwhile, in Germany, Austria, Hungary, Denmark, and perhaps one or two other countries, the socialist chess clubs retained their own organizations, and refused to affiliate to the national bodies. Instead, at Hamburg in 1923 they formed the 'Worker's Chess International', which survived until 1931 and organized a number of events for its own members.

Nevertheless, the national groupings did make a start towards a more orderly administration of the game, and this process was further advanced in 1924. Following a meeting the previous year at Zurich, where a draft constitution was drawn up, delegates from fifteen countries met in Paris, in July 1924, and set up an international chess association: the Fédération Internationale des Échecs (FIDE). The fifteen founding countries were Argentina, Belgium, Canada, Czechoslovakia, Finland, France, Great Britain, Holland, Hungary, Italy, Poland, Rumania, Spain, Switzerland and Yugoslavia. There were important omissions here, but gradually other countries joined in, with the exception of the Soviet Union, which held aloof until after the Second World War, forming relations only with committed socialist bodies or setting up its own satellite organizations. If some of the national associations were precarious, then FIDE was no less so; its income from subscriptions was made too low to enable it to undertake anything very ambitious. But the Federation did hold regular annual conferences from 1924 down to 1939, which constituted an important forum for the exchange of views and ideas. Staunton's plan for a 'Constituent Assembly' of chess, first put forward in 1851, now seemed to have been realized.

The limitations of these changes in the 1920s become apparent when attention is directed to the players themselves and their activities. At one extreme, casual players often avoided the embrace of organizations which seemed designed only to extract subscriptions from them; at the other, professional masters were liable to be jealous of anything which threatened their own independence. Thus, while national championships proliferated and were increasingly run on a regular year-to-year basis, the world title itself remained firmly out of the reach of FIDE and subject to private negotiation. In 1918 Capablanca had emerged as the most powerful challenger to Emanuel Lasker, and he also had the hope of sponsorship for a match, from America or from his countrymen in Cuba. Lasker hesitated for two years, and then in 1920, when a contest seemed to be imminent and most of the practical arrangements had been made, he suddenly decided he could not play and resigned his championship to Capablanca, so treating it exactly like a piece of private property. Capablanca, anxious not to become champion by default, found Cuban backers who would jointly raise the purse from the intended $8000 to $20,000, as long as Lasker would play in Havana; the match duly took place in 1921 and Capablanca won by four games to none with ten draws. But none of the basic attitudes had changed.

At the London tournament of 1922, a group of the players tried to draw up a code of rules by which the world champion would acknowledge any reasonable challenge and undertake to play within a year. Secure in his pre-eminence, Capablanca replied with his own 'London conditions', the chief of which was that any challenger must first put up a stake of $10,000. This kept all comers at bay until 1926, when the Russian *émigré* Alexander Alekhine found backers in the Argentine who could provide the sum demanded. The match took place in Buenos Aires in 1927 and Alekhine won a famous and prolonged encounter by six games to three, with no less than twenty-five draws. Then history promptly repeated itself, as Alekhine entered negotiations for a return match, but found one excuse or another to break them off, evidently more afraid of his rival than he cared to admit. Instead, in 1929 and 1934, he played matches against another Russian *émigré*, Efim Bogolyubov, whom he could defeat without too much trouble. Relations between Alekhine and Capablanca grew so bad that they could not even play each other in tournaments because they refused to meet at all. In the middle of this dispute Capablanca did ask the United States Chess Federation to intercede on his behalf, but again, merely as an intermediary between two individuals. Only public opinion could constrain the champion to put his title at risk when he did not wish to, and public opinion did not support Capablanca's last desperate throw, of claiming that Alekhine had forfeited his championship by default.

Such attitudes were not confined to world champions. The leading group of accepted chess masters, who could earn a living from playing in tournaments and writing about the game, tended also to be cosmopolitan individualists, impatient of constraints on their mobility and freedom to accept invitations where they pleased. A professional 'circuit' of this kind had been taking shape since the late nineteenth century, but it was now more sharply marked off from the rest of organized chess. These men were a caste apart, continually involved in mutual rivalries over their current ranking order, but even more suspicious of newcomers trying to break into the magic circle, until they had proved their worth. Harold Schonberg characterizes this rather well in his book of biographical studies of leading players:

> From city to city they went, like the members of an opera company on tour, playing Hastings this month, Baden-Baden the next, Munich after that. And these players were as egocentric, temperamental and bizarre a group as the members of any opera company: they regarded anybody else in the troupe as Mme Adelina Patti regarded Mme Etelka Gerster: definitely unsound; overblown reputation; what does the public see in *her*; what *can* the public see in her?[3]

There were not very many players in this category, perhaps fifteen to twenty at the most, and almost all of them were based in Europe where the majority of the tournaments were held. If Capablanca and Frank Marshall (the champion of the United States since 1906) lived largely in America, then Alekhine had left Russia in 1921 to live in France, while Bogolyubov had settled at Triberg in southern Germany ever since the war, though he only renounced his Soviet citizenship in 1926. Otherwise, apart from the old guard headed by Lasker, tournament chess tended to be dominated by the generation of players who had first appeared between 1900 and 1914, and had now arrived at their full strength: men like Spielmann,

Nimzowitsch, Réti and Tartakower, all of them with central European backgrounds that cut across the new national frontiers. Once established, the distribution of players in Europe remained fairly consistent, until the rise of Nazism in the 1930s displaced many of them all over again.

The main check on the independence of chess masters did not arise from international regulation, but from crude financial pressures. They were almost entirely at the mercy of their continued ability to play well, to receive enough invitations, and to find a market for their books and articles. When Akiba Rubinstein withdrew from competitive chess in 1932, because of a mental breakdown, he sank almost at once into destitution and an appeal was launched to support him. World champions certainly did well out of the game, after the successive efforts of Lasker and Capablanca to raise prizes and appearance fees, but it is notable that, before he gained the title, Alekhine took time off from tournaments to qualify as a French Doctor of Law in 1925, as a sort of insurance policy. Nor was Capablanca, with his sinecure in the Cuban diplomatic service, at all typical of the problems faced by others. Some masters, like Milan Vidmar of Yugoslavia who was a professor of electrical engineering, were genuinely devoted to another profession and played the best chess they could in their spare time. But others, like the American Reuben Fine in the 1940s, gave up chess for another profession just because they could make a better living at it.

If this was true of the small group of leading masters, it applied with redoubled force to the minor masters and lesser players on the fringes of international chess, who received invitations only to small tournaments and those held in their own countries. The number of men in this category constantly fluctuated and it is hard to assess how many there were at any one time (perhaps one to two hundred, perhaps more?). At this level there were some genuine amateurs, like the English baronet Sir George Thomas and the Italian marquess Rosselli del Turco, but they were very few. Most tried to live from chess, but they had to descend to very repetitive and unattractive work to do it. This meant not only giving lectures and displays, which the top players did too, though for larger fees, but acting as club professionals, giving lessons, playing games with clients for small stakes and so on.

The English master William Winter, who lived this kind of life from 1925 to 1938, while also suffering from the added social odium of being a professed communist, preserved a lively though hardly unbiased account of it in his *Memoirs*. National and local championships were important to such players, but the real hope of security was an appointment to write a regular chess column for a large newspaper. Winter eventually found himself a post like this with the *Manchester Guardian*, but in the meantime he was bitter about 'pin-money amateurs' who deprived the struggling professionals of some of their sources of income. He wrote of the professional game that he could not 'conscientiously advise any young player to take it up under the conditions prevailing in England unless he has either small private means, or the definite promise of a column in a National paper. Otherwise he will find the hurdles too difficult.'[4] The post-war expansion which was to bring respectable prosperity to a much larger number of chess players was not possible in the 1920s and 30s, when the number of international tournaments of any kind was hardly ever more than twenty in a year, and frequently much less.

In view of this, it is hardly surprising that attempts to re-organize world chess took so long to produce results. Though they were themselves economically vulnerable, the ideas and opinions of the leading masters counted for most, and it was they who tacitly admitted newcomers to their ranks. The 'Worker's Chess International' never commanded the allegiance of any master players, except those from Russia during the few years (1926–29) in which the Soviet chess organization subscribed to it. The Fédération Internationale des Échecs in its early years made the opposite mistake of trying to organize events restricted solely to amateurs, partly because the first FIDE congress at Paris in 1924 was in touch with the organizers of the Eighth Olympic Games, held there at the same time. The result in 1924 was a chess 'Olympiad', in which each of the countries present contributed three *bona fide* amateur players, who then contested a large individual tournament, the winner of which was Hermann Mattison of Latvia. The whole plan was misconceived, because no clear distinction between amateur and professional had ever existed in chess; as William Winter remarked 'all chess players, even the dear old ladies who come up to receive the last prize in a third class contest at Hastings, are professionals according to the Olympic rules'.[5] At Budapest in 1926 conditions were changed to bring about a genuine team tournament, run as a series of matches between the competing countries, but unfortunately only four teams (Hungary, Yugoslavia, Rumania and Germany) turned up to play. At last, in 1927 at London, the British Chess Federation took the initiative in organizing a successful event, with sixteen countries represented by four-man teams, and the amateur stipulation removed. This 'First Chess Olympiad' was followed by seven more before 1939, with individual member countries of FIDE being nominated in turn to arrange and finance the tournaments. But this was really the limit of the Federation's attempt to direct world chess in the 1920s and '30s, and it produced a useful supplement to the existing forms of competition but hardly much more.

There was, however, a hint of future developments in the influence exercised by FIDE over the women's world championship, which first appeared in 1927 at London. The very first women's tournament had also been held in England, in 1884, and there was a much larger contest at London in 1897 with substantial prizes, but thereafter the international movement had languished somewhat, though British Ladies' Championships were held regularly from 1904 onwards. In 1927 the women's tournament was associated with the First Olympiad, and from 1930 to 1939 each successive Olympiad and FIDE congress was accompanied by another women's championship in the same way. Here was a title with no powerful vested interests at stake, little private sponsorship available, and altogether an excellent opportunity for the Federation to assume control. But even here they could not guarantee to keep it. The winner of every one of the pre-war tournaments was Vera Menchik, by far the outstanding woman player of the period, who had considerable success competing in open play with leading masters. In 1934 and again in 1937 she put her title at stake in matches privately arranged against one of her leading rivals, Sonia Graf, so the issue of who really disposed of the women's championship, FIDE or the incumbent herself, remained undecided.

From a technical point of view the 1920s are often described as the 'Age of the Hypermoderns', a phrase which perhaps deserves a little explanation. An important group of the younger players who came to the fore after 1918 set themselves in conscious opposition to the ideas of their predecessors, particularly older contemporaries like Tarrasch. These men, they considered, had tried to restrict chess skill to an unprofitably dogmatic set of principles. They had narrowed down the inheritance of ideas from the nineteenth century and, in particular, restricted the exploration of new opening formations, by rejecting anything unfamiliar as unsound without adequate trials. The 'Hypermoderns', as Savielly Tartakower called them, reacted by trying to identify a much wider range of principles, each suited to different kinds of position in varying degrees. More practically, they pioneered a number of new openings, in which they tried to replace the 'classical' notion of controlling the centre of the board by a more subtle and indirect approach, of exerting influence on key squares from a distance. Besides their games, they proclaimed these ideas in a series of influential books, of which the first and most important was Richard Réti's *Die Neuen Ideen im Schachspiel*, published at Vienna in 1922 and translated into English the following year. It was followed by Tartakower's *Die Hypermoderne Schachpartie* (Vienna 1925), Aron Nimzowitsch's two famous books *Mein System* (Berlin 1925) and *Die Praxis meines Systems* (Berlin 1929), and Réti's posthumous work *Die Meister des Schachbretts* (Mährisch-Ostrau 1930). These too were rapidly translated and circulated round the chess world. According to a once common interpretation of the period, the 1920s thus saw a struggle for mastery in chess between this group of masters and their diehard 'classicist' opponents, who ridiculed their new theories. In the course of the decade the Hypermoderns came out on top, by virtue of their practical results as well as their ideas. As Réti himself wrote, 'Chess is a domain in which criticism has not so much influence as in art; for in the domain of chess the results of games decide, ultimately and finally.'[6] His victory over Capablanca in the New York tournament of 1924, at a time when Capablanca had not lost a serious game for eight years, did more to advertise the new style of play than anything else, and there were other victories almost as famous over older players like Rubinstein.

Inevitably perhaps, recent research has shown (as some critics have always been aware) that this picture is an oversimplification. Certainly there was a distinct hypermodern group, and many contemporaries were very conscious of belonging to it or opposing it, but it did not divide the entire chess world into two camps. Many players were uncommitted and easily adopted an eclectic approach, taking from the arsenal of new ideas just those elements which were valuable to them in improving their own results, in accordance with Réti's dictum quoted above. These included the very strongest masters, notably Capablanca and Alekhine. Secondly, the decade of the 1920s, which saw so many of the hypermodern theories accepted into the mainstream of chess theory, was really the culmination of changes which began before 1914, when the 'proto-hypermoderns' were less numerous and less certain of their own ideas. This has been pointed out by Raymond Keene in his biographical study of Nimzo-witsch:

> As soon as the hypermodern ideas were introduced and seen to work they won rapid general acceptance. The polemic campaign conducted by the victorious hypermoderns, themselves now in control of the chess media, was directed against a monster that had, in fact, only been rampant before the First War.[7]

Accordingly, the tone of the polemical writing in the 1920s, which occasionally descends to personal abuse, can be ascribed more to old enmities and rivalries than to the issues at stake. But whatever else they did, the theoretical disputes introduced the chess-playing public to a wider range of ideas.

The popular image of chess in the inter-war years was still in many ways a contradictory one. It has already been made clear that the game gradually took on the character of an organized sport, with its clubs and national associations, tournaments and championships, all sustained by the contributions and subscriptions of devotees. This was as necessary for chess as it was for other games, because those who took it up seriously now wanted to be in touch with national and international events. They followed tournament results and game scores through the continually increasing numbers of books and magazines, which now appeared in minor languages and most parts of the world. They began to identify themselves with the performances of their countrymen in the manner of the authentic sports supporter, though for a time this tendency was held in check by the cosmopolitan nature of top-class chess. Thus the Polish team which won the Third Chess Olympiad, at Hamburg in 1930, included Savielly Tartakower, who was educated in Vienna, lived in Paris, and spoke no Polish. British complaints about the decline of national prestige in chess, which had been proliferating since the turn of the century, largely derived from the fact that London no longer attracted the *émigrés* who had made it the chess capital of the world in the nineteenth century. While the number of established masters remained comparatively small, a change in the allegiance of a few individuals could rapidly alter the world 'balance of power'. It was by this means that Argentina emerged as a great force in chess, coming second in each of the first post-war Olympiads of 1950, 1952 and 1954 with a team bolstered up by refugees of the 1930s. The Australian chess community profited by a similar process, acquiring among others the leading Hungarian master Lajos Steiner. There were special features in the structure of chess as well, such as the lack of distinction between professionals and amateurs which kept it out of the Olympic movement, but none of these prevented the game from becoming more like an international sport. After all, other sports had their peculiarities too. The real contradiction arose from the obvious fact that chess was an intellectual and not a physical pursuit. That, and its lack of spectator appeal, still prevented it from being popularly regarded as a sport in the West; attitudes in Russia were already different, but they spread slowly and incompletely to the rest of the world.

Below the level of organized competition, chess as recreation still appealed to the same social groups as in the nineteenth century, that is to the middle class, middle-aged and male. There were signs that the popularity of the game now extended beyond this home territory, but the change was a gradual one. Thus the socialist chess organizations like the 'Worker's Chess International' did not take permanent root in western Europe and largely collapsed in the 1930s, but ordinary chess clubs in countries like England became less exclusive and bourgeois in tone. Many background changes – from public transport and electric lighting to better education and cheap books – helped to widen the range of working class recreation, though no one would argue that chess took more than a small share in this general development. More obviously, chess began to appeal to younger age groups. Talented players like Morphy, Pillsbury and Capablanca had always matured young, but not by playing with their own contemporaries. Before 1914, even university students were considered to be too immature, as a rule, to make strong chess players. Teams from Oxford and Cambridge attended a chess week in London every Easter, but they met only the third and fourth teams of the metropolitan clubs, and without any great success. In the 1920s the transition began which was to turn the universities into important centres for the game and prime recruiting grounds for international talent, as they were already in other sports.

Chess also began to be played more widely in schools, though the junior chess movement was still at an experimental stage. The reaction given to the young Samuel Reshevsky (born 1911) when he toured Europe and America in 1919–21, giving simultaneous displays and holding his own with strong adult opposition, reflected not merely his extraordinary ability but public astonishment that a child should play chess at all. Yet from 1923 there was an annual boys (under eighteen) tournament held in Hastings, and a formal British boys championship from 1933, while other countries soon followed the same path. Of all the social barriers to the further spread of chess, the sexual one proved perhaps the most persistent. Despite the efforts of Vera Menchik and other outstanding individuals in various countries, the proportion of women among active players remained very low indeed, probably less than one per cent. Whether the explanation for this should be sought in inherent psychological tendencies or in social conditioning is still largely a matter of taste. There was certainly no substantial increase in the popularity of chess as a domestic or social pastime, nothing to compare with the dramatic advance of contract bridge in England and America, which took shape during the 1930s.

None of these main features of inter-war chess showed any real signs of changing in the years immediately before 1939. Tournament and match play continued to be run along the lines established in the 1920s. Even when slightly increased financial support became available, as there is some evidence that it did in the late 1930s, the result was a larger number of relatively small tournaments rather than a return to the mammoth events of the nineteenth century. The main exceptions to this were championship tournaments in the Soviet Union, where chess was sponsored in an entirely different way, by the state.

The world championship itself remained a matter of private agreement. In 1935, to general surprise, Alekhine managed to lose his title to a Dutchman, Max Euwe, by the narrow margin of nine wins to eight with thirteen draws. The common view that Alekhine would not have lost the match if he had prepared for it more seriously (he was actually drunk during some of the games) was largely confirmed in 1937 when he beat Euwe by the convincing score of ten wins to four with eleven draws. But it was only Euwe's sportsmanship which gave Alekhine the chance to play the match at all; the contrast with his own treatment of Capablanca was only too obvious. Once back in control, Alekhine soon reverted to type, and responded with extreme wariness to suggestions that FIDE might nominate the Czech master Salo Flohr as his official challenger. In 1938 a strong tournament organized by the Dutch Broadcasting Company (AVRO) was widely regarded as an elimination contest for the world championship, because Alekhine had agreed to play a subsequent match against the winner. But before the tournament even began, he went out of his way to dispel these expectations.

> He stated that he retained the right to first play for the world title with others, and that the AVRO contract clause had not created new rights or preferences. He placed himself on record as believing that a tournament, no matter how strong the players, cannot be a preponderant factor in deciding the question of the world championship . . . he feels free at present to accept a challenge from any recognised master.[8]

The life styles and livelihoods of the ordinary chess masters did not alter very much either, though their numbers increased somewhat. There were obviously changes in personalities, with the rise of a new generation of young players, led by Salo Flohr, the Americans Samuel Reshevsky and Reuben Fine, and the Estonian Paul Keres, all of them born between 1908 and 1916. Another member of this generation was the leading Russian Mikhail Botvinnik, who began to compete in western tournaments from 1934 onwards as a result of a new Soviet willingness to initiate sporting links with capitalist countries, albeit on a highly selective basis. At the same time, the rise of Nazism in Germany affected the loyalties of the many chess players of Jewish origin, and was a foretaste of the greater national upheavals to follow in the 1940s. The ex-world champion Emanuel Lasker was among those who fled, losing nearly all of his property. Though he was now well over sixty years old and last participated in a tournament in 1925, he was forced to take up competitive play once more, and held his own remarkably well in four events between 1934 and 1936. Then he was persuaded to stay in Moscow as an honoured guest, until he began to appreciate what was happening in contemporary Russia and hastily moved on to New York, where he died in 1941. Lasker's troubled career, or aspects of it, can be paralleled in the fortunes of many other European masters.

So while the claims of Soviet propagandists in the 1930s about the decline of bourgeois chess do not seem to have carried much conviction (except to themselves), it was nevertheless true that technical progress in the game and the continual growth of its social and geographical appeal was offset by persistent financial and organizational weakness. The sponsorship of rich individuals was declining, and only very slowly made good by assistance from companies and governments, or subscriptions from the members of national associations. Higher standards of play inevitably professionalized competitive chess, but at the same time it was still far from easy to make a living out of the game. Other sports too experienced these social pressures, but for chess, which was not yet universally accepted as a sport at all and had little spectator appeal, the problems were particularly acute.

The Soviet phenomenon

The development of chess in Soviet Russia after 1920 followed a path so different from that in the West that it is best treated as a separate subject. There were of course many links with the outside world, particularly in the realm of technical chess theory, where western works like those of the Hypermoderns were translated and studied. There were also some competitive ties, though these were thin in the early 1920s, and virtually non-existent in the decade 1925–35. But the special position which chess assumed in Russian society and in the policies of Soviet governments was in no way imposed by external pressures, as was the need to compete militarily or economically. There was nothing about the way in which chess was regarded in the West to single it out as a vital area for ideological confrontation. Nevertheless, the Soviet leadership began to invest heavily in the game from at least the mid 1920s, and persisted in this course despite the fact that it was many years before it showed any real return in terms of propaganda value or international prestige. Clearly the reasons for this were in large part internal, to do with the attitudes of the Bolsheviks and their successors towards the development of Russian society itself.

Yet it remains a paradox that the Soviet leaders chose a bourgeois pastime, as chess was then generally regarded, to further their ends. It is also extremely difficult to establish why they did so, or how consciously the decision was taken, as little evidence survives from the early formative period of 1920–24, and what there is has been heavily overlaid by later propaganda and rationalization. Already by the late 1920s, in such works as M.S. Kogan's 'History of Chess in Russia' (Moscow, 1927) and 'Outline of the History of Chess' (Moscow, 1931), a 'party line' was being pieced together from various policy statements made by influential figures, defining official attitudes to the nature of chess and its historical development. This was added to over the years, until it culminated in the notion of The Soviet School of Chess, the title of an influential book by A. Kotov and M. Yudovich which first appeared in 1951. So far as it can be grasped through the obscurities of the language and the subtle shifts of emphasis which resulted from the ideologists' attempts to keep up with changes in policy, the official view advanced three main reasons for the adoption of chess as a characteristic Soviet pursuit. The first was its practical value in education and political training. The second was the supposed dialectical nature of the game, because it implied the application of logic to a dynamic struggle. These qualities made chess both useful and appropriate to a socialist society. The third reason was the simple patriotic idea that chess had always possessed a special appeal for Russians, and that they were specially gifted when it came to playing it. The uncommitted western critic, trying to discover what actually happened in the early years after the Revolution, is bound to add a fourth reason: pure chance and the personal tastes of a few influential men.

Early in 1920 chess-playing activities in Russia were largely suspended, many of the leading players were going abroad or remaining there, and there was no sign that this was a matter of any concern to the government. A change in the situation was initiated by one man, Alexander Ilyin-Zhenevsky (1894–1941) a chess master who held a number of important party posts after 1917. He used his position as chief commisar in the headquarters of the General Reservists' Organization to have chess included in training programmes for conscripts:

> The chief value of sport, it was claimed, is that it develops in a man mental qualities which are of supreme importance in a soldier. Here a parallel with chess involuntarily suggested itself. After all, chess too – and in some ways even more than sport – develops in a man boldness, presence of mind, composure, a strong will and, most important, something which sport cannot, a sense of strategy. My proposal was accepted.[9]

The immediate appeal to the usefulness of the game is significant, though it is ironic that the germ of the Soviet chess movement should have lain in such an anachronistic notion. The idea that chess was of value in military training had been vigorously debunked at least as early as the eighteenth century and hardly seemed likely to be revived in the 1920s. But the Reservists' Organization (*Vsevobuch*), though it held the first state-sponsored Russian chess tournament in 1920 (won by Alekhine) was a temporary expedient with no powers to promote civilian activities, and it was wound up in 1923. By this stage chess clubs had begun to revive all over Russia, some run along pre-Revolutionary lines as private associations, others attached to communes, trade unions and bodies aided by the state. There followed a short struggle for control of the chess movement, in which again the government played little part until its aid was enlisted by interested individuals.

The Petrograd chess club announced a conference in 1923 to revive the old All-Russian Chess Federation of 1914, financed by the traditional means of subscriptions and displays given by leading players. This 'apolitical Federation' was quite contrary to Ilyin-Zhenevsky's ambitions, but its intended constitution was nevertheless approved by the Ministry of Internal Affairs in January 1924, and clubs from twenty-seven towns affiliated to it. But Ilyin-Zhenevsky and his allies were already preparing a resistance movement through the Moscow trades unions, urging all union members to withdraw from the Petrograd federation and lobbying political leaders to support their stand. As most clubs depended on union facilities or at least on official tolerance for their survival, the Moscow campaign was rapidly successful and the Petrograd committee conceded defeat. At a second conference, held at Moscow in 1924, an All-Union Chess Section was formed, attached to the Supreme Council for Physical Culture of the Russian socialist republics. N.V. Krylenko (1885–1938), an old Bolshevik and a really senior member of the party hierarchy was chairman. Chess had now been formally incorporated in the institutions of the Soviet state.

But the scope of the role to be assigned to chess players, or claimed by them, was still extremely unclear. At the 1924 conference, and in the following years, the emphasis was still placed heavily on the usefulness of the game as a means of promoting social change. Chess players at least tended to be literate and to be members of organized clubs through which they could be educated and brought to a state of political consciousness. As Krylenko wrote in the introduction to the book of the 1925 Moscow international tournament: 'In our country, where the cultural level is comparatively low, where up to now a typical pastime of the masses has been brewing liquor, drunkenness and brawling, chess is a powerful means of raising the general cultural level.' In his *'Chess and Culture'* (Leningrad, 1929) Y.G. Rokhlin proudly recorded an account of incorrigible illiterates brought to see the light by their interest in chess, and added hopefully, 'This example is very typical.' And literacy itself was only the first step, because 'in the right conditions the steps from chess to literature, then to education, then to political awareness can be taken automatically'.[10] All of this seems far from plausible to the western observer, but the Chess Section produced sufficient results to keep the authorities convinced. The number of officially registered players rose from 1,000 in 1923 to 24,000 in 1924 as the registration system was extended, but then it continued to rise, and had reached 150,000 by 1929. The task of spreading chess across the Soviet Union was taken quite seriously, as the master Fyodor Dus-Khotimirsky later recalled in his memoirs: 'During the next seven years, from 1924 to 1931, I travelled through almost the entire Soviet Union – from the White Sea to the Caucasus, from the Baltic to Vladivostok – passing on my experience and knowledge to the young people of eight Soviet republics, the Ukraine, White Russia, Uzbekistan, Kazakhstan, Turkmenia, Georgia, Armenia and Azerbaidzhan.'[11] There was a similar expansion in chess publishing, and Krylenko himself edited a popular magazine called *'64'* from 1924 onwards. The slogans coined during the 1924 All-Union Congress (no congress was really complete without a slogan) were similarly practical: 'Chess is a powerful weapon of intellectual culture!' 'Take chess to the workers!' and 'Chess must become a feature of every club and every peasant reading room!'

As the leaders of Russian chess began to convince the Soviet authorities that they could perform important tasks in education and in promoting new social attitudes, they also developed theories to explain why their game was such an appropriate training for socialist man. Already in 1924, the Moscow Committee which organized the All-Union Congress issued a statement of principles in which they claimed that chess should not be seen merely as a game, because it stimulates and disciplines thought and willpower. 'All this together develops in the player persistence, insight and caution and the ability quickly to orientate himself in various circumstances. These qualities taken together show all the attributes of an intellectually and psychologically perfect type of individual.'[12] The researches of three Soviet psychologists, who submitted twelve of the contestants in the Moscow international tournament of 1925 to a battery of tests, helped to confirm such optimistic assertions, by concluding that chess is 'a powerful method of self-discipline and self-development, which brings benefit not only to those who are capable of becoming masters, but also to those who do not possess such gifts; chess furthers the development of educationally valuable qualities.' This verdict was a generous one, since the tests did not really show that the players had above-average abilities in many things except chess, or that chess skills could ever be applied to other kinds of activity, which was the key assumption underlying the whole Soviet promotion of the game. Elsewhere in their report too, the psychologists showed themselves willing to be guided by the newly emerging orthodoxy: 'What word can convey all the essential features of chess, indicating both its complexity and its unity? The only word able to satisfy these demands is *dialectics*.'[13]

The impression left by this evidence is that chess was first accepted as a weapon in the socialist arsenal rather than a mere bourgeois diversion because of its usefulness, and that the ideological theories summarized above were introduced as subsequent rationalizations. But many of those involved may have believed them; chess players were certainly prepared to welcome the news that within the whole range of sports currently being harnessed to the needs of proletarian society, their own game took the foremost place. And it was naturally impossible for any institution to have practical status in the Russia of the 1920s, still less the 1930s, without ideological justification. Chess therefore became part of the Soviet state apparatus and a considerable force in Russian society. The chess movement was an instrument of political control, but also a vested interest group headed by highly privileged individuals, which would fight to defend the place it had assumed within the system. These circumstances influenced the development of the game in Russia down to the outbreak of war in 1941 and beyond, as the leaders and theorists continued to promote chess, but also trimmed their activities in accordance with government policies.

Thus in foreign affairs the All-Union Chess Section would have nothing to do with the bourgeois Fédération Internationale des Échecs and instead, in 1926, affiliated to the German based Worker's Chess International. But that body was then torn by conflict between socialists and communists, and in 1929 the Soviet Union withdrew to set up its own international movement, a chess section attached to the Red Sport International, which was a Comintern satellite organization. This was to be devoted, according to a declaration accepted at its inaugural meeting in Leningrad, to unambiguous class war, the defence of the USSR as the motherland of the proletariat, and unremitting struggle against reformist as well as bourgeois chess. But only a few communist-controlled workers' chess clubs, mostly in Germany, would subscribe to such an obvious front organization, and links with them were severed after Hitler's rise to power in 1933. By 1934, the year in which the Soviet Union joined the League of Nations and began to renew contacts with potential allies in western Europe, the Red Sport International was beginning to be a potential embarrassment and its activities were held in check. Once again Soviet chess leaders reacted to changed circumstances, this time by permitting the best Russian masters to compete abroad, and organizing international tournaments at Moscow in 1935 and 1936.

In domestic affairs too, there was a similar adaptability. The launching of the first Five-Year Plan (1928–32) led to calls for chess players to become Stakhanovites, an élite group who would inspire others by their example to raise production and fulfil the plan. 'The present widespread interest in chess and chess tournaments must be transformed into competitions to raise productivity', Rokhlin argued in 1929. This implausible transition was to be assisted by reorganizing sports activities away from social clubs and into factories and workplaces, in order to encourage team spirit in a large number of 'collectives', each one based on a work brigade or shift. A propaganda booklet appeared in 1932 suggesting how chess should adapt to these new conditions, and the seventh All-Union Chess Congress of 1931 contributed a new slogan, 'Saturate chess with a political content!'. Already in 1930 the trades unions had been purged and their sports activities, previously independent, were put under the control of a strengthened All-Union Council for Physical Culture, to which Krylenko's Chess Section was still attached. As the first Five-Year Plan was followed by the second (1932–37), such controls were tightened rather than relaxed, while Stalinist exhortations were backed up by ever increasing threats of discipline and punishment.

In these circumstances, the Soviet chess movement survived and prospered by giving the Leadership what it wanted. Successive campaigns increased the number of registered players to over half a million by the end of 1934. In 1929 there were twenty-five recognized Soviet chess masters, and by 1934 forty-three. But this by itself was not enough. In the 1930s the emphasis of party policy changed from socialism to nationalism; and internal development was now pursued in much closer alliance with the aim of making the Soviet Union a world power, 'catching up and surpassing' the leading western nations. At the same time, potential allies in the West were encouraged in the belief that Russian society was still developing in accordance with their own ideals. Here, international chess contacts played a useful role by generating favourable publicity. Western masters, living free but insecure lives, were perhaps easily impressed by the novel phenomena of state sponsorship, mass publishing, and the large interested crowds which regularly appeared to watch chess events. These things attracted favourable comments from the foreign competitors even during the first Soviet international tournament, at Moscow in 1925; in the 1930s such encomiums were repeated and disseminated through chess magazines and newspapers all over the world. The Czech master Salo Flohr, who first broke the ice by proposing a match between himself and Mikhail Botvinnik, which took place in Moscow in 1933, later recorded his astonishment that when the two chess players went to the Bolshoi theatre the whole audience rose to applaud the Russian champion. Just as important, Russian representatives almost always performed creditably in their matches and tournaments, so upholding the honour of the Soviet Union and encouraging the authorities to permit further contacts.

Botvinnik played a vital part in these developments. In particular, his victory in the Nottingham tournament of 1936, equal with Capablanca and ahead of the then world champion Euwe and ex-champions Lasker and Alekhine, was an important turning point. News of this result produced a leading article in *Pravda* (on 29 August 1936) entitled 'The Chess Players of our Homeland', reaffirming the state commitment to chess in ringing terms: 'Nowadays in the most distant corners of our land, in remote villages, collective farms, from the mountain settlements of Dagestan to the villages of Central Asia there are chess clubs . . . . The USSR is becoming the classical land of chess.' The explanation lay in 'the unity of feelings and will of the whole country, the careful attention and care paid to people by the Soviet government, the Communist party, and, above all, by Comrade Stalin'. Botvinnik himself echoed these sentiments in a telegram sent to Stalin, which is hardly surprising since as he has recently revealed in his memoirs, the whole text beginning 'Dear beloved teacher and leader' was dictated to him from Moscow at the instigation of Krylenko.[14] After this Botvinnik was talked of as a candidate for the world championship, and the Russian authorities fully supported his attempts to arrange a match with Alekhine in 1938–39. The chess movement had produced one of the first tangible signs that it really was possible to overtake the West in competitive activities. Furthermore, this could not have come at a better time, as in the late 1930s the Stalinist purges reached epidemic proportions and many powerful Soviet institutions were exposed to criticism and attack. As it was, Krylenko was arrested and executed in 1938 on the usual assortment of trumped-up charges, including in his case plotting to subvert the truly popular nature of Soviet chess.

But in general, compared with other branches of the sports and cultural hierarchy, chess escaped relatively lightly. It was certainly a time for the utmost caution in expressing theoretical views. In accordance with the general shift in ideology, successes in chess were regarded as tokens, not only of the superiority of socialist society, but also of the ancestral qualities of the Russian people. More attention was devoted to the Russian masters of the nineteenth century, above all the one really great player among them, Mikhail Tchigorin. The public, accustomed to being told that Marx and Lenin had a high regard for chess, were now informed that Pushkin, Turgenev and Tolstoy shared the same view.[15] Naturally this emphasis on the patriotic strand in Soviet thinking was not without its dangers. Too great an insistence on the supposed fact that Russia had always been a great chess nation might blur the distinction between pre- and post-revolutionary society. The state was a demanding taskmaster where orthodoxy was concerned.

But in return Soviet governments did support chess in a way unparalleled in the rest of the world. Clubs were provided with free facilities and equipment. Though it was an axiom of party policy that leading players all had socially useful jobs and were not 'professionals' in the western sense, masters were in practice salaried by the state. Books and magazines were published in large subsidized editions by state publishing houses. State funding was provided for tournaments, including the twelve Russian championships held between 1920 and 1940, and many lesser events. In all of this there was a refreshing straight-forwardness compared with the ambiguous way in which the game was regarded in the West. Though there were certainly debates in Russia about the nature of chess: the ways in which it resembled science or art, its ideological and psychological qualities and so on, from an organizational point of view it was unquestionably a sport. Chess players took part in the *spartakiady* and other sports festivals, they competed for the same titles as physical sportsmen, and they were rewarded with the same privileges and salary scales. The only difference, in this period at least, was that they were more successful.

The question of what sort of contacts ought to be permitted with western bourgeois masters was a delicate one, especially in the years before 1934. The *émigré* master Efim Bogolyubov, who still retained his

Soviet citizenship, was encouraged to participate in the early Russian championships of 1924 and 1925, and in 1925 the new All-Union Chess Section announced that it 'admits the possibility of the proletarian chess organization's participating in international tournaments, in order through victories over bourgeois masters to increase among the proletarian masses self-respect and faith in their strength and youthful talents'.[16] The result was that Ilya Rabinovich was allowed to play in a tournament at Baden-Baden, and also in 1925 there followed the much greater experiment of holding an international event at Moscow, in which ten foreign masters (led by Capablanca and Lasker) competed together with eleven Soviet representatives. Bogolyubov's victory was hailed as a great Russian triumph. Nevertheless there were no further contacts with western masters for almost another ten years; partly because of changes in overall foreign policy, but also because Krylenko and others decided that Russian players were not yet ready to achieve the hoped-for results. Bogolyubov actually renounced his Soviet citizenship in 1926, and was declared a renegade. There was a flutter of hope in 1927, when Alekhine won the world championship, in a match which received much publicity in Russia, but the new champion soon declared his opposition to the Soviet *régime* and made it clear that he had no intention of returning home. This must have been the final straw. Foreign competition in the next few years was confined to unrepresentative events organized by the Worker's Chess International and the Red Sport International, until the new-found confidence generated by Botvinnik's successes in the mid-1930s began to take effect.

There was, however, no reluctance to learn from the West in technical matters. Key books by Capablanca, Lasker, Alekhine, Réti and others were translated in the 1920s and made available to Soviet players. More reservations were expressed about western ideas on the nature of chess, but even here there are a number of discernible links. The hypermodern theorists, central European intellectuals to a man in their outlook, developed ideas about the similarity between chess and artistic expression which later Soviet writers found sympathetic. Emanuel Lasker went even further and concocted his own patent Germanic philosophy based on the concept of 'struggle' (*Kampf*), derived in large part from his chess experiences.[17] Marxist critics could hardly swallow all of this, but they admired Lasker's emphasis on psychology and constructive thinking almost without reservation.

It remains difficult to distinguish ideological reasons advanced for the growth of Soviet chess from the 'real' ones, insofar as the two diverge. Government support and encouragement alone will not serve as an explanation, because government support had to have something to work on, and it was drawn in largely by the hope of success. It is thus of critical importance that chess was established in Russia before 1917, though the extent of this establishment can be exaggerated. The game there was probably less broadly based and more dependent on a few wealthy patrons than it was in most of western Europe. Some commentators have emphasized that the All-Russian Chess Federation of 1914 recognized twenty-two masters, 'more than any other country', as though to suggest a sort of emerging pre-eminence even in Czarist times, but the inference is false; there were as yet no standard tests by which playing strength was assessed, and with the exception of a few outstanding individuals who travelled widely in the West, Russia remained peripheral to the chess world. Nevertheless the spread of the game in the pre-revolutionary period was important even if it made for ideological confusion (was chess desirable because it was Russian or because it was socialist?) It is possible that the existing popularity of native and Asiatic forms of chess in many outlying republics of the USSR made it easier for Soviet educators to promote the European game there. Chess had also certain practical advantages: it could be played all the year round and did not require elaborate training or equipment. Such factors, combined with active promotional campaigns, do help to explain the large numbers of registered chess players to be found by the 1930s. But it is doubtful how many of those hundreds of thousands of people were seriously devoted to the game, or indeed to the political ideals of the whole movement. Chess clubs had a tendency to become little more than social meeting places, a fact well appreciated by the ideologues who tried to 'saturate chess with a political content' in the early 1930s.

The production of a much smaller, but still impressive, number of strong players is another matter. Perhaps to explain this it is sufficient to point to the fact that so many came into contact with the game, and that a clear-cut system of incentives unknown anywhere else in the world was deployed to encourage any who showed talent. In the West, to become a chess player was probably to opt out of the rewards of conventional success, while in Soviet Russia it was increasingly an attractive route by which such success might be achieved. Other explanations are also possible. Attempts to link chess with Russian national psychology inevitably founder on the polyglot nature of the Soviet population, but D.J. Richards has more plausibly linked the game with social attitudes of the Russian and Soviet intelligentsia: 'It is the caste characteristics of that group, rather than the national characteristics of the Great Russians, which find satisfaction in chess.'[18] Finally it might be suggested that checks on artistic and academic activity, particularly in the 1930s, encouraged gifted individuals to take up chess as one of the few forms of self-expression largely free of censorship and control.

The impetus given to the chess movement by its successes in the mid-

1930s persisted down to the outbreak of war in 1941. Even afterwards, there were a surprising number of training tournaments and other events during the critical war years, including the thirteenth Russian championship, held at Moscow in 1944. These years also witnessed what appeared to be the final break with the *émigrés* Alekhine and Bogolyubov, who both appeared playing in Nazi-sponsored tournaments in Germany and occupied eastern Europe. Under pressure from the German authorities, Alekhine even lent his name to two articles in the *Pariser Zeitung* during 1941,[19] arguing that only Aryans were capable of playing artistic chess and attacking many Jewish masters for their materialism and defensive mentality. Some of these pieces, such as those in which the non-Aryans were accused of playing chess only to make money, read almost like malicious parodies of standard Soviet arguments, and it is ironic that Nazi Germany should have been the only other country up to that date to ascribe a political role to chess.

Post-war change

In the years immediately after the end of the war in 1945 world chess was affected by two major forces which have continued to dominate it down to the 1970s, when they were both exposed to attack from the turbulent genius of the American Robert Fischer, an attack they seem for the time being to have survived. The first was the new domination of the Soviet Union over almost every form of international competition, and the second was the extension of the supervisory powers of FIDE to achieve a new kind of regulation of world chess affairs. Both of these came together in the World Championship Tournament of 1948, designed and run by FIDE to find a worthy successor for the vacant world championship, and won by the Russian Mikhail Botvinnik, who held the title, with short breaks in 1957–8 and 1960–1, until he finally lost it in 1963.

After a generation of Russian hegemony in chess it is hard to grasp that early in 1945 very few outsiders had much conception of the Soviet Union's strength. Botvinnik was known to be a world-class player and so were Paul Keres and Salo Flohr, who had become Soviet citizens during or after the war. Andrea Lilienthal and one or two others had established reputations as powerful players in the 1930s. But it was not yet appreciated that the younger generation of Russian players, men born in the 1920s, headed by Vassily Smyslov and David Bronstein who were to be Botvinnik's greatest rivals in the 1950s, had already reached the same class. They had yet to play outside the Soviet Union. Inklings of the truth began to dawn soon after the conclusion of peace when a match was played by radio between Russia and America in September 1945. The Soviet victory by $15\frac{1}{2}:4\frac{1}{2}$ was a shattering blow to the Americans, who had won the last four Olympiads in which they had competed before the war, and were widely regarded as the world's strongest team. In 1946 they accepted an invitation to Moscow for a return match, but only succeeded in narrowing the margin of defeat, to $12\frac{1}{2}:7\frac{1}{2}$. Before very long this second disappointing result was to seem like a major achievement, as the Russians henceforth became invincible. The next USA–USSR matches occurred only in 1954 (New York) and 1955 (Moscow), with Russian victories by 20:12 and 25:7, after which the Americans understandably abandoned the whole fixture. Similar victories over Britain (1947, 1954) and other countries drove home the point.

When in the 1950s FIDE revived its series of Olympiad team tournaments, run biennially along the same lines as before the war, it set the scene for further Russian triumphs. The Soviet Union did not compete at Dubrovnik in 1950 because of the 1948 split between Stalin and Tito, but Helsinki 1952 inaugurated a series of twelve consecutive victories for them, which only ended in 1976 because they boycotted an Olympiad held in Israel. During the 1950s the supply of new Russian talent seemed inexhaustible, as Smyslov and Bronstein were followed by Efim Geller, Tigran Petrosian and Mark Taimanov, all of them world class players. It began to seem as if almost any Russian team could defeat other countries; as early as 1952 the world champion Botvinnik was not even selected for the Olympiad, much to his annoyance. Not until 1956 did the Russians lose so much as a single four-game match in one of these events, and losses by individual Soviet players were rarities. This is probably the longest period of dominance ever established by one country in a competitive sport of comparable popularity.

In individual competitions the trend was very much the same. Alekhine died in March 1946 in Portugal, just as he was about to set out for England to play his long awaited match with Botvinnik. Once again, the match had been arranged by private negotiation, though the British Chess Federation agreed to act as organizer and stakeholder. Alekhine was anxious to rehabilitate himself after his wartime experiences, particularly as there were suggestions from some quarters, notably in America, that he should be boycotted or deprived of his title as champion. His death created an unprecedented situation, and at first no one was quite sure how to resolve it. Some even considered that as the only living ex-champion (Capablanca had died in 1942) Max Euwe should recover the title, as it were by inheritance. But FIDE was not likely to let slip such a rare opportunity to take control of the world's most important chess competition, and at its congress in 1946, the first since before the war, it was decided that a tournament should be held among a small group of leading players to select the new champion. Just as important for the Federation, the issue served as a lure to attract the long-isolated USSR to its ranks. The Soviet authorities, desperately anxious that their claim might go by default if they were not represented and conscious of their new strength, at last accepted the invitation to become FIDE members in 1947. After this, though there was wrangling about the details, it was not too difficult to draw up rules for a World Championship Tournament, to be held in 1948, partly in The Hague and partly in Moscow. The contestants were to be Botvinnik, Smyslov and Keres from the USSR, Reshevsky and Fine from the USA, and Euwe from Holland. Fine declined his invitation so only the other five took part, Botvinnik emerging as a convincing winner. But this was not all. From the best of motives the FIDE delegates also took steps to ensure that the old system was not restored. In future there were to be regular championship matches every three years, with the intervening period taken up by qualifying events to select the next challenger: preliminary events, then the 'Interzonal' tournament and then a 'Candidates' competition between a smaller number who had qualified from that stage.

The triennial cycle has survived until the present day, and serves as a kind of regulating mechanism in top-class chess, much like the Olympic cycle in athletics. It brought Botvinnik challenges from David Bronstein in 1951 and Vassily Smyslov in 1954 and 1957. In 1957 Smyslov won (the two previous twenty-four game encounters were drawn), but the FIDE rules allowed the defeated champion a return match and Botvinnik took advantage of this to recover his title in 1958. Almost the same thing happened in 1960–61, when the challenger was the much younger Soviet master Mikhail Tal (born 1936); Botvinnik lost the first match and then won the second. Only in 1963, after FIDE had abolished the right to a return encounter, did Botvinnik accept his defeat at the hands of Tigran Petrosian and announce his retirement from championship play. Petrosian lost to Boris Spassky in 1969, and Spassky was defeated in 1972 by Robert Fischer, the first non-Soviet master ever to challenge for the world title under the post-war rules.

Meanwhile, as a genuinely representative world body, FIDE was able to preside over the revival and growth of international chess in the 1950s and '60s, instituting new rules or competitions where these seemed appropriate. The women's world championship was brought under control in much the same way as the men's, Vera Menchik having been killed in a German air raid on London in 1944. A world championship tournament in 1949–50 was followed by matches and candidates tournaments at two or three year intervals, though these were never held with quite the same regularity as in the open event. Next a world junior (under twenty) championship began in 1951 and was run as a series of tournaments at two year intervals. In this the Russians were not able to exert quite the same dominance as in the men's and women's matches, taking only two titles between 1951 and 1971. It was beyond the power of even the Soviet organization to produce the world's best junior player every alternate year. The Olympiad team tournaments were revived in 1950, and followed by 'student' Olympiads (in effect team tournaments for players aged below twenty-seven) from 1954, and women's Olympiads from 1957. The Federation also acted to regularize the system of 'master' and 'grandmaster' titles which served as the main way of recognizing status in competitive chess, quite indispensable for anyone who wished to make a living out of the game. These had previously been left at the mercy of public opinion and the tacit consent of established masters, though some national associations, as in the Soviet Union, had begun to confer titles on its own players more formally. In 1950 the FIDE congress set up the new ranks of 'international master' (and grandmaster) and proceeded to decide who was worthy of them by debate among the delegates present. A prolonged and harrowing session of international horse-trading produced 27 grandmasters, 11 of them Russians, and 94 masters, of whom 22 came from the USSR. Not all of these were active players, as some of the awards were almost in the nature of posthumous recognition. Among the grandmasters for instance, Oldrich Duras had not played in an international tournament since Mannheim 1914, and Rubinstein had been in a catatonic state since before the war. But future aspirants had to satisfy standard requirements or 'norms' laid down by the congress and, though these have been subject to periodic complaints and adjustments ever since, the principle has never been questioned.[20]

Accordingly, as international relations headed into the trough of the Cold War at the beginning of the 1950s, world chess was largely dominated by the Soviet Union, but there did exist a basic minimum of ground rules to ensure reasonably orderly competition. Individual players everywhere now had to take much greater notice of their national associations, which held great influence over their careers. Chess was more widely recognized as a genuine international sport, and there was undoubtedly much technical progress; a great many chess books of theoretical importance were published, especially in Russia, and in Holland where Euwe inspired systematic research into the game. Nevertheless, for the following twenty years down to the early 1970s the situation was a curious one, perhaps inevitably so in a competitive sport dominated by one country for so long. It can be regarded from three main points of view: the problems caused in Russia itself by the aftermath of success, and the need to adjust to the political climate before and after Stalin's death; the spread of Russian attitudes and treatment of chess to other countries in eastern Europe; and the consequent reaction in the West and the rest of the world.

In Russia the victories of 1946–48 reaffirmed the status of the chess movement in Soviet culture, and ensured that the state would continue to support it. The winning of the world championship in the match tournament of 1948 was of course the greatest prize of all. Botvinnik in his memoirs recalled an episode which demonstrates just how seriously the Soviet leadership viewed the outcome. After the first half of the tournament, and just before the second half began (in Moscow), he was summoned to a meeting of the Party Central Committee; worrying reports had reached them that the American Samuel Reshevsky, then placed second, was a likely final winner. Botvinnik managed to convince the committee that he could win, was assured of full support, and went on to the greatest triumph of his career.[21] The reader is left wondering what action the Party might have taken if Reshevsky had posed a greater threat. Within the USSR the number of registered players passed the million mark in 1951. Soviet writing of these years, as the European nations struggled to recover from the devastation of the war, reflected the real hope and faith that triumphs in chess were only tokens of greater triumphs to follow. 'That', as Botvinnik remarked, 'is only natural; chess is a part of culture and if a culture is declining then chess too will go downhill.'[22] All the threads of the chess movement's ideology were drawn together in the notion of '*The Soviet School of Chess*', the title of a short book published by Botvinnik in 1951, and based on a paper, '*Our Native School of Chess*', which he read to a plenary session of the Russian Chess Section as early as 1948. The theme was taken up and developed at greater length in another book, by Alexander Kotov and Mikhail Yudovich, also issued in 1951, and destined to become the classic statement of Soviet doctrines on chess. Its arguments rested on the same blend of socialist and nationalist ideas as before the war, but the authors were even more prepared to emphasize pre-Revolutionary achievements.

Tchigorin especially, as the founder of the 'Soviet School', was regarded with almost Lenin-like veneration. But even early and minor figures received similar treatment. Petrov, whose '*Game of Chess*' of 1824 was heavily based on Philidor's *Analyze* but showed some little knowledge of later criticisms of Philidor's work, was now suddenly credited with demonstrating 'that Philidor's views were based on abstract principles divorced from reality, and that his dogmatic assertions hindered progress in chess thinking.'[23] Some strands of thought from the 1930s were also developed further and more confidently than before. The authors of *The Soviet School* were particularly inclined to find parallels between Soviet ideals and the actual chess styles of Russian masters: aggressive, determined, based on intensive theoretical preparations and so on. Though some western commentators unfamiliar with chess have taken this kind of thing seriously, it really amounted to claiming the whole technical progress of the game in the twentieth century as a Soviet achievement, a highly dubious proposition unlikely to convince anyone with a wider knowledge of the game.

Thus in another of his books Kotov insisted that Russian chess is *uniquely* based not on abstract principles but on a concrete analysis of each position: 'In every game of chess the players must repeatedly take concrete decisions, often based not on the principles but on exceptions to them'. This is almost a direct quotation from the anti-dogmatic writings of the Hypermoderns in the 1920s; for instance Réti's assertion that: 'chess rules must be subjected to careful consideration in each particular instance of their intended application. The Hyper-moderns are the greatest opponents of routine play'.[24] But in the early 1950s almost no concessions were made to the idea of learning from bourgeois masters, past or present. Western books were hardly ever translated or published in the Soviet Union, and figures like Steinitz were only mentioned as foils to their all-powerful Russian opponents. Even chess openings named after their (non-Russian) inventors were systematically retitled in Soviet literature.

But, around the time of Stalin's death in 1953, it became more apparent that the West was not going to collapse of its own accord, and the emphasis of Russian foreign policy shifted towards 'cultural diplomacy' in selected fields. Chess was a natural choice for this, and the new policy at once began to have practical effects, as Russian masters were allowed to compete abroad in more than just the bare minimum of FIDE championship events. In 1954 Soviet teams toured the world to play matches against the USA, England, Argentina, Uruguay, France and Sweden, winning them all with great ease, but reporting the results in the new fraternal spirit, under headings like 'Strengthen International Sporting Ties'. The special effort of that year was not repeated, but thereafter the authorities showed themselves willing to nominate selected masters to take part in foreign tournaments, there being naturally no shortage of invitations. The new conditions also affected the internal organization of sport, including chess, in the USSR. In 1957 and 1958 many of the industrially based sports societies dating from the period of the first Five-Year Plan were wound up, and much more scope was allowed for local fund-raising and initiatives in promoting sports events. A new and perhaps slightly more independent Soviet Chess Federation was set up in 1959. There were also some notable reversals in the official line put forward by chess writers and historians. Some of these were simply handed down from above, like the rehabilitation of Krylenko in the early 1960s, but others were re-interpretations brought about by chess players themselves.

Debts owed to western masters of the past were now more freely admitted. The most startling of all was the rehabilitation of Alekhine, from fascist renegade to 'Russia's Greatest Player', as he was described in the third edition of Kotov and Yudovich's *Soviet School*, published in 1958. As early as 1951 or before Botvinnik had emphasized Alekhine's qualities as a player, though admitting his personal weaknesses, and gradually this line became more acceptable. 1956, the year of the Twentieth Party Congress and Khrushchev's denunciation of Stalin, also saw an Alekhine Memorial Tournament in Moscow and plans, which came to nothing, to bring back his remains to the Soviet Union for burial. Other writers, particularly Alexander Kotov in a whole series of books, pushed the Botvinnik line much further. In Kotov's biography of 1973, Alekhine appears as a tragic figure who 'did not for one minute break his connections with Soviet chess players', suffered a crisis in the 1930s because of 'a longing desire to return and see his native land,' and, of course, 'was the direct successor to Tchigorin – the founder of the Russian chess school'. The final chapter, which portrays him dying alone and neglected in a Portuguese hotel with a folk song of his homeland running through his head, inevitably reminds the reader of the Russian penchant for literary sentimentality administered in generous doses.[25] Such re-interpretations, though understandable, were double-edged. A 'Soviet School' with Alekhine as its greatest player might have gained in prestige, but it had lost what theoretical coherence it once possessed.

More practically, the whole Soviet chess movement in the 1950s and '60s was suffering from the problems of success. Through the memoirs and reminiscences of the players who established Russian dominance in the years after 1945, there runs something like a genuine idealism, whatever its patriotic or ideological make-up. The Soviet master, like Botvinnik at Nottingham in 1936

> could not fail to sense that the whole country was watching every move of the wooden pieces on the board and that the whole country, from the most remote corners to the Kremlin towers, was wishing him success and giving him moral support. He could not fail to sense the powerful breathing of his great motherland.[26]

But this put a burden of responsibility on players that was overwhelming, and soon became very one-sided, for once Soviet dominance was securely established anything short of complete victory was liable to serve as grounds for criticism. In these circumstances the 'powerful breathing' of the authorities down the necks of their representatives could be less than welcome. The 1952 Olympiad team were already being criticized for winning by too narrow a margin. Also, as the Soviet movement grew to include most of the world's leading masters, the divergence of styles between them became greater, and it required elaborate casuistry to claim that they *all* played 'in the style of Tchigorin and Alekhine'. This was particularly obvious at the time of the Botvinnik-Tal matches in 1960–61, and the rise of Petrosian, who built his success on caution and the avoidance of defeat, qualities long regarded as typical of bourgeois professionals. In a real sense of course, the Soviet masters were professionals, and the Soviet Chess Federation had become a vast and influential patronage organization able to reward them with affluent careers, foreign travel and other privileges. In 1957 a large number of chess players were awarded state decorations, Botvinnik and Smyslov receiving the Order of Lenin.

Yet in the years of all these successes, speeches at Soviet congresses and editorials in chess magazines continually harped on the shortcomings of the movement and the prevalence of elitism. Masters approached the system with an eye to what they could get out of it; uninteresting tasks like coaching young players or making tours to distant parts of the USSR were assigned to those who had poor results or were out of favour with the authorities. Junior and women's chess were particularly neglected. These criticisms, which appeared in the paper '*On the State of Chess Work in Physical Culture Organizations and Means of Improving it*' (1953), were repeated again and again in subsequent years. Though the number of registered players passed the three million mark in 1964, it remains unclear how many of them are serious about the game, and it is possible that other sports are making inroads into the popularity of chess as leisure opportunities in the Soviet Union expand. The priorities of the 1920s thus seem to have been reversed: chess is now valued by the Soviet authorities primarily for purposes of international prestige, and the organization within Russia is judged by its ability to achieve good results in external competition.

The *émigré* grandmaster Viktor Korchnoi frankly described the role of state support in his own career in his autobiography of 1977, *Chess is My Life*. He first went 'on a stipend' in the early 1950s after some good results during his university career: 'The fixing and withdrawing of stipends is carried out by secret departments of the sports organizations; officially there is no professionalism! The athletes arrive once a month, sign the pay-roll, leave their trade-union and Party dues, and then disappear'. Stipends were not high and more privileges came only with further success (victory in the 1959 Soviet Championship brought Korchnoi a private flat), 'but even so, the success of Soviet chess players can be explained chiefly in terms of state support, and the introduction of stipends for chess players has played a virtually decisive role in their development'.[27] Back in 1935, Botvinnik had been rewarded for his success in the Moscow tournament of that year with an increased student grant and a motor car donated by the Commissar for Heavy Industry; he not only described this incident in his memoirs but even reproduced a photograph of himself driving the vehicle. Botvinnik's memoirs too teem with incidents in which he overcame official obstruction by the adroit use of political influence and the prestige of Soviet chess. In 1943, for instance, he secured time off work to study chess by writing directly to Molotov.[28] Korchnoi's account of the 1950s and '60s more often describes such influence being used for cynical purposes: to secure foreign travel and other privileges, to deprive rivals of aid and support, even to 'fix' the results of games and tournaments. His story is a selective and at times embittered one, but most observers think it has a core of truth. Fixing of results and the distribution of prize money by mutual agreement is of course not unknown in the West, but official sources would indignantly deny that such things happen in the Soviet Union. In these circumstances it is easy to see why Soviet masters felt vulnerable in the 1960s, when their superiority in tournament play was challenged by a younger group of western masters headed by Robert Fischer of the USA and Bent Larsen of Denmark. They were in an exposed position.

The USSR has had rather similar problems in dealing with its *protégés* in eastern Europe. After 1945 state-supported sports and cultural organizations were set up in each of these countries as their integration into a Soviet 'bloc' went ahead. Because of the importance of the Russian model chess was given a leading place and, beginning with the Moscow–Prague match of 1946, many tournaments and other events took place in eastern Europe. The Czech grandmaster Ludek Pachman, who in 1945 was a sincere communist as well as a chess player, has described how eager he and his colleagues were to make contact with chess in the Soviet Union, and in effect to imitate it.[29] However, imitation could have its dangers, of which there was a foretaste in the 1948 break with Yugoslavia, and subsequent severing of cultural links. This merely encouraged the Yugoslav leaders to promote sports like chess in their own country along Soviet lines, and in 1950 Yugoslavia held the first post-war chess Olympiad, carrying off the gold medal in the absence of the Russians, who boycotted the event. Relations with Yugoslavia were resumed in 1954, but as elsewhere in eastern Europe, ideals of socialist cooperation often thinly concealed popular nationalism, and even anti-Soviet feelings. When Svetozar Gligoric, the leading Yugoslav master, defeated Tigran Petrosian at a tournament in Belgrade in 1954, the enthusiasm of the crowd spilled over into a riot which took some time to suppress. In 1957 Yugoslavia even defeated the Russians in a ten-board match. Since then eastern European countries have always been among the Soviet Union's most dangerous rivals in international events, and their successes have usually been regarded as threats rather than fraternal socialist achievements by the leaders of the 'Soviet School'.

The western reaction to the Russian dominance of post-war chess is another matter. For a long time it appeared to be extremely half-hearted, a question of a few individuals struggling against almost insuperable odds, lack of money and other obstacles. Already in 1939 the United States Federation did not send a team to the Olympiad in Buenos Aires because it was not possible to raise funds to defray their expenses. In 1950 the State Department would not issue visas for Reshevsky and Fine to travel to Budapest, even for so important an event as the Candidates Tournament, which was organized by FIDE and not by a communist country. This lack of support arose partly from the confusion of values already evident in the 1920s and 30s: uncertainty over whether chess really was a sport, how seriously it should be taken, how plausible a career it was. Once Russian superiority became overwhelming, it must also have seemed much easier to minimize the importance of chess in international competition than to take it more seriously in hopes of making a better showing. Only gradually in the 1960s did this situation turn around, so that chess began to attract the kind of private sponsorship essential to most organized sport and culture in non-socialist countries.

From the 1960s to the 1980s

The growing popularity of chess outside Russia and eastern Europe since the 1960s is closely associated with the stormy career of one man: Robert James ('Bobby') Fischer. His influence has lasted, though he has played no serious chess since the final game of the match against Boris Spassky which brought him the world championship in 1972. Merely by becoming the first non-Soviet champion in more than twenty-five years, Fischer set his seal on the revival of western chess during the 1960s and blazed a trail which younger players have set themselves to follow since his premature retirement. A summary of his path to the world title will be followed here by an attempt to assess the importance of the 'Fischer phenomenon' and what can be learned from it about the status of modern chess in America, Russia and elsewhere.

Robert Fischer was born at Chicago in 1943. He and his sister were brought up by his mother after her divorce in 1945; she was a schoolteacher and a nurse who, curiously, had worked in Russia from 1933 to 1938. The family were never in serious need but neither were they wealthy, and Fischer's early search for financial sponsorship to develop his chess career, which he found demeaning, probably accounts for his much-criticized mercenary approach later on. His serious interest in chess began after they moved to New York, and he played in his first tournament, the Brooklyn chess club championship, in 1953 at the age of ten. Steady progress led to his victory in the US championship by 1958, when he was not yet fifteen. Later in the same year he was placed fifth in the FIDE Interzonal tournament and qualified for the Candidates final, becoming in the process the youngest ever grandmaster. Child prodigies can always fizzle out, but by now Fischer was exceptional; already in 1957 the Russian chess authorities were sufficiently intrigued (or alarmed) to invite him to the USSR for a visit. Thereafter he became almost unbeatable in America, winning the US national championship on all eight occasions when he competed, but there were inevitable setbacks in world competition. The big crisis came in 1962. Having once again qualified for the Candidates event, this time with a realistic chance of winning and going on to a match for the world title, Fischer could only come fourth behind three Russians. In the long eight-man tournament, with five Russians taking part, he had obviously felt under pressure and he did not take his comparative failure lightly; later in the year he wrote an article called 'The Russians have fixed world chess' which was widely republished.[30] His argument was that the leading Russians had agreed to quick draws amongst themselves to conserve their energy for the two-month competition. Viktor Korchnoi, who played in the event but was not part of the 'pact', has since confirmed its existence,[31] and although many critics have maintained that the accusation (even if true) was irrelevant, that Fischer was not yet strong enough to win such a tournament, he was also the last person to explain failure by his own shortcomings.

After 1962 Fischer increasingly saw the Russians as not just the greatest obstacle to his ambitions, which was self-evident fact, but as an unscrupulous conspiracy against him, colluding with his enemies in FIDE and elsewhere. He adopted Cold War rhetoric and became famous, or infamous, for his remarks about 'commie cheating'. Even his friends and supporters began to think that he was too unstable to fulfil his potential, as he absented himself from the qualifying tournaments for the 1966 world championship match, and prematurely withdrew from those for the 1969 match. But though Fischer hardly played chess for periods of a year or more he never stopped studying the game and perfecting his technique. The results became apparent when he returned to serious competition in 1970 and qualified for the Candidates event for the third time.[32] In 1971 he brushed aside his world-class opponents, two Russians and the Dane Bent Larsen, with alarming ease and earned the right to play Boris Spassky for the world title. The 1972 match in Reykjavik which followed was not merely the culmination of Fischer's career but the most widely publicized chess event of all time. There seemed no end to its surprising twists and turns: the arguments over finance that eventually boosted the prize fund to an unprecedented $250,000 (Spassky's prize in 1969 had been $1,500), the doubts over whether Fischer would play at all, the default in the second game that left him with a 2 : 0 deficit to make up, his final triumphant victory. A press corps of almost presidential proportions followed every move on and off the board; the writers in attendance included Arthur Koestler (*Sunday Times*) and George Steiner (*New Yorker*). Fischer had never much resembled the mild-mannered Clark Kent, but during those heady days he seemed to take on some of the attributes of Superman. Secretary of State Henry Kissinger twice appealed to him to continue the match on patriotic grounds, and President Nixon praised him for his fighting qualities. After he had won, his success was endorsed by other public figures as a triumph for the individual against the Russian 'chess machine', a sort of vindication of western values.

Could such artificial and distorted publicity really do anything to alter the status of chess itself? Surely any effects would be short-lived, especially when Fischer, like Morphy before him, withdrew into seclusion after his victory. After all, Fischer as an individual had always been the subject of press and media attention, at first merely for his ability and precocity, then increasingly because of his quarrels with organizers, his lonely and obsessive life style, his defiant egotism. He himself may have been deeply ambivalent about whether he really wanted such publicity, much of it critical; many other players and supporters found it merely irritating and embarrassing. But such judgements were premature. Around the period 1970–72 sales of chess sets and chess books in America and western Europe markedly increased. Sponsors and publishers reacted to this new popularity of chess and in their turn promoted it; the quality and diversity of western chess literature now rivalled or even surpassed that of Russia. Some at least of these gains in the appeal of chess and the seriousness with which it is treated have outlasted the 1970s and led to new advances. The conclusion must be that Fischer's career was not an isolated influence. In part at least, it served more as a kind of catalyst to draw out a potential interest in chess which already existed in western society. It is hard to say exactly how this happened. Some people who had never encountered chess at all were now brought into contact with it. The Fischer image of youth and rebellion fitted in well with the game's growing popularity among the young. His example of fame and wealth encouraged talented players to take chess more seriously as a potential career. All these things together apparently did have the power to change the game's status: what often had been seen as a bloodless pastime, appealing mostly to college professors and internationally dominated by Russia, was now presented as a ruthlessly competitive (though unusual) kind of sport, with all the attractions which sport generally possesses for the amateur and the professional. This value-shift in some ways resembled the one which had taken place earlier in Soviet Russia; if it continues it will demonstrate that chess can also grow and develop in western capitalistic societies, without the kind of state aid which Russia has provided.

From the Russian point of view, the events of 1970–72 were naturally little short of disastrous. It has already been pointed out that the Soviet chess establishment was rather defensive-minded by the 1960s, and extremely sensitive to accusations of failure. Weaknesses of organization, vested interests or complacency, all might be overlooked if the results were still right, but any slipping in external competition might bring on an uncomfortable re-appraisal for those involved. Fischer's 1972 victory was thus followed by an upheaval in the Soviet Chess Federation far greater than anything produced by years of pious exhortation to pay attention to socialist goals. The 41st USSR Championship in 1973 was organized on a new principle, with several divisions of different strengths and strict relegation rules for those who failed to perform well in the section to which they were assigned. No exceptions were allowed, even for the most senior and respected figures. The result, as Korchnoi has recorded in his memoirs, was a rare collective protest by the grandmasters to the Chairman of the USSR Sports Committee, which met with no response.[33] The new rules, which have since been softened, were undoubtedly part of the response to the previous year's defeat, inspired by the imperative need to show that the lesson had been taken to heart and remedial action was under way. There had been warning signs that the flood of post-war victories might be drying up, even before 1972. One of the worries of the Russian chess leadership in the 1960s was that the new generation of younger players (with the exception of the future world champion Anatoly Karpov) were not so strong as their predecessors ten or twenty years before. A series of special training tournaments was inaugurated to try and improve the situation. In 1970 the Soviet Chess Federation were still confident enough to float a proposal for a ten board match between the USSR and the Rest of the World, but they soon regretted this grandiloquent gesture. Eventually, after many alarms, the Russian team won the four-round event by $20\frac{1}{2}:19\frac{1}{2}$; to no one's surprise, the fixture was not repeated until 1984.

From some points of view it might seem that Fischer's ascent to the world championship could have been taken philosophically: chess is an individualistic game and Fischer had simply shown himself to be an unstoppable individual talent. Soviet players themselves do seem to have shrugged off his victories in this way, pointing out that Fischer had learned Russian specially to read their chess literature, and joking among themselves that he was now the finest representative of the Soviet school of chess. One of the ironies of the 1972 match was the way in which Spassky emerged as a 'gentleman' rather than an organization man in the eyes of western commentators, insisting on playing the match when he could have claimed a win by default, seeking no excuses to explain his defeat, and having little to do with the legal manoeuvering of his own Soviet delegation. Inside the USSR Fischer's achievement could hardly be ignored and lessons had to be learned from his play, so his impressive book *My 60 Memorable Games*, first published in 1969, came out in a Russian edition even before the 1972 match and was widely read. But official ideologists could hardly afford to be so phlegmatic, for it was their own insistence over many years that victories at chess proved the superiority of the Soviet social system that had fashioned the trap in which they were now ensnared. Thus, following Fischer's failure in the 1962 Candidates tournament, grandmaster Yefim Geller wrote complacently:

> Fischer's trouble is that he looks at the game only from the point of view of business. It is unclear how his chess career will develop but one thing is clear: the strongest of this world can only be a person of high conviction, of deep moral fibre, of high intellect, a person free from the faults and ulcers of the rotten capitalist system.[34]

Though western commentators have often found Fischer's political views naive, and his assertions that he saw himself as the champion of western freedom unconvincing, his claims had an undeniable impact on the Soviet establishment, for he was simply taking their own arguments and turning them against their inventors.

Nevertheless, though many observers in 1972 shared his own view that he could remain world champion for many years, Fischer proceeded to withdraw from serious play and failed to agree terms for a match against his Soviet challenger Anatoly Karpov in 1975, so losing the title by default. Karpov has retained it for almost a decade. Accordingly, it might be argued that post-war chess has resumed its accustomed course under Russian hegemony, but this would be a one-sided view for several reasons. First, western competition, even without Fischer, has remained at a much higher level than before. Secondly, the strains in the Soviet chess movement shown up by the events of the early 1970s were not suddenly dispelled by the recovery of the championship. One obvious symptom of internal tension has been the steady trickle of emigration and defection from the ranks of leading players, something that has also affected other parts of the cultural establishment. The most celebrated example is Viktor Korchnoi, who decided in 1974, during his match with Karpov for the right to meet Fischer, that 'the authorities' had determined the result in advance and were using every kind of formal and informal pressure to ensure that he lost. For a time he was openly at odds with officialdom, but though his discontent became widely known even in the West he was again permitted to travel abroad at the end of 1975. In July 1976, typically after playing his last game in (and winning) a tournament in Holland, he asked for political asylum. The resultant furore could have been a nine-day wonder, but Korchnoi soon proved himself to be Fischer's nearest successor, both in competitive results and in flair for publicity. His demands that his wife and son be permitted to leave Russia were backed up by victories which kept his name firmly in the public eye. In both 1978 and 1981 Korchnoi earned the right to meet Karpov, defeating other Soviet players in the process. He lost both matches, but the 1978 one was extremely close, and outdid even 1972 in its extravagant atmosphere of rumour, intrigue and propaganda.

It is important also to realize that Korchnoi was not the only chess refugee of these years: some preceded him and others followed. The trend goes back at least to the American grandmaster Pal Benko, who left Hungary after 1956, but it became really significant in the 1970s. A list only of prominent grandmasters who left eastern Europe in this period would have to include Anatoly Lein, Vladimir Liberzon, Gennadi Sosonko and Leonid Shamkovich (USSR), Lubomir Kavalek and Ludek Pachman (Czechoslovakia), as well as Korchnoi. In addition there are those like Boris Spassky and the Czech Vlastimil Hort who have been permitted to marry or live abroad without loss of citizenship. The socialist countries have increasingly faced the dilemma that, if they want the international prestige that comes from such star performers, they may well have to retain their loyalty by permitting them more freedom as well as material rewards.

What of the wider popularity of chess in the world as a whole? It is hard to measure the distribution of interest in the game, let alone to explain it, but one partial source of information lies in the figures submitted to the world chess federation, FIDE, by its member states, covering not just titled players (international masters and grandmasters) but registered players of any strength. Whenever these can be compared over time they show a dramatic growth. In 1950, when the title system was first standardized by FIDE, there were 27 grandmasters and 94 masters; by 1977 there were 157 grandmasters and 355 masters. Part of this growth can be put down to the statistical devaluation of the titles, as opportunities to gain them have become more widespread, but most of it reflects a real increase in the game's popularity and the standards of competition. There has been a similar increase in the number of countries affiliated to FIDE, now approaching one hundred, organized in twelve worldwide zones. Table 3 gives a breakdown by area of some of the 1977 figures.[35]

The figures are hardly reliable in detail, as even the FIDE statistician Arpad Elo admits, for not every country provides reliable data. In addition, social pressures for chess players to become officially registered differ enormously, being greatest in the socialist countries, with their publicly-funded sports organizations. The USSR thus has a massively boosted figure for enrolled players, but disproportionately few international title holders because of its restrictions on travel and competition. In the USA, on the other hand, sales of chess sets and chess books suggest

	Population (in thousands)	Chess Players (in thousands)	Titled Players (masters and grandmasters)
USSR	250,900	4,180	84
Eastern Europe (7 countries)	126,900	209	168
USA	212,900	50	39
Western Europe (15 countries)	328,500	153	103

Table 3

The eastern European countries are: Hungary, Yugoslavia, Czechoslovakia, East Germany, Bulgaria, Poland and Rumania. The western European countries are: France, West Germany, Belgium, Holland, Luxembourg, Italy, Denmark, Greece, Spain, Portugal, Switzerland, Austria, Norway, Ireland and Great Britain. (The total could be increased by two, as England, Wales and Scotland compete as separate countries.)

that there are many more players than appear in the official total. It would be unprofitable to analyze these sample statistics in more detail, but they provide some indication of parameters within which it is possible to assess the current world popularity of the game and its potential for future growth. Changes since 1977 have not been dramatic, though the number of titled players in western Europe, above all in England, has shown a marked increase.[36]

Potentially an even more dramatic development for the future than this re-alignment of forces between the chess powers, has been the continuing expansion of the game's appeal into other parts of the world. Two stages of the process can be identified. First, countries with well-established but isolated chess communities like Australia and New Zealand have been brought into closer contact with international competition. Once chess was more popular and better funded, the 'tyranny of distance' could in part be overcome; promising players could more easily travel abroad and leading foreign masters be attracted. Improved results followed, and the success of the Australian team in coming 15th out of 60 participants in the 1970 chess Olympiad was a striking example, though there is still a feeling that really outstanding players can only pursue their careers by moving temporarily or permanently to Europe or America. Secondly, modern competitive chess has spread into other countries where previously it hardly existed. Some of these, like China which began to participate in international events in the mid-1970s, have vast potential for growth. The number of countries involved is reflected in entries for the FIDE Olympiad tournaments since the war: 16 in 1950 but 40 by 1960 and 60 by 1970. As with the Olympic Games themselves, organizational problems have become so great that some sort of qualifying system has been proposed. Future world champions are perhaps unlikely to emerge from Andorra or the Virgin Islands (both recent participants in the Olympiads), but they may well come from some currently unfashionable parts of the chess world. Like the Russians before them, the International Chess Federation are realizing that the promotion of chess in outlying areas, at times an uphill struggle, may in the end yield unexpected returns.

An account of twentieth-century chess becomes naturally an analysis of its progress in the Soviet Union, which has indeed been extraordinary, and the subsequent reaction or imitation in eastern Europe and the West. But it is wrong to leave the impression that chess has served always as a battleground in modern international relations. The spread of the game around the world, and the comradeship which can spring up among chess players almost anywhere, give slightly more credibility to the optimistic FIDE motto: *Gens Una Summus.*

Conclusion

It is not primarily the task of the historian to make predictions. The history of chess is long and instructive, but it does not enable us to visualize where the game will stand a decade or a generation ahead with any confidence. Already there are new influences to be taken into account, such as the development of sophisticated chess computer programs. Computing will not make the human player redundant, but its association with chess may well change attitudes to the game and its popular appeal (as well as providing competition for it in the form of new 'computer games'). Nevertheless, some qualities of chess have been so persistent through the long history outlined in this book that they are likely to exercise a continuing influence over its development.

What are these qualities? First, as a complex game chess has proved extraordinarily stable. Hundreds of years have passed, bringing with them new patterns of thought and leisure, and yet the rules of chess have altered hardly at all. In a thousand years of well-documented history there has been only one such major change, the one which took place *c.* 1475–95. The game has moved geographically from culture to culture and remained similarly impervious; hence it was played in an almost identical way across the great expanse of the divided Christian and Muslim civilizations in the middle ages. Variant forms of chess have grown up in China, Japan and parts of south India and south-east Asia, but hardly at all elsewhere. With these exceptions chess has remained essentially a single game, and has not been fragmented into many games each with its own local currency. This fixity of rule must testify to a constant element in the appeal of chess, something it has always been: an intriguing puzzle. Yet though chess has shown great stability as a game, even in different surroundings, its outward form – that of conflict between two forces, both with a complex hierarchy of different pieces – has proved almost equally open to having external cultural meanings read into it. The chessmen symbolized the major elements of an army in early India and Islam; the ranks and degrees of feudal society and the state in the western middle ages. More recently some Soviet ideologists have seen in chess-playing a model for the ideal qualities of socialism and socialist man. In contemporary thought interest in chess is polarized in different directions: towards psychologists, psycho-analysts or philosophers who find in the game evidence for the structure of human thought and motivation, or towards computer designers and programmers who have used it as a test in the development of artificial intelligence. This chameleon-like adaptability as a focus of cultural interest perhaps explains the historic popularity and importance of chess almost as much as its enduring game qualities.

In recent times though, competitive chess has been stripped of some of its ambiguities. Though it sometimes retains in the popular mind the image of a highbrow and exclusive mystery, it is increasingly treated as a variant of a more familiar modern institution: the organized sport. Press and media portrayals of 'typical' chess players have abandoned the once-popular stereotype of the eccentric old gentleman, lingered fondly over the newsworthy attractions of monomaniac or cold warrior (Fischer, Korchnoi), before settling down to showing simply competitive people who happen to be good at chess rather than tennis, swimming or something else. Many of the world's leading chess players, it must be admitted, are so incorrigibly ordinary that it would be hard to portray them in any other way. But the status of chess as a sport raises another major theme in the game's history: the interrelation between popularity ('quantity') and technical or competitive progress ('quality') in its development. An obvious example is economic: professional players provide entertainment and instruction for an audience of less serious players, receiving support and patronage in return. Historically the relationship has been more complex than this, and it is often very hard to say why the game has been popular in one place or time rather than another. Certainly a chess master's career can be frustrated for lack of a sufficiently numerous or educated public, just as much as that of an artist. It has been said that a great novelist should himself 'create the taste by which he is appreciated', and build up his own following, but often this is simply not possible; in chess terms even Morphy or Fischer (or the promoters of the Russian chess movement after 1917) needed a favourable environment in which to work if their individual examples were to have a lasting effect.

Arpad Elo's correlation of recent international chess federation statistics on the number of masters and registered players in different countries provides no definitive answer to such problems, but it does show clearly that there are now more players and more very strong players than in the whole previous history of the game. This is not just a reflection of increases in national populations. Chess has spread rapidly outside its previous heartland of eastern Europe and the industrialized countries into the rest of the world. So far at least, its involvement with computing has only aided its growth; computer programs have attracted new players without becoming so strong as to inspire the discouraging thought that the machine is unbeatable. At the time of writing, the higher reaches of competition are still well outside the computer's range. The world championship is now again firmly in Russian hands, but after Fischer's success in 1972 western opposition has been much stronger than in the 1950s and 1960s. In almost every respect, chess is better established now than ever before in the paradoxical position it occupies in modern life: the only generally acknowledged sedentary (and cerebral) sport.

Chess Books
and
Chess Notation

The growth of modern chess literature, and hence of modern competitive chess, would hardly have been possible without the devising of a concise and accurate notation to record the moves of chess games. Similar problems have had to be solved in the development of music and mathematics. The symbolic language of chess is simpler, because it deals only with the disposition of thirty-two men on a two-dimensional board of sixty-four squares, but its evolution has nevertheless been a slow and halting process.

There are still two systems of chess notation in current use. The more common 'algebraic' system, which is gradually becoming dominant in world chess, gives every square on the board its own designation by letter and number. The horizontal 'ranks' are numbered 1–8 and the vertical 'files' lettered a–h.

8	a8	b8	c8	d8	e8	f8	g8	h8
7	a7	b7	c7	d7	e7	f7	g7	h7
6	a6	b6	c6	d6	e6	f6	g6	h6
5	a5	b5	c5	d5	e5	f5	g5	h5
4	a4	b4	c4	d4	e4	f4	g4	h4
3	a3	b3	c3	d3	e3	f3	g3	h3
2	a2	b2	c2	d2	e2	f2	g2	h2
1	a1	b1	c1	d1	e1	f1	g1	h1
	a	b	c	d	e	f	g	h

White plays always up the board, beginning with his men on ranks 1 and 2; Black plays down the board, beginning with his men on ranks 7 and 8.

199

The move of any piece can be described by the square it leaves and the square it reaches, e.g. B (Bishop) f1–c4, or in abbreviated form Bc4. Symbols for the different pieces naturally vary from language to language; in English usually K = King, Q = Queen, B = Bishop, N = Knight, R = Rook, P = Pawn. It has become common in recent chess literature to use pictorial figurine symbols instead, so achieving a genuinely international chess notation, as pioneered by the Yugoslavian journal *Informator* (now an official FIDE publication) since 1966.

The rival 'descriptive' system, though it has lost ground steadily in the last twenty years, survives in English- and Spanish-speaking countries. In this system the squares are designated according to the initial position of the pieces.

Starting again from White's position at the bottom of the diagram, the files are named from left to right: QR (Queen's Rook), QN, QB, Q, K, KB, KN, KR. The ranks are numbered as before 1–8. Moves are described usually by reference to the square a piece arrives at, e.g. Q–Q4, P–K4. This system is more cumbersome, and also two-sided, for White's QR6 is Black's QR3 and so on. Black begins with his men on White's ranks 7 and 8, but his own ranks 1 and 2, and his moves are described from his point of view. So the ranks (though not the files) must be re-calibrated by the reader, depending on whether he is dealing with a white or a black move. It is a big advantage of algebraic notation that each square retains its unique designation; g5 is always g5. Many players thus find algebraically recorded moves easier to visualize, which is why this system may come to have in Britain and America the dominance it already exerts in Russia and most of Europe.

The curious thing about the recorded history of chess notation is that these two systems appear always to have been rivals; at least both can be found in western medieval manuscripts and in the earliest Arabic texts. It seems strange that one system did not long ago drive out the other, for no one uses two solutions to the same technical problem impartially for very long. Part of the answer lies in the limited circulation of written chess works before printing. Much knowledge of the game was circulated orally, so that notation was sometimes re-invented independently when the need to write moves down arose. Algebraic and descriptive systems could thus have evolved by fits and starts, without the emergence of a steady tradition. Endless variations in the conventions used, from text to text and country to country, reinforce the impression that this was the case.

Secondly, almost all early chess books were collections of problems, which made only limited demands on the system of notation. A symptom of this was the occasional appearance alongside algebraic and descriptive of a third system in which all the squares were simply numbered from 1 to 64. The resultant strings of numbers might suffice for the three or four moves of a problem solution, but were intolerably burdensome for complete recorded games. More commonly the compilers of problem collections avoided the need for precise notation at all by describing their solutions in general terms, with the aid of letters, crosses or other signs drawn in on the pictorial diagrams. This habit, further evidence of the tendency for real notation to fall out of use from time to time, was attributed by Murray, not altogether fairly, to 'the indolence . . . characteristic of the medieval chess player'.[1]

But when from the late fifteenth century onwards changes in the rules of chess made analysis of openings and whole games more popular, descriptive notation was clearly preferred for recording them. The earliest printed chess books, those of Lucena (1496/7) and Damiano (1512) used it for their chapters on the openings, though they retained the annotated diagrams of the medieval manuscripts for their problem collections. Plate 12, the title page of Lucena's book, shows one of these diagrams, with only six white and black pieces, but eight other squares marked with symbols. The letters A to E show the squares occupied in succession by the white pieces in the five-move solution.

The difficulty with the notation is that there was no generally accepted way of abbreviating it, or arranging punctuation and layout so that each move stood out clearly from the rest. Play was recorded in a kind of continuous prose narration, seen at its clumsiest in Plate 13, the 1562 English translation of Damiano attributed to James Rowbothum. One diagram and two or three single moves was all that could be fitted onto each (admittedly small) page. The 1656 English edition of Greco, *The Royall Game of Chesse-Play*, shows a more businesslike arrangement, with the moves set out one to a line, though the words still take up a lot of space. Similar styles lasted until the early nineteenth century, and certainly Plate 15, Bertin's *Noble Game of Chess* of 1735, shows no advance except for a slightly modernized vocabulary. Philidor used an almost identical system in the various editions of the *Analyze des Echecs* from 1749 onwards. Yet as early as 1737, Stamma in his *Essai sur le Jeu des Echecs* had attempted to introduce, or reintroduce, a form of algebraic notation. Plate 16, taken from the subsequent English edition, *The Noble Game of Chess* of 1745, clearly shows the greater economy he achieved. This notation, more than anything else in Stamma's book, may have derived from his knowledge of Arabic chess. But though he had at least one imitator, the author of the anonymous *Chess Made Easy* of 1750 (mostly an edition of Greco, though also plagiarized from Philidor), Stamma's system never really caught on. The growing popularity of Philidor's *Analyze* helped to preserve descriptive notation as the dominant form into the nineteenth century, and in England until recent times.

Meanwhile, from the first appearance of printed chess books, there was also a whole series of problems to be overcome for the adequate reproduction of chessboard diagrams. The printers of Lucena and Damiano used a separate woodcut for each position, which was an extremely expensive and time-consuming process. One sign of this was the re-use of the woodcut blocks through five successive editions of Damiano down to 1564.[2] When Damiano was published in French and English translations, in 1560 and 1562,[3] the problems were omitted entirely and the diagrams in the rest of the text were reduced to a simple grid with pieces identified by initial letters, as shown in Plate 13. The printer's preface to the French version makes it quite clear that this was done for reasons of economy, and the point is echoed in the literal translation of the English preface: 'And in the mean time content your self with this, for I assure you the difficulty to express or set out the types and figures of the men is so much and the charges so great, that as yet no man would ever gladly take in hand to print them . . . And therefore (curiosity set apart) take in good worth these types and figures here presented until some better invention be found'.

There was also the purely technical difficulty of portraying white and black squares with white and black pieces on them, which was certainly not overcome in the Lucena or Damiano diagrams, as the confusion of white and black men in Plate 12 demonstrates, but this was less serious. As early as 1557, in his book *De Varietate Rerum*, Girolamo Cardano had proposed the solution still used in modern chess books: cross-hatching the black squares instead of inking them as solid blocks, so that black pieces would stand out against them. The real problem remained the one of cost. For this reason diagrams virtually disappeared from chess books until the first decade of the nineteenth century when they began to be printed with moveable type, potentially a more modern and economical process. But it was still necessary for the printer to make the initial investment in a special fount of type, and many chess books lacked diagrams down to the 1840s, after which they at last became common.

Little work has been done as yet on the printing and production of chess books in the machine press age of the nineteenth and twentieth centuries.

APPENDIX TWO
A Note
on Chess Problems

Perhaps more precisely one should speak of chess 'problems' or 'studies'. In modern terms a problem is a composed position with a specific task or solution attached to it, such as: *White to play and mate in two moves against any defence*. Nothing else matters except this specific task, so that the position can be far removed from normal play; there can be a vast disparity in material such that in a real game one of the players would long ago have resigned. In the problem this is irrelevant, for anything which frustrates the solution and postpones the mate even for one move, counts as a victory for the defence. The study by contrast has a simpler and broader task: *White to play and win, or draw*. Accordingly, though study positions may still appear (as they are) artificially contrived, there is a kind of dynamic balance between the forces of both sides, and the solutions often resemble episodes from competitive games. Endgame studies in particular can be instructive as well as aesthetically pleasing, and often find a place in practical handbooks for players.

Historically, however, all these distinctions are of recent origin and have grown up only during the last hundred years or so; in earlier times 'problem' was a generic term which covered all kinds of chess composition. The first known examples are the Arabic *mansubat* (singular *mansuba*), usually with specific direct-mate tasks, but still regarded as valuable training for the practical player. The reduced mobility of the muslim game compared with modern chess made mating patterns much harder to achieve, and problems were a way of practising this elusive skill. Compilers of problem collections thus believed, or affected to believe, that they were recording episodes from real games rather than contrived positions. Much the same may be said of problems in medieval western chess, which developed from the Arabic models, though western problems were also used for other purposes, notably gambling, with onlookers betting on the outcome of each position as it was shown. This is thought to be the reason why quite a number of medieval problems were made deliberately unsound or incapable of solution, to catch the unwary.

Once the rules of chess changed, around the years 1475–95, the game became much more rapid and decisive from its first moves onward, and the attention of most players steadily shifted away from problems towards opening analysis and the study of complete recorded games. The earliest modern-chess books, those of Lucena (1496/7) and Damiano (1512) combine primitive opening analysis with collections of problems; Ruy Lopez in 1561 and Greco by the early seventeenth century dispensed with the problems altogether, as did Philidor in his *Analyze* (1749, and subsequent editions). Yet the interest in problems never quite died, and something of a revival began with Philip Stamma's *Essai sur le Jeu des Echecs* of 1737, which consisted essentially of a hundred composed positions. They included both direct-mate problems and winning-play studies, with some re-workings of old classic themes and some new settings dressed up to look like real games. Though Stamma was contributing to the eventual revival of the chess problem as an art form, he still felt obliged to insist on its practical value: 'These reasons, joined to the requests of my chess-playing friends, have led me to put before the public the hundred *parties* which must be regarded as equivalent to the secrets of this game . . . it must not be supposed that these hundred *parties* are exceptional cases, for in the ordinary games I have played, I have encountered such situations every day'.[1] Despite its implausibility, this claim may stand as a classic statement of the pre-nineteenth-century view of the chess problem, as an outgrowth of the ordinary game, to which it must remain closely linked in order to survive.

By the time Stamma's *Essai* was re-issued in 1745 as *The Noble Game of Chess*, his chess-playing friends had encouraged him to augment the problems with some opening analysis, but his collection of positions still retained an appeal of its own, and was reprinted at least fifteen times in the century down to 1840. Perhaps influenced by Stamma's example, the Italian Modenese writers del Rio (1750), Lolli (1763) and Ponziani (1769) also included some problems in their chess treatises, though only incidentally. The future of the chess problem however remained uncertain and its status ambiguous. As the claim that studying problems was the best way to study the game became harder to defend, chess composition could develop in either of two directions: it could restrict itself to those areas where there was still a real overlap between contrived effects and practical play, or it could seek to justify problems as a separate pursuit, a minor art form increasingly emancipated from the parent game. Broadly speaking, these developments have led to the endgame study and the 'art' problem respectively, but the process took time. In the terms of H. Weenink's classic study, *The Chess Problem*,[2] the 'Old School' of experimental composition (*c.* 1820–45) was followed by the 'Transition

School' (1845–62) in which a repertoire of artistic themes and principles was laid down. After this there grew up a number of so-called national schools, 'English', 'Bohemian', 'German' and so on, each of them drawing on the repertoire selectively in accordance with their own ideas and priorities. Through all this, the severance between problems and the ordinary game became more and more apparent. It is symptomatic that the leading player Adolf Anderssen (1818–79) was the author of two collections of problems, but gave up composing entirely in favour of competitive play after 1852. Others made their choice in the opposite direction.

Without pursuing this further, it is clear that the modern chess problem has a technical history of its own, and also that it has arisen almost as an antagonistic reaction to the development of the modern game. Increasingly, players have opted for pragmatism and organized competition, with aesthetic effects incidental to the pursuit of victory. 'Brilliancy prizes' for the most artistic games are common in chess tournaments, but hardly anyone plays specifically to win them. Problemists meanwhile have refined their themes and principles of purity, economy and accuracy for their own sake. An increasing number of twentieth-century composers, inspired by the example of T.R. Dawson (1889–1951) have not scrupled to vary the rules of the game, inventing new chess pieces and new tasks in order to achieve original artistic effects. Chess problems are still frequently composed for submission to problem tourneys, but the prizes are awarded, as in literary or musical competitions, according to the taste of the judges. It is therefore a crowning irony that the International Chess Federation (FIDE), in its desire to supervise all chess activities, has set up a Commission for Chess Compositions, which since 1956 has acknowledged arbiters, and then subsequently masters (1959) and grandmasters (1972) of chess composition, in direct imitation of the competitive game. Title-holders are to be found listed according to their country of origin. Even in the rarefied world of the chess problem, beauty and truth must sometimes walk hand-in-hand with national prestige.

Bibliography

This bibliography is intended to serve as a guide to further reading, as well as an indication of the sources used in the present work. It is therefore highly selective:

(i) Full references have already been given in the text for the dates and places of publication of most pre-1850 sources. These are anyway accessible only in large libraries and specialist collections. Only modern reprint editions are separately listed below, where they happen to be available.

(ii) A very large number of books have been consulted for background information or passing allusions to chess, and it would be impracticable to cite them all here. A list of useful works on medieval Islam alone would run to dozens of items. In such cases I have tried to avoid the problem by quoting a few representative books, which themselves contain specialist bibliographies.

General

The indispensable guide to the materials for the history of chess is H.J.R. Murray, *A History of Chess*, Oxford 1913, though it is long (890 pages), curiously unbalanced (only 115 pages on the post-1500 period), and makes no concessions to the general reader. Murray also wrote a large number of articles on specific points of chess history. Most of these are listed in E. Meissenburg, 'H.J.R. Murray (1868–1955): bibliography of a chess historian', *British Chess Magazine*, 1980, pp. 249–52. Only the real enthusiast will go to the works of Murray's predecessors: A. van der Linde, *Geschichte und Litteratur des Schachspiels*, 2 vols., Berlin 1874, and *Quellenstudien*, Berlin 1881; T. von der Lasa, *Forschungen zur Geschichte und Literatur des Schachspiels*, Leipzig 1897.

Among more compact accounts H.J.R. Murray, *A Shorter History of Chess*, Oxford 1963, is not really satisfactory. Murray himself never passed it for publication, and it was published posthumously without adequate re-editing. Harry Golombek, *A History of Chess*, 1976, is a readable and well-illustrated introductory account. Most other popular histories of chess are either entirely derivative or do not go back much before the nineteenth century.

There are a number of chess encyclopedias useful for historical purposes. The most up-to-date in English is *The Encyclopedia of Chess*, ed. Harry Golombek, 1977 (revised and abridged as *The Penguin Encyclopedia of Chess*, 1981), but *The Encyclopaedia of Chess*, ed. Anne Sunnucks, 1970, and the Italian *Dizionario Enciclopedico Degli Scacchi*, ed. Adriano Chicco and Giorgio Porreca, Milan 1971, are still valuable.

The best guides for research purposes are the catalogues of the famous chess libraries, in particular *Bibliotheca Van Der Linde – Niemeijeriana: A Catalogue of the Chess Collection in the Royal Library, The Hague*, The Hague 1955, and *The Cleveland Public Library, John G. White Department, Catalog of the Chess Collection*, 2 vols., Boston 1964. See also D.A. Betts, *Chess: an annotated bibliography of works published in the English Language 1850–1968*, Boston 1974. H.J.R. Murray, *A History of Board-Games Other Than Chess*, Oxford 1952, is valuable for comparative purposes. Elliott M. Avedon and Brian Sutton-Smith, *The Study of Games*, New York 1971, though a variable collection, includes useful bibliographies of anthropological materials. But Jacques Dextreit and Norbert Engel, *Jeu d'Echecs et sciences humaines*, Paris 1981, is now the best bibliography on chess and psychology, education, sociology, and kindred disciplines.

Specific studies of chess and psychology include W.R. Hartston and P.C. Wason, *The Psychology of Chess*, 1983, which is a lucid survey. Earlier books on this subject have usually adopted a very partial approach, for instance N. Krogius, *The Psychology in Chess*, New York 1976, concentrates on practical training for players; Reuben Fine, *The Psychology of the Chess Player*, New York 1967 (first published 1956), is largely taken up with psycho-analytical vignettes of leading masters. But the major empirical study of how chess players think is A.D. de Groot, *Thought and Choice in Chess*, The Hague 1965, first published in Dutch in 1946. In the growing list of works on chess and computers, two items stand out for their historical interest: Claude Shannon, 'A Chess Playing Machine', *Scientific American*, 1950, widely regarded as the seminal article which initiated modern work on chess programs, and M.M. Botvinnik, *Achieving the Aim*, 1981, which recounts the ex-world champion's interest in chess computers after his retirement from active play. See also D. Levy, *Chess and Computers*, 1976; A. Bell, *The Machine Plays Chess*, 1978.

On the fringes of chess history there are a number of anthologies and impressionistic studies of chess and culture. See for instance G.

Abrahams, *Not Only Chess*, 1974, and Alexander Cockburn, *Idle Passion: Chess and the Dance of Death*, New York 1974. *Chess Pieces*, ed. N. Knight, 1949, and *King, Queen and Knight*, ed. N. Knight and W. Guy, 1975, are both agreeable anthologies, though uncritically edited. *Oxford Encyclopedia of Chess Games*, vol. 1, 1485–1866, ed. D. Levy and K. O'Connell, Oxford 1981, (only one volume published), is a complete collection of early recorded games. The historical circumstances in which the games were played or composed is not discussed. C.H.O'D Alexander, *A Book of Chess*, 1973, is a varied and engaging introduction to the game. See also *Chess in Poetry*, ed. A. Waterman, 1981; and *The Oxford Companion to Chess*, ed. D. Hooper and K. Whyld, 1984.

Books about chess pieces provide interesting insights into the game, though they are sometimes no more than collectors' guides. F. Lanier Graham, *Chess Sets*, 1968, is lucid and intelligent. Hans and Siegfried Wichmann, *Chess, the story of chesspieces from ancient to modern times*, 1964, is an impressive collection of material, but the general introduction is disappointing. Donald M. Liddell, *Chessmen*, New York 1937, is now a little out of date though reprinted in 1976.

1 Origins in the East

Murray, *History of Chess*, is a thorough guide to all the material collected by nineteenth-century scholarship. Earlier stages in his research are shown in some of his articles: 'The Ta'biyat and Other Battle Arrays', *British Chess Magazine*, 1900, pp. 169–76; 'Modern Discoveries in Chess History', *ibid.*, pp. 429–35: 'The Oldest Recorded Games of Chess. A Discovery', *ibid.*, 1903, pp. 441–9.

For more recent controversies see the following articles: P. Thieme, 'Chess and Backgammon in Sanskrit Literature', in *Indological Studies*, ed. E. Bender, New Haven 1962; A.S.M. Dickins, 'Did Chess Originate in China?', *British Chess Magazine*, 1973, pp. 163–5, and subsequent correspondence, *ibid.*, pp. 186–8, 254, 292–8; P. Bidev, 'Did Chess Originate in China?', *ibid.*, 1978, pp. 295–8; I.M. Linder, 'The Mystery of the Origin of Chess', *Shakhmatny v SSSR*, 1975. R. Wieber, *Das Schachspiel in der Arabischen Literatur von den Anfangen*, Walldorf 1972, is the most important work on Arabic sources since Murray. His conclusions are summarized in, 'Aufkommen, Weg und Verbreitung des Schachspiels in der arabisch – islamischen Welt,' *Schachwissenschaftliche Forschungen*, 1974, pp. 94–101. See also P. Bidev, 'Geschichte der Entdeckung des Schach im magischen Quadrat', *ibid.*, 1975, pp. 120–31; I.M. Linder, 'Schach und Archäologie', *ibid.*, pp. 142–6.

The following provide useful background and guides to further reading. For Islam: D.N. Dunlop, *Arab Civilization to* AD *1500*, 1971;

BIBLIOGRAPHY

Norman Daniel, *The Arabs and Mediaeval Europe*, 1975. For Persia: *The Cambridge History of Iran*, vol. 6, 'The Period from the Arab Invasion to the Saljuqs', ed. R.N. Frye, Cambridge 1975; J. Rypka, *History of Iranian Literature*, Dordrecht 1968. For India: *A Cultural History of India*, ed. A.L. Basham, Oxford 1975; and the same author's *The Wonder That Was India*, 1967. For China: Joseph Needham, *Science and Civilization in China*, Cambridge 1954 onwards; there is an abridged version of the first two volumes by Colin A. Ronan, *The Shorter Science and Civilization in China*, vol. 1, Cambridge 1978.

2 The symbolic game of the Middle Ages

A considerable selection of the documentary sources for medieval chess is summarized or quoted in Murray, *History of Chess*. Consultation of the original manuscripts has almost always confirmed the accuracy of Murray's work, but since his time some new sources have become available and historical understanding of medieval society has been much advanced.

There are modern editions of a few works of medieval chess, notably the Castilian manuscript of 1283, and a number of versions of Jacobus de Cessolis. *Alfonso el Sabio: Libros de Acedrex Dados e Tablas*, ed. Arnald Steiger, Geneva and Zurich 1941 (the original Spanish text appears with a German translation). *Jacobus de Cessolis*, ed. Ernst Köpke, 'Mittheilungen aus den Handschriften der Ritter-Akademie zu Brandenburg', Brandenburg 1879 (the Latin text); *Das Schachzabelbuch Kunrats von Ammenhausen*, ed. F. Vetter, Frauenfeld 1892 (the German translation of 1337, with extracts from other versions); *Das Schachzabelbuch des Jacobus de Cessolis*, ed. G.F. Schmidt, Berlin 1961 (the German prose translation); *Caxton's Game and Playe of the Chesse, 1474. A Verbatim Reprint of the First Edition*, ed. W.E.A. Axon, 1883, recently re-issued by the *British Chess Magazine*.

Other studies of aspects of medieval chess include: Helena M. Gamer, 'The Earliest Evidence of Chess in Western Literature: The Einsiedeln Verses', *Speculum*, 1954, pp. 740–4; Lynn Thorndike, 'All the World's a Chess-board', *ibid.*, 1931, pp. 461–5; H.J.R. Murray, 'Chess in Western Europe in the Middle Ages', *British Chess Magazine*, 1950, pp. 80–1; A. Chicco, 'The Tractatus Schachorum of the Estense Library Modena', *ibid.*, pp. 82–5. On Viking chess and chess on the fringes of Europe: H.J.R. Murray, 'Chess in Central and Northern Asia', *ibid.*, 1904, pp. 181–3; 'On the History of Chess in the Russian Empire', *ibid.*, 1907, pp. 1–5, 49–53; Willard Fiske, *Chess in Iceland and in Icelandic Literature*, Florence 1905; O.M. Dalton, 'Early Chessmen of Whale's Bone Excavated in Dorset', *Archaeologia*, 1927, pp. 77–86; Michael Taylor, *The Lewis Chessmen*, 1978.

J.M. Mehl, 'Le Roi de L'Echiquier', *Revue d'Histoire et de Philosophie Religieuses*, 1978, pp. 145–61, is an indication of recent research on the symbolism of chess in the Middle Ages. On Jacobus de Cessolis and his chess book see: Thomas Kaeppeli, 'Pour la Biographie de Jacques de Cessole', *Archivum Fratrum Praedicatorum*, 1960, pp. 149–62; C. Knowles, 'Caxton and His Two French Sources', *Modern Language Review*, 1954, pp. 417–23; J. Rychner, 'Les Traductions Françaises de Jacques de Cessoles', in *Receuil de travaux offert à M. Clovis Brunel*, Paris 1955, pp. 64–71; F. Lecoy, 'Guillaume de Saint-André et son Jeu des Echecs Moralisés', *Romania*, 1942, pp. 491–503; George D. Painter, *William Caxton*, 1976, pp. 64–71. See also H.J.R. Murray, 'Lydgate's References to Chess', *British Chess Magazine*, 1905, pp. 213–8; F. Lecoy, 'Le Jeu des Echecs d'Engreban d'Arras', *Mélanges offerts à Ernest Hoepffner*, Paris 1949, pp. 307–12; L.F. Flutre, 'La partie d'échecs de Dieudonné de Hongrie,' *Mélanges offerts à Rita Lejeune*, Gembloux 1969, pp. 757–68; P. Jonin, 'La partie d'échecs dans l'épopée médiévale', *Mélanges offerts à Jean Frappier*, Geneva 1970, pp. 483–97. There has been no general study of chess in medieval literature since Murray.

For other board games in the Middle Ages: H.J.R. Murray, 'The Mediaeval Games of Tables', *Medium Aevum*, 1941, pp. 57–69; C.G. Lewin, 'The Philosophers' Game', *Games and Puzzles*, 1973, pp. 14–19; Frank Lewis, 'Gwerin Ffristial a Thawlbwrdd', *Transactions of the Honourable Society of Cymmrodorion*, 1941, pp. 185–205.

Alexander Murray, *Reason and Society in the Middle Ages*, Oxford 1978, contains a wide variety of references to aspects of medieval culture linked with chess.

3 The new chess and its patrons, c. 1475–1650

Among the influential books of this period, there are facsimile or reprint editions of those by Lucena (1496/7), Damiano (1512), Arthur Saul (1614) and 'Gustavus Selenus' (1616). *Repeticion de Amores y Arte de Ajedrez de Luis Ramirez de Lucena*, ed. J.M. de Cossio, Madrid 1953 (this is actually a reprint with facsimiles of the original diagrams); *Damiano Portugese: Libro da Imparare Giocare a Scachi*, 'Homo Ludens', vol. 1, Nieuwkoop 1967; *Arthur Saul: The Famous Game of Chesse-Play*, 'The English Experience', Number 691, Amsterdam and Norwood New Jersey 1974; *Gustavus Selenus: Das Schach- oder König-Spiel*, Edition Olms, Zurich 1978. L. Hoffman, *The Games of Greco*, 1900, is entirely uncritical, except for the bibliography by J.A. Leon, which is excellent.

For critical studies see: A. van der Linde, *Das Schachspiel des XVI. Jahrhunderts*, Berlin 1874; J.A. Leon, 'Notes on a recently-discovered Polerio Ms.', *British Chess Magazine*, 1894, pp. 317–36; 'The Old Masters of Modern Chess', *ibid.*, pp. 393–7 (Lopez), 429–37 (Damiano),

1895, pp. 1–8 (Salvio), 9–12 (Greco): Ross Pinsent, 'The Various Editions of Damiano', *ibid.*, pp. 229–39, 285, 423–7; Ross Pinsent, 'Damiano and Carreras', *ibid.*, 1907, pp. 98–105; H.J.R. Murray, 'An Early Work of Modern Chess', *ibid.*, 1909, pp. 283–7; Ross Pinsent, 'Some Notes on the Ruy Lopez Article', *ibid.*, 1895, pp. 155–60; John G. White, *Greco and His Manuscripts*, Philadelphia 1919. Also the recent work of F.C. Görschen, 'Entstehung und Ursprung des neuen Schachs', *Schach-Echo*, 1975, pp. 74–6, 91–2, 105–8; 'Sprache und Bedeutung der Göttinger Schach-handschrift', *Schachwissenschaftliche Forschungen*, 1975, pp. 163–70.

Work on chess and literature in this period includes M.A. Di Cesare's research on Vida's chess poem, which has shown that four (rather than two) variant versions survive. Mario A. Di Cesare, *The Game of Chess: Marco Girolamo Vida's Scacchia Ludus*, Nieuwkoop 1974; 'Vida's Game of Chess: A Bibliography', *Bulletin of the New York Public Library*, 1964, pp. 493–516. Thomas Middleton's play, *A Game at Chess* of 1624, is edited by J.W. Harper in the 'New Mermaid' Series, 1966. J.R. Moore, 'The Contemporary Significance of Middleton's *Game at Chesse*', *Proceedings of the Modern Languages Association (P.M.L.A.)*, 1935, pp. 761–8 discusses the chess content of the play, though not without some inaccuracies. Florence Weinberg, 'Chess as a Literary Idea in Colonna's Hypnerotomachia and in Rabelais' Cinquiesme Livre', *Romance Review*, 1979, pp. 321–35, is another literary study.

Among more general books D. Brailsford, *Sport and Society: Elizabeth to Anne*, 1969, is a useful guide though its interpretations are sometimes unconvincing. Marcia Vale, *The Gentleman's Recreations: Accomplishments and pastimes of the English gentleman 1580–1630*, Cambridge 1977, covers a more limited area impressively.

4 The game of the intellectuals 1650–1800

The most important books of this period (those of Greco, Stamma and Philidor) appeared in many editions, most of which are cited in the text. There are no critical modern editions of any of them, though Edition Olms of Zurich have reprinted some other eighteenth-century works: Giambattista Lolli, *Osservazioni teorico-practiche sopra il Giuoco degli Scacchi* of 1763; Moses Hirschel, *Das Schach des Herrn Gioachino Greco Calabrois und die Schachspiel- Geheimnisse des Arabers Philipp Stamma*, a compilation of 1784. Also a minor Philidor edition, the German *Die Kunst im Schachspiel ein Meister zu werden* of 1754.

Chess writers of the eighteenth century are discussed in outline in J.A. Leon, 'The Old Masters of Modern Chess', *British Chess Magazine*, 1895, pp. 149–55 (Bertin), 245–52 (Stamma), 453–60 and 501–8 (Philidor), 1896, pp. 1–7 (del Rio and Lolli), 217–9 (Cozio). A number of minor texts are discussed in articles by H.J.R. Murray: 'M. Caze's MS. on the King's Gambits', *British Chess Magaine*, 1914, pp. 129–32; 'English Chess in the Early Eighteenth Century', *ibid.*, 1903, pp. 1–2; 'Some Fresh Light on Cunningham of the Gambit', *ibid.*, 1912, pp. 145–9.

George Allen, *The Life of Philidor*, Philadelphia 1863, has now been effectively superseded by the research of C.M. Carroll, *François-André Danican Philidor: His Life and Dramatic Art*, unpublished Ph.D. thesis, Florida State University, 1960. Carroll's work is accessible in his articles, 'Philidor in London', *British Chess Magazine*, 1961, pp. 11–13, 76–9, 102–4, 152–5; and 'Philidor', in *Die Musik in Geschichte und Gegenwart*, ed. F. Blume, Basle 1962. See also Ludwig Bachmann, *Aus Vergangenen Zeiten*, Band 1 Heft I 'Philidor und seine Zeitgenossen', Berlin 1920; R. Harwell, 'Books, Opera, Chess and the Gout: A Bibliographical Excursion', *Huntington Library Quarterly*, 1969, pp. 1–19; H.J.R. Murray, 'Parsloe's in January and February 1795', *British Chess Magazine*, 1907, pp. 445–9.

On the chess automaton there is C.M. Carroll, *The Great Chess Automaton*, New York 1975. The best thing about the article on this subject by Donald M. Fiene, 'Kempelen's Turk and the Mystery of the Legless Pole', *British Chess Magazine*, 1977, pp. 372–7, 396–404, is its title.

For the origins of serious work on the history of chess see: T. Hyde, *De Ludis Orientalibus*, Oxford 1694; N. Fréret, 'L'origine du jeu des eschecs', *Histoire de l'Académie royale des inscriptions et belles lettres*, vol. 5, Paris 1729, pp. 250–59; Daines Barrington, 'An Historical Disquisition on the Game of Chess', *Archaeologia*, vol. 9, 1787, pp. 14–38. R. Lambe, *The History of Chess*, 1764, is an eccentric but engaging compilation.

Finally two items are worth mentioning, from a great deal of potentially relevant social history: *Le Jeu au XVIIIe Siècle: Colloque d'Aix-en-Provence*, ed. H. Coulet, Aix-en-Provence 1976; J.H. Plumb, *The Commercialisation of Leisure in Eighteenth-Century England* (the Stenton Lecture for 1972 at the University of Reading), Reading 1973, a valuable preliminary synthesis.

5 The beginnings of popularity 1800–1914

In the nineteenth century the number of chess books increased rapidly with the advent of mass printing, and they became steadily more technical. Periodicals and magazines often give a better impression of the game's social appeal, e.g., *Bell's Life in London*, 1835–1873 (a column written by George Walker); *The Illustrated London News*, 1842–1874 (Staunton's Column); *The Chess Player's Chronicle*, three series, 1841–1852, 1853–1856, 1859–1862; *Deutsche Schachzeitung*, from 1846; *Le*

Palamède, 1836–1839 (edited by Labourdonnais), 1842–1847 (edited by Saint-Amant). Among later magazines the most notable are *The Chess Monthly*, 1879–1896, with which Zukertort and Leopold Hoffer were involved; and the *British Chess Magazine*, from 1881.

Books of individual chess tournaments often give clues to how such events were organized. Two of the best from this point of view are: *The Book of the First American Chess Congress: containing the Proceedings of that celebrated Assemblage, held in New York, in the year 1857*, by Daniel Willard Fiske, New York 1859; and *The Hastings Chess Tournament 1895*, ed. Horace F. Cheshire, 1896. Among contemporary memoirs F.M. Edge, *The Exploits and Triumphs in Europe of Paul Morphy*, New York 1859 (another version published in London 1859 as *Paul Morphy the Chess Champion*) is racy though biased.

Biographies of chess masters tend to concentrate on the games at the expense of the life, but R.D. Keene and R.N. Coles, *Howard Staunton: The English World Chess Champion*, St. Leonard's on Sea 1975, is a very honourable exception. D.N.L. Levy, *Howard Staunton*, Nottingham 1975, is also useful and includes much material relating to the Staunton-Morphy contretemps. The standard biography of Morphy is now David Lawson, *Paul Morphy: The Pride and Sorrow of Chess*, New York 1976; but Morphy's mental problems have always attracted attention. Ernest Jones, 'The Problem of Paul Morphy: A Contribution to the Psychology of Chess', *Essays in Applied Psycho-Analysis*, vol. I, 1951, pp. 165–96, first published in the *International Journal of Psycho-Analysis* in 1931, was the starting point for a great deal of speculative writing, much of it corrected by Lawson. There are a number of articles on minor figures by H.J.R. Murray: 'William Lewis', *British Chess Magazine*, 1906, pp. 8–12, 49–53; 'George Walker', *ibid.*, pp. 189–94; 'The Berlin Pleiades', *ibid.*, 1907, pp. 407–14. See also R.N. Coles, 'An Unknown Manuscript Revealed', *British Chess Magazine*, 1981, pp. 69–71 (about Augustus Mongredien, president of the London chess club); J. Levy, 'Women in Chess: mid-nineteenth to early twentieth century', *ibid.*, pp. 402–5; J. Edmund Peckover, 'The Ajeeb Exhibit', *ibid.*, 1979, pp. 299–303 (on the revived chess automaton).

Among more general books P.W. Sergeant, *A Century of British Chess*, 1936, is a mine of useful information. Ralph K. Hagedorn, *Benjamin Franklin and Chess in Early America*, Philadelphia 1958, is thin but has a useful bibliography. P. Bailey, *Leisure and Class in Victorian England*, 1978, is a guide to a great deal of comparative evidence. For reference purposes there are the valuable collections of tournament and match results by P. Feenstra Kuiper, *Hundert Jahre Schachturniere 1851–1950*, Amsterdam 1964, and *Hundert Jahre Schachzweikämpfe 1851–1950*, Amsterdam 1967. Jeremy Gaige, *Chess Tournament Crosstables*, vol. I

(1851–1900), Philadelphia 1969, vol. 2 (1901–1910), Philadelphia 1971, gives even more results of chess events, but hardly any other information about them. Finally, Bernard P. Kiernan, *A History of International Master Chess 1851–1914*, unpublished Ph.D. thesis, The American University Washington D.C., 1957, is a thorough narrative account.

6 The sedentary sport 1914–1980

The sheer volume of writing about chess in the twentieth century has become almost overwhelming. The reference books of P. Feenstra Kuiper (already referred to) cover the period down to 1950. See also Jeremy Gaige, *Chess Tournament Crosstables*, vol. 3 (1911–1920), Philadelphia 1972, vol. 4 (1921–1930), Philadelphia 1974. For other events, and particularly those since 1950, B. Kazic, *International Championship Chess: a complete record of FIDE events*, 1974; and S. Gligoric, *The World Chess Championship*, 1972, are similarly useful. A. Elo, *The Rating of Chessplayers, Past and Present*, 1978, collects a mass of information and analyses the persistent debate about the relative strengths of chess players from different periods. Otherwise, information can be found easily in the back numbers of a whole range of chess magazines, including the English ones: *Chess* (since 1935) and the *British Chess Magazine*.

For those who can follow game scores there are 'career biographies' of most important twentieth-century masters. One which gives a great deal of contextual information, including Nimzowitsch's own autobiographical sketch, is Raymond Keene, *Aron Nimzowitsch: A Reappraisal*, 1974. J. Hannak, *Emanuel Lasker, the life of a chess master*, trans. Heinrich Fraenkel, 1959, is also an interesting biography, though somewhat marred by the author's adulation of his subject. Frank Brady, *Bobby Fischer*, New York 1965, second (and much revised) edition New York 1973, is a sympathetic account of the most extraordinary career in modern chess. Harold C. Schonberg, *Grandmasters of Chess*, 1974, tackles no difficult issues but is a lively series of biographical sketches, terminating with Fischer. There are dozens of similar works.

The best source for the ideology of the chess movement in Russia is A. Kotov and M. Yudovich, *The Soviet School of Chess*, Moscow 1958. This is actually the third edition of the book (though the first in English), and much changed from its original text of 1951. D.J. Richards, *Soviet Chess*, Oxford 1965, is an excellent monograph. J. Riordan, *Sport in Soviet Society*, Cambridge 1977, is a useful background study. Much of this information is conveniently summarized in *The Cambridge Encyclopedia of Russia and the Soviet Union*, Cambridge 1982: articles on sporting organizations by J. Riordan and on chess by D.J. Richards. See also John Barber, 'The Establishment of Intellectual Orthodoxy in the U.S.S.R.

1928–1934', *Past and Present*, 1979, pp. 141–64, and references there given.

Otherwise, there are revealing autobiographies and memoirs by a number of Soviet masters. See for instance Efim Geller's remarks on the post-war period in *Grandmaster Geller at the Chessboard*, trans. B. Cafferty, Nottingham 1969; and M.M. Botvinnik, *Achieving the Aim*, 1981 (original Russian edition 1978), the autobiography of the leading figure in the Soviet chess movement from the 1930s to the 1960s. These can be contrasted with the 'dissident' memoirs of Viktor Korchnoi, *Chess is My Life*, 1977; and L. Pachman, *Checkmate in Prague*, 1975 (Pachman is a Czech grandmaster who was imprisoned and expelled from his country after 1968). Finally, A. Kotov, *Alexander Alekhine*, 1975, trans. K.P. Neat, from the Russian edition of 1973, is a good example of 'revisionism' in chess history.

There is no really thorough survey of the place of chess in twentieth-century art and literature. Alexander Cockburn, *Idle Passion: Chess and the Dance of Death*, New York 1974, serves as an introduction, but the best account is now in Jacques Dextreit and Norbert Engel, *Jeu d'Echecs et sciences humaines*, Paris 1981. The best known 'chess novels' are Vladimir Nabokov, *The Defence* (first published in Russian in 1930); Stefan Zweig, *Schachnovelle*, Stockholm 1943 (trans. as *The Royal Game*, 1944); and the celebrated chess game in Samuel Beckett, *Murphy*, 1938, complete with parodies of chess annotation. There are many other works which contain chess themes or chess episodes. Among artists Marcel Duchamp stands out as the only major figure who played chess seriously (he took part in several tournaments and represented France in the Olympiads of 1928, 1930, 1931 and 1933). Critical studies of Duchamp take account of his absorption in chess, and mention the book on chess endgame studies he wrote with V. Halberstadt, *L'opposition et les cases conjuguées sont réconciliées*, published in 1932. See especially F. Le Lionnais, 'Marcel Duchamp as a chess player and one or two related matters', *Studio International*, 1975, pp. 23–5. Others, like Man Ray and Max Ernst, shared this interest in chess, but without taking it so seriously. There is much scope here for further research by art historians and critics.

Appendix One: Chess books and chess notation

Little can be added to Murray, *History of Chess*, on the technical evolution of the game and its rules up to the eighteenth century, though many of his conclusions about chess style ('schools of play') and the appeal of the game at different periods are open to question. See however H. Suwe, 'Die historische Entwicklung der Rochade', *Schachwissenschaftliche Forschungen*, 1975, on the castling move. W. Glinski, *The First Theories of*

Hexagonal Chess, 1974, is a guide to the best-known (if not yet popular) contemporary chess variant, by its inventor.

Appendix Two: A note on chess problems

Almost all modern histories of chess problems closely follow the account of H. Weenink, *The Chess Problem*, Stroud 1926 (a much expanded version of a book first published in Dutch in 1921). The more complex and eclectic developments of the last fifty years are harder to describe, but for a general guide see: M. Lipton, R.C.O. Matthews and J.M. Rice, *Chess Problems: Introduction to an Art*, 1963; J.M. Rice, *An ABC of Chess Problems*, 1970. The tendency of some problemists to invent not merely new tasks, as in the Helpmate (in which Black and White co-operate to bring about a mating position) but new pieces, and so break through the artistic constraints of chess rules, is surveyed in A.S.M. Dickins, *A Guide to Fairy Chess*, 1967.

References

Introduction (pages 11–18)

1 Johan Huizinga, *Homo Ludens: A Study of the Play Element in Culture*, 1949. The book was first published in Dutch
2 Stewart Culin, 'Chess and Playing Cards', *Annual Report of the U.S. National Museum*, Washington 1898, pp. 665–942. For a survey and bibliography of Culin's work see E.M. Aveden, and B. Sutton-Smith, *The Study of Games*, New York 1971, Chapter 3
3 Joseph Needham, *Science and Civilization in China*, Vol. 4, Part I, Cambridge 1962, pp. 314–34
4 *Wittgenstein and the Vienna Circle*, ed. B. McGuinness, Oxford 1979, p. 104. A. Kenny, *Wittgenstein*, 1973, pursues parallels between chess and Wittgenstein's thought further than most commentators
5 P. Stamma, *The Noble Game of Chess*, 1745, pp. iii–iv
6 A.D. Philidor, *L'Analyze des Echecs*, 1749, pp. xii–xiii. The quotation is taken from the first English edition, *Chess Analysed*, 1750, which is a literal translation of the French
7 A.D. Philidor, *Analysis of the Game of Chess*, 'A New Edition Greatly Enlarged', 1777, Preface
8 Daines Barrington, 'An Historical Disquisition on the Game of Chess', *Archaeologia*, Vol. IX, 1787, p. 19
9 Royal Asiatic Society, Persian Ms., Codrington 211. H.J.R. Murray, *A History of Chess*, Oxford 1913, p. 177, gives a description of the manuscript. H. Golombek, *A History of Chess*, 1976, pp. 31, 36, 53, reproduces three miniatures from it
10 H.J.R. Murray, 'Modern Discoveries in Chess History', *British Chess Magazine*, 1900, pp. 429–30
11 Most, though not all, of these articles are listed in E. Meissenburg, 'H.J.R. Murray (1868–1955): bibliography of a chess historian', *British Chess Magazine*, 1980, pp. 249–52. K.M.E. Murray, *Caught in the Web of Words*, 1977, is a sensitive family history, a biography of H.J.R. Murray's father written by his own daughter

REFERENCES

1 Origins in the East (pages 19–38)

1 H.J.R. Murray, *A History of Chess*, Oxford 1913, p. 194

2 The following passages have been translated by Murray, *History of Chess*, pp. 156–7; and by Reuben Levy, *The Epic of the Kings*, 1967, pp. 327–9. I have made use of both versions

3 The common features of these myths have also been pointed out in non-historical studies like those of psycho-analysts. See J. Dextreit and N. Engel *Jeu d' Echecs et sciences humaines*, Paris 1981, pp. 44–7

4 P. Thieme, 'Chess and Backgammon in Sanskrit Literature', in *Indological Studies*, ed. E. Bender, New Haven 1962, tried to revive the idea that 'chess' can be traced back at least to texts of Patanjali, in the second century BC. But his argument, which relies on the assumption that any reference to a game of skill (however vague or indefinite) must be a reference to chess, is not convincing.

5 Even Thieme, *op. cit.*, does not quote this as a chess reference

6 See especially Murray, *History of Chess*, pp. 45–77. The idea that the primitive chess was a four-handed game is often still assumed by historians of India, e.g. A.L. Basham, *The Wonder that was India*, 1954 (1971 ed., p. 210).

7 Murray, *History of Chess*, pp. 47–8

8 *Ibid.*, pp. 32–42, 61–3

9 I.M. Linder, 'The Mystery of the Origin of Chess', *Shakhmatny v SSSR*, 1975. This is one of a series of articles by Linder in the leading Russian chess magazine. Pictures of the Uzkekistan finds were published in *British Chess Magazine*, 1973, p. 254, and H. Golombek, *A History of Chess*, 1976, p. 13

10 The evidence is summarized in A. Chicco and G. Porreca, *Dizionario Enciclopedico degli Scacchi*, Milan 1971, pp. 447–8, with an illustration. The authors do not query the archaeological dating

11 Joseph Needham, *Science and Civilization in China*, Vol. 4, Part I, Cambridge 1962, pp. 314–34. Various attempts have been made to rewrite the early history of chess along these lines: A.S.M. Dickins, 'Did Chess Originate in China?', *British Chess Magazine*, 1973, pp. 163–5, and subsequent correspondence, *ibid.*, pp. 186–8, 254, 292–8. See also P. Bidev, 'Did Chess Originate in China?', *ibid.*, 1978, pp. 295–8, with copious references, mostly to the author's other works. But Linder, 'Mystery of the Origin of Chess', is sceptical about these ideas. He also gives references to the Russian writer N.M. Rudin, whose theories about chess and numerical symbolism he finds equally unconvincing.

12 Needham, *Science and Civilization*, p. 320

13 *Ibid.*, p. 324

14 Stewart Culin, 'Chess and Playing Cards', *Annual Report of the U.S. National Museum*, Washington 1898, p. 858

15 Needham, *Science and Civilization*, p. 325

2 The symbolic game of the Middle Ages (pages 39–70)

1 H.J.R. Murray, *A History of Chess*, Oxford 1913, p. 402

2 *Ibid.*, pp. 161–8

3 *Ibid.*, p. 166. *The Alexiad of the Princess Anna Comnena*, trans. E.A.S. Dawes, 1928, p. 312

4 Murray, *History of Chess*, pp. 411, 497–9, 512–4. Helena M. Gamer, 'The Earliest Evidence of Chess in Western Literature: The Einsiedeln Verses', *Speculum*, 1954, pp. 740–44

5 Murray, *History of Chess*, p. 403

6 *Ibid.*, pp. 425–6

7 Michael Taylor, *The Lewis Chessmen*, 1978, p. 15

8 A. Elo put forward this thesis in a paper given to the conference on Chess and Humanities, University of Nebraska 1978. The idea that the Jewish communities of Poland and elsewhere were largely made up of 'Khazars', famously propounded by Arthur Koestler, *The Thirteenth Tribe*, 1976, is itself open to question

9 Murray, *History of Chess*, p. 394

10 H.J.R. Murray, 'The Mediaeval Games of Tables', *Medium Aevum*, 1941, pp. 57–69

11 Murray, *History of Chess*, pp. 445–6. H.J.R. Murray, *A History of Board-Games other than Chess*, Oxford 1952

12 See *Dialogus de Scaccario*, ed. and trans. Charles Johnson, 1950, pp. 6–7. I have altered one or two phrases

13 *The Disciplina Clericalis of Petrus Alfonsi*, ed. and trans. E. Hermes, 1977, p. 115 and n.63

14 *The London Eyre of 1276*, ed. Martin Weinbaum, London Record Society, 1976, pp. 14–15, 42

15 *Paston Letters and Papers of the Fifteenth Century*, ed. N. Davis, Part I, 1971, p. 257

16 Peter Dronke, *Poetic Individuality in the Middle Ages*, Oxford 1970, pp. 42–4, discusses the chess passage in Ruodlieb. See also Murray, *History of Chess*, pp. 411–6

17 Murray, *History of Chess*, p. 428

18 G.R. Owst, *Literature and Pulpit in Medieval England*, Second ed. 1961, p. 363

19 See Murray, *History of Chess*, pp. 408–9, 414–5

20 *The English Works of Wyclif*, ed. F.D. Matthew, Early English Text Society, Revised ed. 1902, p. 152. It has never been demonstrated conclusively that the 'English Works' were by Wyclif, and probably they were written by disciples on the basis of his Latin works or known opinions. See *Selections from English Wycliffite Writings*, ed. A. Hudson, Cambridge 1978. Introduction

21 Murray, *History of Chess*, pp. 750–51. I have also consulted a number of modern translations

22 *The Works of Geoffrey Chaucer*, ed. F.N. Robinson, Oxford 1966, pp. 273–4, 776

23 Some critics have tended to make a sharp rather than a relative distinction between symbolism and allegory. See for instance C.S. Lewis, *The Allegory of Love*, 1936, pp. 44–7. But it is increasingly recognized that in practice they blurred together and overlapped. Dronke, *Poetic Individuality*, pp. 193–201, illustrates this approach

24 Murray, *History of Chess*, pp. 530–34, 559–61. Lynn Thorndike, 'All the World's a Chess-board', *Speculum*, 1931, pp. 461–5, prints a manuscript unknown to Murray and revises some of his conclusions

25 Murray, *History of Chess*, pp. 550–54, 561–3. *Gesta Romanorum*, ed. S.J.H. Herrtage, Early English Text Society, 1879, pp. 70–72

26 A. Van der Linde, *Geschichte und Litteratur des Schachspiels*, Vol. 1, Berlin 1874, Beilagen, pp. 34–112

27 *Das Schachzabelbuch des Jacobus de Cessolis* 'in mittelhochdeutscher Prosa-Ubersetzung,' ed. G.F. Schmidt, Berlin 1961

28 All these documents were printed in Thomas Kaeppeli, 'Pour la Biographie de Jacques de Cessole', *Archivum Fratrum Praedicatorum*, 1960, pp. 149–62. They make the earlier dating of the *Liber de Moribus* to *c.* 1259–1273 unlikely, though it is accepted by J.M. Mehl, 'Le Roi de L'Echiquier', *Revue d' Histoire et de Philosophie Religieuses*, 1978, pp. 145–61

29 See especially Jill Mann, *Chaucer and Medieval Estates Satire*, Cambridge 1973

30 *Thomas Hoccleve's Regement of Princes*, ed. F.J. Furnivall, Early English Text Society, 1897, p. 77. The 'liber de ludo Scaccorum' in a list of books owned by Henry V in 1422 is probably also de Cessolis. See K.B. McFarlane, *Lancastrian Kings and Lollard Knights*, Oxford 1972, p. 235

31 W. Blades, *William Caxton*, Vol. I, 1861, pp. 277–9. Davis, *Paston Letters*, Part I, 1971, pp. 516–8

32 Sir Thomas Elyot, *The Book named the Governor*, Everyman series, 1962, p.91

3 The new chess and its patrons, c. 1475–1650 (pages 71–93)

1 Juan Remirez de Lucena was a scholar and diplomat, member of a wealthy family of *conversos*, or descendants of Jewish converts. Despite his successful career and royal patronage, some of his works were condemned by the Spanish Inquisition towards the end of his life. See J.N. Hillgarth, *The Spanish Kingdoms 1250–1516*, Vol. 2, Oxford 1978, pp. 153, 454–5

2 Luis de Lucena, *Repeticion de Amores: E arte de axedrez*, Salamanca 1496–1497. See the modern edition by J.M. de Cossio, Madrid 1953, p. 73

3 F.C. Görschen, 'Entstehung and Ursprung des neuen Schachs,' *Schach-Echo*, 1975, pp. 74–6, 91–2, 105–8; 'Sprache und Bedeutung der Göttinger Schachhandschrift', *Schachwissenschaftliche Forschungen*, 1975, pp. 163–70

4 H.J.R. Murray, *A History of Chess*, Oxford 1913, p. 782

5 See *Catalogue of Books printed in the XVth Century now in the British Museum*, Vol. X (Spain and Portugal), 1971, p. xxv, and references

6 Murray, *History of Chess*, p. 778

7 Baldesar Castiglione, *The Book of the Courtier*, ed. and trans. G. Bull, 1967, pp. 140, 165

8 Jacob Ornstein, *Luis de Lucena, Repeticion de Amores*, University of North Carolina Studies in the Romance Languages and Literatures 23, Chapel Hill, 1954, p. 1

9 Hans and Siegfried Wichmann, *Chess, The story of chesspieces from ancient to modern times*, 1964, p. 46. The translator of the original German edition is primarily responsible for the prose

10 K.M. Colby, 'Gentlemen, the Queen!', *Psychoanalytic Review*, 1953, pp. 144–8, proposes Catherine Sforza (1462–1507), having previously argued on psychoanalytic grounds that the inventor of the new chess was probably a weak man fascinated by female power. This is not a historical argument

11 Castiglione, *Book of the Courtier*, p. 140

12 See James's collected works: *The Workes of the Most High and Mightie Prince, James*, 1616, pp. 186–7

13 Robert Burton, *The Anatomy of Melancholy*, Everyman Series, 1932, Vol. II, p. 83

14 Murray, *History of Chess*, p. 442

15 Arthur Saul, *The Famous Game of Chesse-Play*, 1614, Title Page and Dedication. There is a facsimile reprint in the series 'The English Experience', Amsterdam and Norwood, New Jersey, 1974

16 Thomas Wilcox, *A glasse for gamesters*, 1581. Samuel Clarke, *The lives of thirty-two English divines*, 1677, p. 23. *The Pleasaunt and wittie Playe of the Cheasts renewed*, 1562, (usually catalogued under the name of James Rowbothum), 'To the reader'

17 Saul, *Famous Game*, Chapter 1

18 Miguel de Cervantes, *The Adventures of Don Quixote*, ed. and trans. J.M. Cohen, 1950, p. 539. The Guicciardini manuscript is described in A. van der Linde, *Geschichte* Vol. 1, Berlin 1874, p. 32. A nineteenth-century transcript of the manuscript is in the John G. White Library of Cleveland, Ohio

19 Arthur Saul, *The Famous Game of Chesse-Play*, 1618, 'Now augmented of many material things formerly wanting ... By Jo. Barbier,' Chapter 1. Murray was mistaken in his belief that the Barbier revisions were not added until the edition of 1640: *History of Chess*, pp. 832, 841

20 Mario A. Di Cesare, *The Game of Chess, Marco Girolamo Vida's Scacchia Ludus*, Nieuwkoop 1974

21 Mario A. Di Cesare, 'Vida's Game of Chess: A Bibliography', *Bulletin of the New York Public Library*, 1964, pp. 493–516. See also the additions in the same author's 'Erasmus Pacificator and Girolamo Vida', *Moreana*, 1967, pp. 25–42

22 Johan Huizinga, *The Waning of the Middle Ages*, 1955, p. 204. The book was first published in Dutch in 1919.

4 The game of the intellectuals 1650–1800 (pages 95–123)

1 Pierre Bayle, *Dictionnaire Historique et Critique*, Rotterdam 1697. The quotation is taken from *General Dictionary Historical and Critical*, 1734–1741, which is a literal translation of the French, in these articles

2 H.J.R. Murray, *A History of Chess*, Oxford 1913, pp. 392–3, 483–5, and references

3 H.J.R. Murray, 'M. Caze's MS. on the King's Gambits', *British Chess Magazine*, 1914, pp. 129–32; and the shorter account in *History of Chess*, pp. 844–5. The manuscript is now in the John G. White Library of Cleveland, Ohio

4 G.W. Leibniz, *Opera Omnia*, ed. L. Dutens, Vol. VI, Geneva 1768, pp. 255, 271, 278

5 See *Historical Memoirs of the Duc de Saint-Simon*, ed. and trans. Lucy Norton, 1968, Vol. 1, p. 135, Vol. 2, pp. 214–5, 251

6 Charles Cotton, *The Compleat Gamester*, 1674. See the modern edition by C.H. Hartmann, *Games and Gamesters of the Restoration*, 1930, p. 24

7 Printed in W.B. Boulton, *The History of White's*, Vol. II, 1892, pp. 23, 32

8 *Encyclopédie ou Dictionnaire Raisonné des Sciences, des Arts et des Métiers*, Vol. V, Paris 1755, p. 247

9 *Ibid.*, pp. 247–8

10 Denis Diderot, *Le Neveu de Rameau*. Trans. L.W. Tancock, *Rameau's Nephew and D'Alembert's Dream*, 1966, p. 33

11 Quoted in R. Twiss, *Miscellanies*, Vol. II, 1805, p. 48

12 A.D. Philidor, *L'Analyze des Echecs*, 1749, pp. xv–xvi. Quoted from the English of *Chess Analysed*, 1750

13 Jean-Jacques Rousseau, *Confessions*. Trans. J.M. Cohen, *The Confessions of Jean-Jacques Rousseau*, 1953, p. 271

14 See Bryant Lillywhite, *London Coffee Houses*, 1963, p. 530

15 P. Stamma, *Essai sur le Jeu des Echecs*, Paris 1737, *Préface*. Subsequent quotations are also taken from this preface, and from the dedication to Harrington

16 For an outline of Stamma's official appointment see *Office Holders in Modern Britain*, Vol. 2, ed. J.C. Sainty, 1973, pp. 48, 106

17 R. Twiss, *Chess*, Vol. I, 1787, pp. 149–71

18 *Ibid.*, p. 155

19 J. Biou, 'La Révolution Philidorienne,' in *Le Jeu au XVIIIe Siècle: Colloque d'Aix-en-Provence*, ed. H. Coulet, Aix-en-Provence 1976, pp. 61–7

20 Philidor, *Analyze* 1749, p.xviii. Quoted from the English of *Chess Analysed*, 1750

21 Murray, *History of Chess*, p. 866

22 Rousseau, *Confessions*, p. 211. See also I. Grünberg, 'Rousseau Joueur D'Echecs', *Annales de la Société J.J. Rousseau*, 1907, pp. 157–74; H.J.R. Murray, 'Rousseau and Chess', *British Chess Magazine*, 1908, pp. 329–31

23 Translated from pp. 7–8. Though inscribed 'Philadephie, chez J. Johnson', this edition was published in Europe, probably in the Low Countries, for the American market. See R.K. Hagedorn, *Benjamin Franklin and Chess in Early America*, Philadelphia 1958, p.54

24 *The Early Diary of Frances Burney 1768–1778*, ed. A.R. Ellis, Vol.2, 1907, p.123

25 Murray, *History of Chess*, p. 863

26 Denis Diderot, *Correspondance*, ed. G. Roth and J. Varloot, Vol. 15, Paris 1970, pp. 293–5. The passages from Philidor's letters to his wife are quoted by C.M. Carroll in 'Philidor in London', *British Chess Magazine*, 1961, pp. 77, 153

27 Philidor himself published nine of his games, involving eight opponents, as a supplement to his *Analysis of the Game of Chess*, 1790. George Atwood's manuscript note-book supplies an additional sixty-

two games and four more names of opponents in England. The second manuscript contains six games but no other new information

28 Quoted in Hagedorn, *Benjamin Franklin and Chess in Early America*, p. 30

29 Philidor, *Analyze* 1749, p. xix. Quoted from the English of *Chess Analysed*, 1750

30 Murray, *History of Chess*, p. 868

5 The beginnings of popularity 1800–1914 (pages 125–156)

1 F.M. Edge, *The Exploits and Triumphs in Europe of Paul Morphy*, New York 1859 (reprinted 1973), p. 50. A slightly different version was published in London in 1859, as *Paul Morphy the Chess Champion*

2 Walker's pamphlet, *Chess*, was published in 1837. It is quoted in P.W. Sergeant, *A Century of British Chess*, 1936, p. 41

3 St. Amant's report on his visit to London appeared in the journal *Le Palamède* later in 1836

4 Bryant Lillywhite, *London Coffee Houses*, 1963, p. 482

5 H.J.R. Murray, *A History of Chess*, Oxford 1913, p. 881

6 Quoted in R.D. Keene and R.N. Coles, *Howard Staunton*, 1975, p. 10. Tomlinson's memories were published in the *British Chess Magazine* in 1891

7 Taken from an early number of Staunton's *Chess Player's Chronicle*. See Sergeant, *Century*, p. 51

8 Edge, *Paul Morphy*, p. 28

9 Letter to Charles Tomlinson, 18 June 1858. Published in the *British Chess Magazine*, 1891

10 W.H. Miller, *The Culture of Pleasure*, 1872, p. 64

11 A. Esquiros, *The English at Home*, 1861–1863, Vol. II pp. 52, 63

12 Edge, *Paul Morphy*, p. 24

13 Murray, *History of Chess*, p. 887

14 Edge, *Paul Morphy*, p. 31

15 Keene and Coles, *Howard Staunton*, p. 17

16 Staunton published his reply in the *Illustrated London News*, 3 April 1858

17 Passages quoted in D. Lawson, *Paul Morphy: the pride and sorrow of Chess*, New York 1976, pp. 227, 262–3

18 A. Elo, *The Rating of Chessplayers, past and present*, 1978, pp. 118–26, gives a series of maps showing the birthplaces of master-strength players at various dates. This is a very selective kind of evidence on which to base general conclusions

19 Quoted in the *British Chess Magazine*, 1913, p. 59

20 W. Steinitz, *My advertisement to antisemites in Vienna and elsewhere*, New York 1900. The title is characteristic

21 *British Chess Magazine*, 1914, p. 193
22 Murray, *History of Chess*, p. 890
23 From an article written by Morphy for a New York paper after his return to America in 1859. Quoted in P.M. Sergeant, *Morphy's Games of Chess*, 1915, p. 25
24 Murray, *History of Chess*, p. 889
25 *The Field*, 16 October 1914

6 The sedentary sport 1914–1980 (pages 157–194)

1 P. Feenstra Kuiper, *Hundert Jahre Schachturniere*, Amsterdam 1964, has been used as a guide here. J. Gaige, *Chess Tournament Crosstables*, Vol. 4, 1921–1930, Philadelphia 1974, lists a larger number of minor events of marginal 'international' status
2 P.W. Sergeant, *A Century of British Chess*, 1936, p. 265
3 Harold C. Schonberg, *Grandmasters of Chess*, 1974, p. 149
4 William Winter's 'Memoirs' were edited and published in nine instalments in *Chess*, 1963. This passage appears on p. 112. They were written in the year of his death, 1955
5 *Ibid.*, p. 163
6 Richard Réti, *Modern Ideas in Chess*, 1923, pp. v–vi
7 Raymond Keene, *Aron Nimzowitsch: A Reappraisal*, 1974, pp. 141–3. Some of the same ideas were advanced in R.G. Eales, and A.H. Williams, *Alekhine's Defence*, 1973, p.9
8 A speech by Alekhine reported in the American magazine *Chess Review*, December 1938. See Schonberg, *Grandmasters*, pp. 195–8
9 A.F. Ilyin-Zhenevsky, *'Notes of a Soviet Master'*, Leningrad 1929, pp. 38–9. Translation from D.J. Richards, *Soviet Chess*, Oxford 1965, p. 11
10 *'The International Chess Tournament at Moscow 1925'*, Moscow 1926; Y.G. Rokhlin, *'Chess and Culture'*, Leningrad 1929, pp. 17–18. Translations from Richards, *Soviet Chess*, p. 40
11 F.I. Dus-Khotimirsky, *'Selected Games'*, Moscow 1955, pp. 25–6. Translation from Richards, *Soviet Chess*, p. 21
12 M.S. Kogan, *'History of Chess in Russia'*, Moscow 1927, p. 21. Translation from Richards, *Soviet Chess*, p. 18
13 I.N. Dyakov, N.Y. Petrovksy, and P.A. Rudik, *'Psychology of the Game of Chess'*, Moscow 1926, p. 142. A German edition was published in 1927. For criticism of their findings and methods see Reuben Fine, *The Psychology of the Chess Player*, New York 1967, pp. 2–4, first published in 1956
14 The full texts of the *Pravda* article and the telegram appear in Richards, *Soviet Chess*, pp. 62–5. For the background story see M.M. Botvinnik, *Achieving the Aim*, 1981, p. 60, first published in Russian in 1978

REFERENCES

15 Particularly in M.S. Kogan, '*Chess in the Lives of Russian Writers*', Leningrad 1933. It is, incidentally, a little known fact that after 1885 the president of the British Chess Association was Tennyson, and vice-president Ruskin

16 Quoted in Richards, *Soviet Chess*, p. 25

17 E. Lasker, *Struggle*, New York 1907. The original German version was published simultaneously

18 Richards, *Soviet Chess*, p. 44

19 'Jewish and Aryan chess', *Pariser Zeitung*, 22 and 28 March 1941. An English translation was published in *Chess*, 1941, when details reached England

20 B.M. Kazic, *International Championship Chess: a complete record of FIDE events*, 1974, gives results of most of these events and a list of international title holders. A. Elo, *The Rating of Chessplayers, past and present*, 1978, summarizes the qualification rules and their history

21 Botvinnik, *Achieving the Aim*, pp. 118–9

22 M.M. Botvinnik, '*The Soviet School of Chess*', Moscow 1951, p. 39. Translation in Richards, *Soviet Chess*, p. 142

23 A. Kotov and M. Yudovich, *The Soviet School of Chess*, English edition, Moscow 1958, p. 10

24 A. Kotov, '*Alekhine's Chess Heritage*', Moscow 1953, pp. 35–6. Translation in Richards, *Soviet Chess*, pp. 138–9. Réti, *Modern Ideas*, p. 122. Leopold H. Haimson, 'The Soviet Style of Chess', in *The Study of Culture at a Distance*, ed. Margaret Mead and Rhoda Métraux, Chicago 1953, is a good example of a contemporary western observer trying to make sense of these pronouncements, perhaps not critically enough

25 Alexander Kotov, *Alexander Alekhine*, trans. K.P. Neat, 1975, pp. 13, 46, 117, 199–201. It should be said that this book contains some brilliant analyses of Alekhine's games, and also that in 1935 and 1937 Alekhine did attempt to renew his relations with the Soviet authorities, though very tentatively and without receiving any response. Kotov has subsequently been instrumental in the making of a Soviet film about Alekhine's life

26 From the *Pravda* article cited in 14 above

27 V. Korchnoi, *Chess is my Life*, 1977, pp. 24–5

28 Botvinnik, *Achieving the Aim*, p. 86

29 L. Pachman, *Checkmate in Prague*, 1975

30 Fischer's article first appeared in *Sports Illustrated*, 20 August 1962

31 Korchnoi's account is in *Chess is my Life*, pp. 44–6

32 By this time FIDE had changed the Candidates from one large tournament (as in 1962) to a series of short two-man matches. This is just one piece of evidence to show that the world body was not biased against Fischer

33 Korchnoi, *Chess is my Life*, pp. 88–91
34 Translated in B. Cafferty, *Grandmaster Geller at the Chessboard*, Nottingham 1969, p. 52
35 Calculated from the table in Elo, *The Rating of Chessplayers*, pp. 108–9
36 This is clearly linked with the lead taken by English-based publishers, B.T. Batsford and others (Pergamon, The Chess Player etc.), in promoting high-quality chess literature

Appendix One: Chess books and chess notation (pages 199–203)

1 H.J.R. Murray, *A History of Chess*, Oxford 1913, p. 469
2 See on this Ross Pinsent, 'The Various Editions of Damiano', *British Chess Magazine* 1906, pp. 229–39, 285; and especially the comments of J.G. White, *ibid.*, 423–7. But I do not accept White's suggestion that the diagrams in the 1512 edition were printed with moveable type
3 Claude Gruget, *Le Plaisant Jeu des Eschecz*, Paris 1560. James Rowbothum, *The Pleasaunt and wittie Playe of the Cheasts renewed*, 1562 (another edition 1569). Rowbothum's name appears on the title page, and he wrote the dedication to the earl of Leicester, but the translation itself was probably not his. He wrote in the dedication: 'I was so bold (having found it translated out of French into English after the form and manner in all points as it is here printed) to choose your honour to whom I might offer this simple present'

Appendix Two: A note on chess problems (pages 205–207)

1 P. Stamma, *Essai sur le Jeu des Echecs*, Paris 1737, *Préface*. Compare *The Noble Game of Chess*, 1745, *Preface*: 'I have explained the several Openings, and rules for the beginning of Games, better suited to the Capacity of Beginners, and such as are not strong enough to take a Pleasure in the Parties of my former *Essay*'
2 H. Weenink, *The Chess Problem*, Stroud 1926. Weenink regards the end of the 'Old School' as marked by the publication of the massive collection by A. Alexandre, *Praktische Sammlung bester und höchst interessanter Schachspiel-Probleme*, Leipzig 1846, which contains over 2,000 problems

Index

The Index covers the text, but not the Bibliography or References. *Anonymous and collaborative works are indexed under title; others under the names of their authors*

INDEX

236